Open Mind,
Faithful Heart

Open Mind, Faithful Heart

— Reflections on Following Jesus —

JORGE MARIO BERGOGLIO
POPE FRANCIS

Translated by
Joseph V. Owens, SJ

In cooperation with

CLARETIAN
PUBLICATIONS

A Herder & Herder Book

The Crossroad Publishing Company
www.CrossroadPublishing.com

English translation copyright 2013
by The Crossroad Publishing Company
A Herder&Herder Book
The Crossroad Publishing Company, New York

Originally published as *Mente abierta, corazon creyente.*
Editorial Claretiana, Buenos Aires, Argentina
Chapter titles in the original Spanish publication
have been altered in this English edition.

The stylized crossed letter C logo is a registered trademark of
The Crossroad Publishing Company.

ISBN 978-08245-1997-1 (alk. paper)

Library of Congress Cataloging-in-Publication Data
available from the Library of Congress.

Cover image: *White Crucifixion,* by Marc Chagall.
In the book *El Jesuita,* then Cardinal Bergoglio spoke of
White Crucifixion as his favorite painting.
Cover design by George Foster
Book design by The HK Scriptorium, Inc.

In continuation of our 200-year tradition of independent publishing, The Crossroad
Publishing Company proudly offers a variety of books with strong, original voices
and diverse perspectives. The viewpoints expressed in our books are not necessarily
those of The Crossroad Publishing Company, any of its imprints or of its employees.
No claims are made or responsibility assumed for any health or other benefit.

Books published by The Crossroad Publishing Company may be purchased at special quantity discount rates for classes and institutional use. For information, please
e-mail sales@CrossroadPublishing.com

Printed in the United States of America in 2013.

Contents

Contents

Contents

Contents

Foreword

In 2011, I was making one of my occasional visits to talk with my archbishop when he told me that he was gathering together all his writings and other papers. He wanted to have them in order since he would turn 75 in December and so present his resignation to the Pope according to canonical norms. He told me that to help him in this work he had secured the collaboration of Daniel Pellizzon, a young man who was then studying for a licentiate degree in theology at the Catholic University. The archbishop told me that he would contact me when all was in order so that I could evaluate the materials and see which might be worth publishing.

One thing that impressed me greatly was when Jorge (I always called him by his given name) told me, "Make sure you know what you're doing. I don't want you to *get nailed*"—that's an expression meaning "suffer economic loss." So it was with all the books of his that we published; he invariably repeated that warning to me. He even asked me if I needed help in order to publish the books. We should remember that during the first years of his ministry as the archbishop of Buenos Aires the country was immersed in a serious economic crisis and publishing books was not at all easy.

The editorial team of the Claretian Press went through his many writings and gradually put together various texts that we thought should be published. After we had assembled and edited each work, the final step was to send it to "the cardinal" so that he could give it his final revision and approval. We always reserved the right to give the book its title and an appropriate cover.

With regard to the publishing process, I share with you a little story that caused me some delight. After placing the book in the author's hands, we would anxiously await his reaction. The cardinal did not like to have his photo on the cover, but since we were the "experts" in publishing, we did not always pay him mind. Soon after receiving the copy of a new book, he would telephone me to offer his commentary. I remember one time we had put his photo very prominently on the cover, and I'm not sure if he was really angry, but he certainly wasn't pleased. He told me several things, and all I could do was laugh. Finally, he thanked our press, and we bade each other a fraternal good-bye—he with his unfailing, "Pray for me, and have others pray for me."

It is important to stress that all of the books by him that we published were of decidedly *pastoral* orientation. They were never "self-referential," to use one of his own terms. These materials were used by the author to reinforce and complement his pastoral ministry; they were written for all interested Christians, but especially for the pastoral workers of the archdiocese.

Among the large number of publications that have appeared in the months since the conclave, we do well to distinguish between books "about" the Pope and books "of" the Pope. It's not that some are better and some are worse, but these two types of books really differ in nature. The books about the Pope satisfy the urgent demand for information and background about the new pontiff, while the Pope's own books, of which this is one, come directly from his own hand. For that reason, I think they will be long-lived. These are the books that show us all the depth and breadth of Francis, the new Pope. It is in these books that the author projects his inner self and makes himself visible in his own words.

Once he had finished putting order into Cardinal Bergoglio's papers, Daniel met with me in the office of the Editorial Claretiana. He gave me the materials that he thought would be worth publishing so that our team could evaluate them. Once we had done that, he digitized those that were still only in manuscript form.

What can be said, then, with regard to this book, *Open Mind, Faithful Heart*? First and foremost, we must say that it is a book of spirituality. Let no one be deceived about that. It is written in a simple style using plain language that is accessible to the general public. It is the last book written by Bergoglio as cardinal, and it is the one that he liked best of all. As the bishop who wrote the prologue of the Spanish edition states, "In this book is found the secret of Pope Francis."

There is no question about the quality of this work. Its texts are addressed to a wide audience, not only to priests and religious. Its forty-eight evocative meditations have an "Ignatian flavor" that will help the reader to draw closer to God and to others after the fashion of the "Holy Fathers."

All that remains for me to do is to invite you to get first-hand knowledge of Pope Francis by reading his own writings.

Gustavo Larrazábal, CFM

Prologue

When the editor asked me to write the prologue to this work by Cardinal Jorge Mario Bergoglio, I felt especially grateful. The request meant a lot to me, not only because I feel very close to the cardinal and highly esteem him, but also because it was a kind gesture toward me. Nevertheless, I tried to explain to the editor that I had many urgent things to attend to and would need some time before I could get around to writing the prologue. When he insisted, I ended up accepting the task, and I'm not sorry I did.

As I began to read these pages, I could readily perceive that the work was the result of a long process of reflection, preaching, and spiritual retreats. The fruit of these experiences was now being presented in written form so as to help others in following Jesus Christ. I stress the aspect of personal witness, for the book really sums up many years of the cardinal's life experience and his work as priest, pastor, and spiritual guide. We can discern in these pages the context of a spiritual retreat, or rather several retreats, in which these texts were slowly brought forth and carefully woven together. Even though these reflections arose in diverse times and circumstances, the work is not disjointed; it has a unity that flows both from the author's vision and, above all, from the person of Jesus Christ, the contemplation of whom is the focal point and source of life for Christian spirituality. What is noteworthy is the author's obvious concern to present Christian living as a reality oriented to improving our relations with God, with the world, and with one another. I especially appreciate the cardinal's concrete, down-to-earth approach, which should serve us as a guide in the ways and practices of spirituality and as a basis for a sincere examination of conscience.

Another characteristic important to note is the cardinal's familiarity with scriptural texts, which gives evidence of a solid biblical theology. What I would call his sapiential perspective enriches the texts and allows them to be applied to our daily living. We are not dealing with an exegetical study, even though his handling of the texts reveals profound knowledge of them and theological rigor in their interpretation. The scriptural passages, especially the teachings of Jesus, are shown to relate very closely to concrete human reality; they touch what is deepest within us and what we most hope for. Such qualities give the work a contemporary aspect that will make it accessible to almost any reader who delves into it. This is a work that presents the person and the teaching of Jesus as a way of life that is both human and divine; the divine takes nothing away from the human but rather presupposes, frees, and fulfills it. What is more, the human is shown to be in need of the divine in order to be fully realized as human.

The reader of the text will also take note of the author's informed use of language and his appreciation of the captivating, revelatory power of the word. I think that the reason for this, at least in part, is that the cardinal in his youth taught literature. If I may speak from experience, I remember that once I asked him what he did and where he went during his annual January vacation. I recall that he told me that he stayed at the curia in Buenos Aires and relaxed by praying and by reading (or re-reading) the classics. His answer surprised me, but it also helped me, and since then I have tried to put it in practice. How much we have lost culturally because we have abandoned the classics! This little anecdote also helps to explain his superb Spanish style and the beauty of his prose. Esthetics forms part of the Christian faith; it has its source and its inspiration in God.

This book is a text to be put into practice in the sense that it is oriented to spiritual growth; it is not only for reading but also for meditation. In addition to abundant biblical references and citations from the magisterium, the text contains some wonderful canticles and poems taken from the liturgy and the Church's religious tradition. These add a special note of beauty and color that helps to create an ambience conducive to prayer. Also of great pedagogical value are the sections "For Prayer and Reflection" that are placed at the end of every meditation. We have in our hands, then, a work that not only has profound contents and contemporary relevance but is also easy and pleasant to read. Its goal is to guide readers along the path of spiritual reflection that will enrich their lives.

The work is divided into four parts. All of them have a single goal, as we indicated earlier, but each part has a certain autonomy that allows us to discern its particular identity and value. Although the author has perhaps not directly intended it, the division of the work reveals something of the schema of the *Catechism of the Catholic Church*. It begins with the encounter with Jesus Christ and ends with reflections on prayer, based on the experience of various witnesses taken from the scriptures. Faith and prayer are the two central themes that provide this work with unity and consistency. At the same time, as we shall see, the path of spiritual renewal traced out here does not involve us in game-playing nor does it throw us into alienating activity. Rather, this faith in the God whom we have known in Jesus Christ opens us to a life of loving relationships, and it rouses the Church to missionary dynamism.

PART I ENGAGES US in the encounter with Jesus through a number of dialogues we find in the Gospels. Here we can appreciate how the author's rich Ignatian tradition helps him recreate the circumstances and settings in which Jesus encounters different persons. With great skill he shows the value and the meaning of the words the Lord uses with his interlocutors. These encounters with Jesus help to shed light on the different life situations of Christians, which range from the joy found in encountering Christ—which he defines as vocation—to death on the cross, which entails the experience of suffering and sin. In this way, the author communicates to the reader the profound meaning of the joyous Christian hope, which, through faith in Christ dead and risen, should suffuse the life of every person.

THE LIFE AND THE WORDS of Jesus reveal to us the history of salvation in all its fullness as the setting in which our present-day lives unfold. This theme is developed in Parts II and III, which introduce us into the meaning of revelation: it is a history of love, life, and mission that providentially shows us the way toward the final revelation. Within that framework, Jesus Christ makes the Church present to us as the "epiphany of the Spouse." In this time of the Church, the theme of mission takes on special prominence as an expression of the revelation of the Father's saving love. In my view, Part II should motivate and mobilize us decisively to work for the life of the Church. In recovering the evangelizing import of faith within the framework of Church communion, the author issues us an urgent and challenging call to define our apostolic commitment once and for all.

PART III SPEAKS ABOUT the Church in its concrete life, with all its wonders, weaknesses, and petty problems. I think wise and timely is the author's approach to Church life from the perspective of the word of God, specifically the letters addressed to the seven churches of Asia Minor in the book of the Apocalypse (chapters 1–3). The seriousness with which he has undertaken this reflection is evident in his appeal to theologians such as Romano Guardini and Hans Urs von Balthasar for help in studying and meditating on these very difficult texts. I need say little more in this brief prologue about Part III except to urge a slow and thoughtful reading that will allow us to discover and love our Church—for this Church, whose often inappropriate garments disturb us, is still beautiful and is still the only Spouse of the Lamb. I can only tell you that reading this part has helped me greatly.

THE LAST PART, as we said, is dedicated to prayer as experienced in our concrete lived reality. We should not be surprised, then, that the very first theme is "Our Flesh in Prayer." The various movements through which our prayer moves—closeness, distance, abandonment—are considered in the light of various biblical witnesses. Thus, we encounter Abraham, Moses, David, Job, and Judith, all of whom are asked to share with us their religious experience. A major theme in this part on prayer is one we met before in the meditations on the encounter with Jesus Christ: "letting oneself be led." A sign of the presence of the Spirit is a certain active passivity. Part IV concludes with a meditation on Jesus Christ the Priest offering prayer to the Father, a prayer that is the source and model of all Christian prayer.

I BELIEVE that the work that you have in your hands and I have had the pleasure of introducing is the fruit of a long journey of reflection and prayer. It therefore asks of us an unhurried, reflective reading. The first requirement for advancing in something important is to give ourselves sufficient time. We are accustomed to reading rapidly in order to stay informed and up to date, but this book has a very different purpose. I am grateful to Cardinal Bergoglio for gathering together these diverse texts and unifying them into a useful instrument that will forever enrich our lives.

José María Arancedo
Archbishop of Santa Fe de la Vera Cruz
Argentina

To the Reader of the English Edition

Pope Francis connects with people, especially the young, the forgotten, and the forlorn. The cameras show him in Rome, in Brazil, in Lampedusa reaching out to the crowds, holding infants, embracing the disabled.

What is the source of this septuagenarian's energy? What is the secret of his spiritual vitality? This book is perhaps the best introduction to what makes the Pope the engaging pastor he is.

During his years as the archbishop of Buenos Aires, Jorge Mario Bergoglio gave many conferences to those collaborating with him in pastoral ministry. His constant theme was how to follow Jesus unreservedly, even in the hectic turmoil of our modern world. The texts of these conferences, collected in the present volume, reveal the spiritual depths of Pope Francis as perhaps no other work does.

The strong scriptural orientation of the Pope is evident in the countless references to both Old and New Testaments. To help the reader, this edition has supplemented the original text with appropriate scriptural citations.

Like the Scriptures themselves, the language of these pages speaks to the heart as much as to the mind. These are meditations to be savored rather than just read quickly and filed away.

Many of the themes Pope Francis treats in his almost daily addresses to the public can be traced back to these conferences from earlier years. The materials in this book will help to unlock the deeper meaning of the papal discourses.

This is not just a book for reading—it is a path for prayer and a guide for life.

Joseph V. Owens, SJ

PART I

Encountering Jesus

1. Jesus in Dialogue

APOSTOLIC JOY is nourished by the contemplation of Jesus Christ, that is, by observing how he moved about, how he preached, how he healed, how he saw the world.... The heart of the priest should be steeped in this contemplation and through it resolve the main challenge of his life: his friendship with Jesus Christ. I propose here to contemplate a few of Jesus' dialogues with different types of people. We want to reflect here on how Jesus speaks, first, with those who want to lay down conditions; then, with those who are trying to entrap him; and finally, with those whose heart is open to the hope of salvation.

THERE ARE MANY ACCOUNTS in the Gospels of persons who approach Jesus but only with certain conditions. For example, Luke 9:57-62 mentions three persons who want to follow Jesus, but not unconditionally. In the Gospel of John, we read the stories of Nicodemus (John 3:1-21) and of the Samaritan woman (John 4:1-41), both of whom also approach Jesus with conditions. The three persons in Luke's Gospel seek to limit their commitment to Jesus for particular reasons: concern for wealth, for friends, for parents. The Samaritan woman, on the other hand, attempts to deflect her dialogue with Jesus because she wants to avoid what is crucial; she prefers to speak of theology rather than explain about her husbands. The case of Nicodemus is different but also conditional; he visits Jesus only when he can do so safely, under the cover of night. Jesus realizes that this man is not quite ready and so leaves him wrapped up in his musings, which serve as his refuge to avoid the demands of loyalty.

> *As they were going along the road, someone said to him, "I will follow you wherever you go." And Jesus said to him, "Foxes have holes, and birds of the air have nests; but the Son of Man has nowhere to lay his head." To another he said, "Follow me." But he said, "Lord, first let me go and bury my father." But Jesus said to him, "Let the dead bury their own dead; but as for you, go and proclaim the kingdom of God." Another said, "I will follow you, Lord; but let me first say farewell to those at my home." Jesus said to him, "No one who puts a hand to the plough and looks back is fit for the kingdom of God." (Luke 9:57-62)*

OTHER PERSONS APPROACH Jesus deviously, with the idea of "testing" him to see whether his teaching is coherent with his action or whether cracks can be found in it which will allow religious devotion to remain a profitable business. Such persons seek to exchange faith for security, hope for possessions, love for self-interest.

IN THE SCENE of the woman taken in adultery (John 8:1-11), if Jesus approves the stoning, his mercy is called into doubt; if he disapproves, he goes against the law. In these devious dialogues Jesus usually does two things: he utters words of instruction to those who want to trap him, but he speaks differently to the victim (here, the adulterous woman) and directly addresses the deceitful situation. In this case, Jesus turns the condemnation back on the schemers, telling them to apply it to themselves, and then he restores to the woman her very life, encouraging her to live from that point on responsibly.

SIMILARLY, WE CAN MEDITATE on the devious question about paying tribute to Caesar (Matt 22:15-22), which attempts to implicate Jesus in the Sadducean temptation of collaborating with Rome. To this question and the one about his own authority (Luke 20:1-8) Jesus responds by exhorting his adversaries to pay heed to the "authorities" that God has sent to them but that they have refused to accept.

> *Then the Pharisees went and plotted to entrap him in what he said. So they sent their disciples to him, along with the Herodians, saying, "Teacher, we know that you are sincere, and teach the way of God in accordance with truth, and show deference to no one; for you do not regard people with partiality. Tell us, then, what you think. Is it lawful to pay taxes to the emperor, or not?" But Jesus, aware of their malice, said, "Why are you putting me to the test, you hypocrites? Show me the coin used for the tax." And they brought him a denarius. Then he said to them, "Whose head is this, and whose title?" They answered, "The emperor's." Then he said to them, "Give therefore to the emperor the things that are the emperor's, and to God the things that are God's." When they heard this, they were amazed; and they left him and went away.* (Matt 22:15-22)

To another wily question of the Sadducees, about the woman who was married to seven brothers (Matt 22:23-33), the Lord responds by looking toward the eschatological horizon. When the devious heart becomes irreversibly hardened, then there is sin unto death (1 John 5:16), sin against the Holy Spirit (Matt 12:32), and confusion of spirits. This ploy is so shameful that the Lord doesn't even bother to argue with the tricksters: he responds simply by asserting the sublimity of the glorified life (Luke 20:27-40).

> *Jesus said to them, "Those who belong to this age marry and are given in marriage; but those who are considered worthy of a place*

in that age and in the resurrection from the dead neither marry nor are given in marriage. Indeed they cannot die any more, because they are like angels and are children of God, being children of the resurrection. And the fact that the dead are raised Moses himself showed, in the story about the bush, where he speaks of the Lord as the God of Abraham, the God of Isaac, and the God of Jacob. Now he is God not of the dead, but of the living; for to him all of them are alive." Then some of the scribes answered, "Teacher, you have spoken well." For they no longer dared to ask him another question. (Luke 20:34-40)

AT THE ROOT of every devious dialogue are vainglory, sensuality, pride, and greed. The Lord teaches us to respond to these deceitful provocations by recalling the wondrous story of our faithful people (Matt 4:1-11).

Then Jesus was led up by the Spirit into the wilderness to be tempted by the devil. He fasted for forty days and forty nights, and afterwards he was famished. The tempter came and said to him, "If you are the Son of God, command these stones to become loaves of bread." But he answered, "It is written, 'One does not live by bread alone, but by every word that comes from the mouth of God.'"

Then the devil took him to the holy city and placed him on the pinnacle of the temple, saying to him, "If you are the Son of God, throw yourself down; for it is written, 'He will command his angels concerning you,' and 'On their hands they will bear you up, so that you will not dash your foot against a stone.'" Jesus said to him, "Again it is written, 'Do not put the Lord your God to the test.'"

Again, the devil took him to a very high mountain and showed him all the kingdoms of the world and their splendor; and he said to him, "All these I will give you, if you will fall down and worship me." *Jesus said to him, "Away with you, Satan! for it is written, 'Worship the Lord your God, and serve only him.'" Then the devil left him, and suddenly angels came and waited on him.* (Matt 4:1-11)

FINALLY, A THIRD GROUP of dialogues in which Jesus engages might be called dialogues of loyalty. They take place when people approach Jesus without duplicity or conditions, with a heart open to God's revelation. They put everything on the table. When people draw close to Jesus in this way, his heart overflows with joy (Luke 10:21).

For Prayer and Reflection

With a ready heart and a great desire to encounter the Lord, let us meditate on the dialogue between Jesus and the man born blind in John 9:1-41.

2. Living in Constant Encounter

AN ABYSS SEPARATES the priest from the religious functionary; they are qualitatively different. Sadly, however, the priest can be slowly transformed, little by little, into a religious functionary. When that happens, the priesthood ceases to be a bridge, and the priest is no longer a *pontifex*, a builder of bridges; he ends up simply having a function to perform. He ceases to be a mediator and becomes simply an intermediary. No one chooses to be a priest; it is Jesus Christ who does the choosing. Priestly existence remains true to itself only when it draws deeply on direct encounter with Jesus Christ. The priest must seek the Lord and let himself be sought in return; he must encounter the Lord and allow himself to be encountered in turn. All of this goes together; it is inseparable. John Paul II in his book *Gift and Mystery* speaks of the priest as the person who is in contact with God. He presents the priest as engaged in a twofold movement of seeking to encounter God (ascent) and receiving holiness from God (descent). "It is the holiness of the paschal mystery," he writes. When the priest moves away from this dual movement, he becomes disoriented. Holiness is not just a collection of virtues. Indeed, such a conception of holiness causes great harm; it stifles our hearts, and after a while it fashions us into Pharisees. Holiness means "walking in the presence of God and being perfect"; holiness means living in constant encounter with Jesus Christ.

To begin this prayer, I propose that you meditate on the presentation of Jesus in the temple (Luke 2:22-39). The liturgy for the feast tells us that in this mystery "the Lord goes out to meet the people." There in the temple we find old people and young, Law and Spirit, promise and reality, prophet and God's faithful people. This is Candlemas Day, when we celebrate the small flame that will keep growing until it becomes the fire of the paschal vigil.

> *Now there was a man in Jerusalem whose name was Simeon; this man was righteous and devout, looking forward to the consolation of Israel, and the Holy Spirit rested on him. It had been revealed to him by the Holy Spirit that he would not see death before he had seen the Lord's Messiah. Guided by the Spirit, Simeon came into the temple; and when the parents brought in the child Jesus, to do for him what was customary under the law, Simeon took him in his arms and praised God, saying, "Master, now you are dismissing your servant in peace, according to your word; for my eyes have seen your salvation, which you have prepared in the presence of all peoples, a light for revelation to the Gentiles and for glory to your people Israel." (Luke 2:25-32)*

The Gospels recount many scenes of people searching for Jesus and finding him. In each scene we can see some trait that may help us in our prayer. The encounter with Jesus always involves a call; the call may be a great one or a small one, but it is always there (Matt 4:18-19; 9:9; 10:1-4). The encounter may happen at any time, and it is pure gratuity, totally unmerited (Matt 20:5-6). Sometimes the encounter must be sought out (Matt 8:2-3; 9:9); it may require heroic persistence (Matt 15:21-40) or loud shouts (Matt 8:24-25). The seeking may even entail painful confusion and doubt (Luke 7:18-24; Matt 11:2-7). However it happens, the encounter with Jesus Christ leads us toward ever greater humility (Luke 5:4-10). His invitation can be rejected or half-heartedly accepted (Matt 13:1-23). When it is rejected, pain pierces the heart of Christ (Matt 23:37-39; Matt 11:20-30). Seeking out Christ and finding him is not the anodyne exercise of a Pelagian spirit; rather, it assumes that there is sin and repentance (Matt 21:28-32). The encounter with Jesus Christ takes place in our daily lives, in the direct contact of prayer, in the wise discernment of the signs of the times (Matt 24:32-33; Luke 21:29-32), and in our brothers and sisters (Matt 25:31-46; Luke 10:25-37).

> *Then the king will say to those at his right hand, "Come, you that are blessed by my Father, inherit the kingdom prepared for you from the foundation of the world; for I was hungry and you gave me food, I was thirsty and you gave me something to drink, I was a stranger and you welcomed me, I was naked and you gave me clothing, I was sick and you took care of me, I was in prison and you visited me." (Matt 25:34-36)*

THE LORD HIMSELF RECOMMENDS that we be vigilantly on the lookout for this encounter. Jesus searches for me. He does not view us as part of a crowd but seeks us out one by one, searching our hearts. Vigilance means being receptive to the wisdom that will help us discern Jesus and truly find him. Sometimes the Lord passes by our side and we don't even see him—or else we "know him so well" that we don't recognize him. Our vigilance is the prayerful attitude that makes us want to keep him with us when he seems to want to "continue on his way" (Mark 6:48-50; Luke 24:28-30).

> *As they came near the village to which they were going, he walked ahead as if he were going on. But they urged him strongly, saying, "Stay with us, because it is almost evening and the day is now*

nearly over." So he went in to stay with them. When he was at the table with them, he took bread, blessed and broke it, and gave it to them. (Luke 24:28-30)

For Prayer and Reflection

We can end our prayer with the gesture of the Magi. After discerning heavenly signs and spending long years in search of the child, they finally find him. And when they do, they bow down in adoration (Matt 2:11).

On entering the house, they saw the child with Mary his mother; and they knelt down and paid him homage. Then, opening their treasure-chests, they offered him gifts of gold, frankincense, and myrrh.

3. Believing in Joy

We are writing these things so that our joy may be complete.

(1 John 1:4)

"I have said these things to you so that my joy may be in you, and that your joy may be complete." (John 15:11)

"I speak these things in the world so that they may have my joy made complete in themselves." (John 17:13)

T HE JOY SPOKEN OF HERE is the joy occasioned by the gift of God (Luke 1:10-15; Rom 15:13) and by the visitation of God himself (Luke 1:41-44). It is the joy that grips us when we are able to grasp the whole of salvation history (Luke 1:47) or foresee it in faith (John 8:56; 1 Pet 4:13). Such joy is the fruit of the presence of the Holy Spirit (Luke 10:21). It strengthens us in times of trial (Luke 6:23: Heb 10:34; Rom 12:12; 1 Pet 1:6; 2 Cor 6:12), and it accompanies us, as it did the apostles, in our evangelizing work (Luke 24:52; Acts 13:52) because it is a sign of the Lord's abiding presence. It is a vitally apostolic joy that helps to consolidate the bond of love between founding apostle and local church (Phil 1:25; 4:1; Phlm 7; 1 John 1:4; 2 John 12). Throughout the scriptures, we are urged to let our joy be complete.

Now at the time of the incense offering, the whole assembly of the people was praying outside. Then there appeared to him an angel of the Lord, standing at the right side of the altar of incense. When Zechariah saw him, he was terrified; and fear overwhelmed him. But the angel said to him, "Do not be afraid, Zechariah, for your prayer has been heard. Your wife Elizabeth will bear you a son, and you will name him John. You will have joy and gladness, and many will rejoice at his birth, for he will be great in the sight of the Lord." (Luke 1:10-15)

When Elizabeth heard Mary's greeting, the child leapt in her womb. And Elizabeth was filled with the Holy Spirit and exclaimed with a loud cry, "Blessed are you among women, and blessed is the fruit of your womb. And why has this happened to me, that the mother of my Lord comes to me? For as soon as I heard the sound of your greeting, the child in my womb leapt for joy." (Luke 1:41-44)

OUR JOY IN GOD generates missionary enthusiasm: "Jesus said to them, 'Come and see.' They came and saw where he was staying, and they remained with him that day. It was about four o'clock in the afternoon.... Andrew then found his brother Simon and said to him, 'We have found the Messiah.' He brought Simon to Jesus" (John 1:39-46). "Jesus told Mary Magdalene, 'Go to my brothers,' and she went and announced to the disciples, 'I have seen the Lord!'" (John 20:17-18).

THIS JOY IS CONSOLATION. It is a sign of the harmony and unity realized through love. It is a sign of the unity of the body of the Church. It is a sign of how that body is growing stronger. We need to be faithful to this joy and not just "enjoy" it as something that belongs only to us. The joy is there for our astonishment; it is there for us to communicate it to others.

This joy opens us to the freedom that comes with being children of God. By placing us in God, this joy separates us from things that confine and imprison us and from situations that take away our freedom. That is why the joyful heart is always growing freer.

As a sign of Christ's presence, joy shapes the habitual state of the consecrated person. We therefore naturally seek out consolation not for its own sake, but as a sign of the Lord's presence. Consolation may be sought in many different forms, as Saint Ignatius explains in his Spiritual Exercises: "By consolation I mean that which occurs when some interior motion is caused within the soul through which it comes to be inflamed with love of its Creator and Lord. As a result it can love no created thing on the face of the earth in itself, but only in the Creator of them all. Similarly, this consolation is experienced when the soul sheds tears which move it to love for its Lord—whether they are tears of grief for its own sin, or about the Passion of Christ our Lord, or about other matters directly ordered to his service and praise. Finally, under the word consolation I include every increase in hope, faith, and charity, and every interior joy which calls and attracts one toward heavenly things and to the salvation of one's soul, by bringing it tranquility and peace in its Creator and Lord" (SpEx 316).[1]

THE BASIC ELEMENT of joy, then, is profound peace, that imperturbability in the Spirit that remains with us even in the most painful, excruciating moments. A fourth-century spiritual writer describes well the many different ways in which true Christians are guided by Christ: "Sometimes they weep and grieve over the human race; aflame with spiritual love, they pray for humankind with tears and moans. Other times, the Holy Spirit enkindles in them a joy and a love so great that, if they could, they would embrace in their hearts all the people of the world, without distinction between good and bad. Still other times, a feeling of profound humility makes them place themselves beneath all other human beings and consider themselves the most abject and despicable of creatures. Then again, there are moments when the Spirit communicates to them an indescribable joy. At other times, they are like the courageous soldier who, donning regal armor and rushing into battle, fights bravely against the enemy and overcomes it. Still other times, the soul rests in great silence, peaceful tranquility, and supreme serenity. There are moments when the Spirit grants them sublime intelligence, wisdom, and knowledge, far beyond anything that can be expressed in words. But there are other times when they experience nothing in particular. And so the soul is led by grace through a great variety of states, according to the will of God who shows his favor in diverse ways" (Saint Macarius of Egypt, *Homilies,* in *Patrologia Graeca* 34:639-42). It is clear, then, that what endures through all these changes is the same anointing of the Holy Spirit. This anointing is rooted in joy, and that is why it is expressed in such a variety of ways. Our rootedness in that anointing by the Spirit remains imperturbable; it is what might be called fundamental peace.

WE ARE URGED to ask the Holy Spirit for the gift of happiness and joy. The opposite is sadness, for as Paul VI tells us, "Cold and darkness are above all in the heart of the person who knows sadness" (*Gaudete in Domino*, I). Sadness is the magic weapon of Satan, who hardens and embitters the human heart. When bitterness enters into the heart of a consecrated person, he or she does well to recall the warning of the same Paul VI: "Let the more agitated members of various groups reject the excesses of systematic and destructive criticism! Without abandoning a realistic viewpoint, Christian communities should become centers of optimism where all the members resolutely endeavor to perceive the positive aspect of people and events. 'Love does not rejoice in wrongdoing but rejoices in the truth. It bears all things, believes all things, hopes all things, endures all things' (1 Cor 13:6-7)" (*Gaudete in Domino*, Conclusion).

But the most serious problem with the spirit of sadness is that it bears within itself the sin against hope. Bernanos says it well in his *Diary of a Country Priest:* "The sin against hope ... is the most mortal of all, and yet it is the one most welcomed and honored. Much time is needed for us to recognize it, so sweet is the sadness that announces and precedes it! It is the most precious of the devil's elixirs, his ambrosia."

IN RESPONSE TO THIS, Paul VI states: "Joy which is properly spiritual, the joy which is a fruit of the Holy Spirit (cf. Rom 14:17; Gal 5:22-23), consists in the human spirit's finding repose and a deep satisfaction in the possession of the Triune God, known by faith and loved with the charity that comes from God. Such a joy henceforth characterizes all the Christian virtues."

> *By contrast, the fruit of the Spirit is love, joy, peace, patience, kindness, generosity, faithfulness, gentleness, and self-control.* (Gal 5:22-23)

"The humble human joys in our lives, which are like seeds of a higher reality, are transfigured. Here below, this joy will always include to some extent the painful ordeal of a woman giving birth and a certain apparent abandonment, like an orphan's tears and lamentation, while the world parades its gloating satisfaction. But the disciples' sadness, which is according to

God and not according to the world, will be promptly changed into a spiritual joy that no one will be able to take away from them (cf. John 16:20-22; 2 Cor 1:4)" (*Gaudete in Domino,* III).

Paul VI urges us to ask for the gift of happiness and joy as "a fruit of the Holy Spirit. This Spirit, who dwells fully in the person of Jesus, made him during his earthly life so alert to the joys of daily life and so tactful and persuasive in putting sinners back on the road to a new youthfulness of heart and mind! It is this same Spirit who animated the Blessed Virgin and each of the saints. It is this same Spirit who still today gives to so many Christians the joy of living day by day their particular vocation, in the peace and hope which surpass setbacks and sufferings" (*Gaudete in Domino,* Conclusion).

Joy means fervor. Paul VI concludes his encyclical *Evangelii Nuntiandi* by describing for us this fervor: "Of the obstacles that are still present today, we shall limit ourselves to mentioning the lack of fervor. This is all the more serious because it comes from within. It is manifested in fatigue, disenchantment, compromise, lack of interest, and above all lack of joy and hope. We exhort all those who have the task of evangelizing, by whatever title and at whatever level, always to nourish spiritual fervor (cf. Rom 12:11). Let us therefore preserve our fervor of spirit. Let us preserve the delightful and comforting joy of evangelizing, even when it is in tears that we must sow. May it mean for us ... an interior enthusiasm that nobody and nothing can quench. May it be the great joy of our consecrated lives. And may the world of our own time, which is searching, sometimes with anguish, sometimes with hope, be enabled to receive the Good News not from evangelizers who are dejected, discouraged, impatient, or anxious, but from ministers of the Gospel whose lives glow with fervor, who have first received the joy of Christ" (*Evangelii Nuntiandi*, 80).

For Prayer and Reflection

Our joy is nourished by our contemplation of Jesus Christ, by observing how he moved about, how he preached, how he healed, how he saw the world.... All priests and all consecrated men and women must resolve in their lives the fundamental challenge of their friendship with Jesus Christ, and they must bring their lives to resolution through this friendship with Jesus. I am referring here to the genuine needs of authentic consecrated life. It is through the sharing of our lives that true friendship is born, grows, and gets stronger. At the end of the day, that is why contemplating Jesus is so necessary.

I propose that you dedicate your time of prayer to contemplating the Lord. Choose the passages about his apostolic life that you like most, and just stay with them, watching, listening, walking with him.

4. Joy and Perseverance

I WOULD LIKE TO CONTINUE to reflect on our joy in ministering. True joy is forged in work and in the cross. Joy that has not been "tested" is no more than simple enthusiasm; it is often undiscerning and therefore cannot guarantee fruitful ministry. Jesus prepares us for testing, and he cautions us so that we will stand strong: "You have pain now, but I will see you again, and your hearts will rejoice, and no one will take your joy from you" (John 16:22). Saint Ignatius also exhorts us to persevere in temptation and desolation by remaining constant and trusting that eventually we will again experience consolation and joy: "One who is in desolation should strive to preserve himself or herself in patience. This is the counterattack against the vexations which are being experienced" (SpEx 321). In desolation and times of trial, it may seem that the Lord is far away or fast asleep (as he was in the stern of the boat during the storm [Matt 8:24-25]). Other times, it may be our worldly or sinful attitude that makes the Lord seem distant from our heart. He is always there, but we don't see him—or don't want to see him.

> *And when he got into the boat, his disciples followed him. A windstorm arose on the sea, so great that the boat was being swamped by the waves; but he was asleep. And they went and woke him up, saying, "Lord, save us! We are perishing!"* (Matt 8:24-25)

Those who work in ministry can sometimes suffer from pastoral fatigue. It is usually an effect (and symptom) of inconstancy and spiritual apathy. Doing justice by God's faithful people means being ever constant in pastoral ministry. It means responding eagerly to people's sometimes tiring requests to be anointed (touched) by God at any moment—through blessings, words, and sacraments. It's curious but true: the faithful wear us out because they ask for concrete things. On the other hand, we may sometimes be seduced into the kind of work that allows us to take refuge in fantasy. Within our minds, we are kings and queens, lords and ladies. Those who dedicate themselves solely to cultivating their fantasies will never feel the urgency of concrete reality. The pastoral work in our parishes has nothing of fantasy; it is very concrete. It demands reflection, intellectual effort, and prayer, but the greatest amount of time must be spent basically in doing "works of charity."

WITH CHARITY AND CALMNESS we should attend to people who come seeking all sorts of things: a woman will ask if she can change a promise she has made; another person will request a certificate to baptize a baby in Luján; still another will seek assistance from Caritas; someone will request a memorial Mass for a deceased loved one on one particular day and not another. The people are demanding in matters that relate to religion. Just as they are generally faithful in fulfilling their promises, so they expect those who are responsible for providing pastoral care to be faithful in fulfilling their duties. The priest does not belong to himself. He may sometimes try to escape to other things, but all those "other things" count for little in comparison with the mother who makes him walk many blocks to bless her house. Constancy in our apostolic work will create foundations. I don't think the hands of a priest should simply go through routine gestures when baptizing; rather, they should tremble with emotion because at that moment he is performing decisive gestures that become a foundation.

I WOULD LIKE TO SPEND a moment trying to describe the anti-apostolic vice called apathy. It is a failing that eats away at the apostolic perseverance required in our mission as pastors of God's faithful people. What characterizes every form of apathy is a sort of utopian vision that refuses to take seriously the times, the places, and the persons among whom we carry out our pastoral mission. A philosopher might say that such a person seeks to exist outside space and time. This vice manifests itself in different forms in our lives as pastors, and we must be alert in order to be able to detect it beneath the subtle guises it often wears.

At times, apathy takes the form of paralysis: one simply refuses to accept the rhythms of life. Other times it appears in the clownish priest who in his activities seems incapable of grounding himself in God and in the concrete history in which he must live. Occasionally, it reveals itself in those who elaborate magnificent plans without any concern for the concrete means by which they will be realized. Conversely, it is seen in those who get so wrapped up in the minutiae of each moment that they cannot see beyond them to the grand plan of God. We do well to recall the epigram attributed to Saint Ignatius: *Non coerceri a maximo, contineri tamen a minimo, divinum est*, "Not being overwhelmed by what is greatest, while still being attentive to what is smallest—that is divine."

We have seen many people fall prey to apathy. We have known people dream up unrealizable projects in order not to carry out other projects that were well within their reach. There are those who refuse to allow processes to evolve naturally and instead demand spontaneous generation. Others believe that everything worthwhile has already been said, so there is no need for further questions. Like the disciples of Emmaus, some persons close their hearts off to new "steps of the Lord." They don't know how to hope, and their very failure to hope causes dispersion and dissipation. What unites and gathers together is always life-giving, but these do not accept life; they prefer apathy.

We do well to recognize apathy as a reality that besieges us constantly; it is a daily threat to our lives as pastors, and we need to be humbly aware that it is always with us. That is why we must nourish ourselves with the word of God, which gives us strength to continue moving forward. That is why we must seek the joy that comes only from the Lord when he finds us keeping watch, searching for him in the many moments when he becomes present in our ministry. Only those laborers who have wisely renounced whimsy, apathy, and inconstancy in order to spend themselves all day and every day in pastoral service will understand from their hearts the price Christ paid to rescue us. Their toiling hands will contribute, perhaps even without intending it, to Church unity through cooperation with the bishop and through the collaboration with God that comes from belonging to Holy Mother Church, for these are the qualities that shape us into children of the Father, brothers and sisters among ourselves, and parents of God's faithful people. Only the untiring worker who shows patience, perseverance, and endurance (the Greek notion of *hypomonē*) will know how to preserve what Saint Ignatius of Antioch called the "immaculate unity" of the Church (see his letter to the Ephesians, 2:2). We will accomplish this only when we fix our sight on Jesus, "the pioneer and perfecter of our faith, who for the sake of the joy that was set before him endured the cross, disregarding its shame, and has taken his seat at the right hand of the throne of God" (Heb 12:2).

For Prayer and Reflection

Let us pause a moment and review our lives. What guises does apathy assume in me? In what situations of my life am I tempted to feel weariness and to flag in my resolve, so that I end up almost paralyzed?

5. The Faith That Frees Us

"WHATEVER IS BORN OF GOD conquers the world. And this is the victory that conquers the world, our faith" (1 John 5:3-5). Today more than ever, the questions we ask ourselves about our apostolic effectiveness are difficult ones, and they risk entangling us in the very questions we have about our own fidelity. This matter is so important that we cannot allow ourselves to indulge in any form of improvisation. The same holds true with regard to the different apostolic decisions that we have to make in our pastoral activity. When Paul VI spoke to us about the effort involved in announcing the Gospel to the modern world, he pointed out something extraordinary; in our time, he said, we are "buoyed up by hope but at the same time often oppressed by fear and distress" (*Evangelii Nuntiandi*, 1). Hopes and fears are woven together even in our apostolic lives, especially when we have to choose among the different aspects of our work. We cannot take the risk of deciding such matters without clear discernment of our fears and hopes, for what is asked of us "in this time of uncertainty and confusion" is nothing less than to "accomplish this task with ever increasing love, zeal, and joy" (*Evangelii Nuntiandi*, 1). This is not something that can be improvised. For us who are committed to the Church, this challenge goes far beyond anything the positive sciences envision; it appeals rather to an original vision, to the very originality of the Gospel. Mutually consoled by one another's faith (Rom 1:11-12), we must unite with this vital force, and as apostles we must nourish our hearts with it precisely in order to recover the coherence of our mission, the cohesion of our apostolic body, and the consistency of our feelings and our actions.

> *For I am longing to see you so that I may share with you some spiritual gift to strengthen you—or rather so that we may be mutually encouraged by each other's faith, both yours and mine.* (Rom 1:11-12)

WE MUST ENCOUNTER our faith, the faith of our fathers and mothers, which is liberating in itself, without any added quality or qualification. This is the faith that makes us just before the Father who created us, before the Son who redeemed us and called us to follow him, and before the Spirit who works directly in our hearts. In the moment of making concrete decisions, this faith will lead us, through the Spirit's anointing, to a clear knowledge of the limits of our own role; it will make us wise and intelligent in choosing the means we use; in the end, it will lead us to evangelical effectiveness that is far removed from both emotional ineptitude and easy-going indifference. Our faith is revolutionary; it is a foundation unto itself. Our faith is militant, but not with the aggressiveness of most skirmishes; rather, under the guidance of the Spirit, it gently insists on whatever project it discerns will be for the greater service of the Church. At the same time, its liberating potential comes from its contact with the holy for it is hierophantic: it reveals the sacred. Let us think, for example, of the Virgin and the saints as "intercessors."

BECAUSE THE FAITH is so revolutionary, it will be under constant attack by the enemy, not so much to destroy it as to weaken it, make it inoperative, remove it from contact with the holy, with the Lord of all faith and all life. When our faith is weakened, we find ourselves exposed to positions that we thought were alien to us; and if we carefully examine our apostolic practice, we find that they are actually hidden in our sinful hearts. These simplistic positions would have us excuse ourselves from the hardships and the constancy required in our pastoral labors. We need to take a look at some of these temptations.

A MOST SERIOUS TEMPTATION, one that impedes our contact with the Lord, is defeatism. When the enemy comes up against a faith that is by definition militant, he takes on the semblance of an angel of light and begins to sow seeds of pessimism. To engage effectively in any struggle, one must be fully confident of victory. Those who begin a struggle without robust confidence have already lost half the battle. Christian victory always involves a cross, but a cross that is the banner of victory. We can learn about militant faith and nourish it in ourselves by moving among the poor. During these meditations, we will remember the faces of many people whom we have known in our past pastoral labors. Those faces of the humble folk with their simple piety are always faces of triumph, but they are also almost always accompanied by the cross. In contrast, the faces of the arrogant are always faces of defeat. They do not accept the cross; they want an easy resurrection. They separate what God has united. They want to be like God. The spirit of defeat entices us to commit ourselves to losing causes. It knows nothing of the powerful tenderness that can be seen in the seriousness with which a child blesses himself or in the profundity with which an elderly woman says her prayers. That is faith, and that is the best vaccine against the spirit of defeat (1 John 4:4; 5:4-5).

> *For the love of God is this, that we obey his commandments. And his commandments are not burdensome, for whatever is born of God conquers the world. And this is the victory that conquers the world, our faith. Who is it that conquers the world but the one who believes that Jesus is the Son of God?* (1 John 5:4-5)

ANOTHER TEMPTATION is wanting to separate the wheat from the weeds too quickly. Priests have a privileged experience in hearing confessions. There we see much misery, but there also we behold the best of human hearts in the person who has repented. The penitent is one who is human plain and simply. Sometimes the priest can be stern with the faithful in his preaching, but it is much more difficult for him to be harsh in the confessional. There the wheat cannot be easily separated from the weeds, and God is present there. Confession also gives us a sense of time because it is impossible to force the pace of any human process. And that's the way life is: purity does not exist only in God; there is also purity in human beings. God is not a far-off deity that does not get involved in the world; rather, "he became sin," Saint Paul tells us. The structures of this world are not essentially sinful—that is Manichaeism. The wheat and the weeds grow all together willy-nilly, and perhaps our humble mission consists in nothing more than carefully protecting the wheat while leaving the reaping of the weeds to the angels.

ANOTHER TEMPTATION is to prefer head-values to heart-values. That should not be the case. Only the heart unifies and integrates. Intellect without a sense of piety tends to divide. The heart unites ideas with reality, time with space, life with death and with eternity. The temptation is to dislodge intellect from the place where God our Lord put it. He gave it to us so that we could clarify faith. God did not create human intelligence so that we could set ourselves up as judges of all things. It is a light that has only been lent to us, a mere reflection. Our intellect is not the light of the world; it is simply a flash for illuminating our faith. The worst thing that can happen is for human beings to let themselves be dragged along by the "lights" of reason. They easily become ignorant intellectuals or carefree "sages." The true mission of our minds is to discover the seeds of the Word within humanity, the *logoi spermatikoi*.

FAITH IS SOMETHING we need to ask for. God forbid that we should fail to be importunate with God and with his saints. One of the most refined forms of arrogance consists in claiming that prayer of petition is inferior to other forms of prayer. Only when we become beggars do we realize that we are creatures. When we don't honor the faith of humble folk, who can teach us how to ask for what we need, then we think that what saves us is pure faith; but that is empty faith, a faith devoid of all religion and all piety. In such a state, we are unable to interpret religious experience. Our intellects go astray with their feeble lights, and we resort to explaining the truth of faith with slogans borrowed from cultural ideologies. We are transformed into something like modern Quietists, but we substitute the notion of "faith alone saves" with more trendy formulations such as "justice alone saves" (but with an idea of justice that has no history and seems to start from scratch) or "risk alone saves" (which means not relying on any consciousness of history or any memory of the path that has been trod). Or else we talk about "faith as commitment" and claim that "only committed faith saves" (where commitment is visualized in terms of risk, novelty, etc., and faith is seen as feeble and in need of adjectives to make it stronger). I mention these just as examples, and perhaps I'm caricaturing them a bit. What is important is to recognize that these concrete formulations diminish the role of faith (see *Evangelii Nuntiandi*, 35). What is more, they constitute a confession of weakness: the weakness of those who do not believe that their faith can "move mountains," the weakness of those who fear that their faith is ineffective. Those who are "strong in faith" know exactly where faith is effective: it is effective where the evil one is overcome (1 John 2:14).

> *I write to you, children,*
> *because you know the Father.*
> *I write to you, fathers,*
> *because you know him who is from the beginning.*
> *I write to you, young people,*
> *because you are strong*
> *and the word of God abides in you,*
> *and you have overcome the evil one.* (1 John 2:14)

PERHAPS IN THIS MEDITATION, as we seek the means to recover the faith of our ancestors in order to hand it over intact and fruitful to our children, we do well to recall the Catholic image of our God. Rather than being a distant deity, God is the Father who accompanies all growth; he is the daily bread that nourishes; he is the merciful one who is near at hand in the moments when the enemy would exploit his children. God is the Father who gives his children what they request if it is appropriate; but whether he grants it or not, he is always affectionate toward them. If we accept the reality that God expresses himself within our human limits, then we should also accept the limits of our own pastoral expression. Our honest limitations distance us from the ideas of those who think they have the key to the world, those who know nothing of waiting patiently and working hard, and those who are easily swayed by hysteria and illusion. Jesus, who by his incarnation proclaims that God expresses himself in limited ways, desired to share the life of human beings, and that is redemption. What saves us is not just "the death and resurrection of Christ" but Christ incarnate, Christ being born, Christ fasting, preaching, healing, dying, and rising. The miracles performed, the consolations offered, all the words pronounced by Jesus have saving power (see *Evangelii Nuntiandi, 6*). Christ wanted to show us that syntheses are fashioned; they don't come ready made. He wanted to teach us that serving God's holy and faithful people means accompanying them as we day by day announce salvation; it does not mean getting lost in visions of unattainable peaks that we don't even have the strength to climb ourselves.

IN SUMMARY, THEN, we are confronted with two rival projects. The first is the project of our faith that recognizes God as Father; this is the project that works for justice and makes us all brothers and sisters. The other project is the one proposed to us by the enemy acting as an angel of light; it is the project of the absent God, where humans prey on humans and the law of the strongest prevails: *homo homini lupus.* Which project will I choose? Am I able to distinguish one from the other? If I realize that I cannot discern between them, will I be astute enough to defend myself?

THAT IS WHY our identity as persons of faith involves our belonging to a body; it is not just a matter of affirming our isolated conscience. Baptism means belonging to the institutional Church. Our very existence is related to our belonging. Consequently, our religious sense of belonging will seek out unifying symbols like the Virgin and the saints rather than simply trying to satisfy our individual consciences. And here we take a further step: our faith will be militant, and militant in a way that is fully conscious of the enemy; our aim will be to defend the whole body and not just myself alone. All this gives us a sense of realism: people are known by the struggles they wage, but to the extent that they are ignorant of the reasons for our struggle, their efforts are lost. The first evangelizers on this continent gave the Native Americans knowledge of why they should engage in struggle. Our work as pastors should not neglect this aspect of our faith: we should help people to learn the real reasons for their struggle.

WE SAID THAT along with this militant aspect, our faith also has a hierophantic dimension: contact with the holy. This is different from magical sacramentalism. It involves profound confidence in the power of God that becomes history through sacramental signs. It means making present in our day the specific grace of the incarnation: that physical contact with the Lord who "went about doing good and healing all." The tactic of the enemy is to squelch every combative spirit and cut off all contact with the holy so that our faith ends up devoid of discipline and respect. Indeed, it is only by discipline and respect, which are direct consequences of our faith, that we will able to discern what territories are best for our preaching, for our service of faith, for our promotion of justice.

For Prayer and Reflection

By way of conclusion and as a guide for reflection and prayer, we might ask ourselves what part the faith of our ancestors plays in my life as a pastor:

1. Do I confirm my people in their faith in God the Almighty Father, conscious that in this way I am also confirming the project of the just God?

2. Do I believe in the revolutionary nature of tenderness and affection each time I behold the Virgin or speak about her? Am I convinced that the warmth of hearth and home has a part to play in our project of justice?

3. Am I a pastor who is importunate before God the Father, recognizing him as all-powerful Father who is also all-loving in caring for his faithful people?

4. Do I consciously belong to a body by affirming those unifying symbols—such as doctrine, images, and sacraments—whose religious nature makes them efficacious or nearly efficacious (*Evangelii Nuntiandi*, 23)?

5. Do I have a consciousness of sin that leads me to repentance and the preaching of the commandments? Or have I opted for an ethical doctrine that preaches self-sufficiency?

6. Am I faithful to the mandate of the Church that sends us "to preach not [our] own selves or [our] personal ideas (2 Cor 4:5), but a Gospel of which [we are not] the absolute masters and owners, to dispose of it as [we] wish, but a Gospel of which [we] are the ministers, in order to pass it on with complete fidelity" (*Evangelii Nuntiandi*, 15)?

AND SO WE CAN CONTINUE to question ourselves about our faith as pastors of a people—or conversely, about our attitudes as persons in the clerical state. How deeply do we feel about belonging to the body of our holy Mother the Church, the Spouse of the Lord whom we should love and preserve united?

IN OUR REFLECTION as pastors of God's faithful people, we should realize that the truth by itself is not enough; what is needed is the truth in charity, for only this will build up the unity of the Church. In our adhesion to the best programs, let us not forget the body. Even if the Eucharist is still validly celebrated in certain cases of schism, we should remember that it still derives its power and its value from being the common table. It is our unavoidable duty in justice and as pastors to save people from schism and to help them toward greater communion and unity with Mother Church, remembering always that unity is superior to conflict.[2]

As we prepare for our ministry, let us ask for the grace to be men and women of faith, evangelizers of the faith we have received. Let us hope that in these exercises the Lord will make us understand and realize that evangelization "is not an optional contribution for the Church.... This message is something necessary. It is unique. It cannot be replaced. It does not permit either indifference, syncretism, or accommodation. It is a question of people's salvation. It is the beauty of the Revelation that it represents. It brings with it a wisdom that is not of this world. It is able to stir up by itself faith—faith that rests on the power of God (cf. 1 Cor 2:4-5)." Let us be fully aware that it requires that we, as apostles, "consecrate to it all [our] time and all [our] energies, and ... sacrifice for it, if necessary, our own lives" (*Evangelii Nuntiandi*, 5).

> *My speech and my proclamation were not with plausible words of wisdom, but with a demonstration of the Spirit and of power, so that your faith might rest not on human wisdom but on the power of God.* (1 Cor 2:4-5)

6. Called Despite Our Fears

Y OU WERE CALLED, and now you are preparing to receive the ministry. You may be thinking, "At last we've arrived!" You may experience this preparation from the perspective of the "big moment." This can be harmful for us because, without our being aware of it, it can lead us to relativize the ministry we are going to receive. To avoid doing that, our perspective should be that of the *chairos*, that is, of "God's time," which transcends all the "moments" of our existence. Here, then, our question should be: Where do I stand? What is the foundation of my vocation?

IT WILL HELP US to recall the words of Jesus: "On that day many will say to me, 'Lord, Lord, did we not prophesy in your name, and cast out demons in your name, and do many deeds of power in your name?' Then I will declare to them, 'I never knew you; go away from me, you evildoers.' Therefore, everyone who hears these words of mine and acts on them will be like a wise man who built his house on rock. The rain fell, the floods came, and the winds blew and beat on that house, but it did not fall, because it had been founded on rock. And everyone who hears these words of mine and does not act on them will be like a foolish man who built his house on sand. The rain fell, and the floods came, and the winds blew and beat against that house, and it fell—and great was its fall!" (Matt 7:22-27).

"AND HIS RUIN WAS GREAT." Those words remind me of the Lord's warning about the devil who, after being expelled from a possessed person, attempts to return with seven others so that "the last state of that person was worse than the first" (Luke 11:26). So again we ask the question: What is the foundation of my being?

FOR AN INITIAL MEDITATION, I propose that you consider the ministerial mission you will receive. Having been formally commissioned, you will be confronted yet again with this reality: you are created and saved by the same Jesus who now calls you to serve as ministers, and you will therefore need to exercise the discerning generosity required for greater service in this specific mission.

MUCH TO OUR CONSOLATION, scripture has preserved for us the special relation that was established between the Lord and those he sent on mission: Moses, Isaiah, Jeremiah, John the Baptist, Joseph, and so many others. All of them felt deeply their own inadequacy in the face of the Lord's request: "Who am I that I should go to Pharaoh and bring the children of Israel out of Egypt" (Exod 3:11); "Woe is me! For I am lost; for I am a man of unclean lips" (Isa 6:5); "Ah, Lord God! Behold, I do not know how to speak for I am only a youth" (Jer 1:6); "I need to be baptized by you, and do you come to me?" (Matt 3:14); even Joseph, who made plans "to dismiss Mary quietly" (Matt 1:19). There is the initial resistance, the inability to comprehend the magnitude of the call, the fear of the mission. This sign is from the good spirit, especially if it does not stop there but allows the Lord's strength to express itself through human weakness and to infuse that weakness with consistency and solidity. "I will be with you, and this shall be the sign that I have sent you:

when you have brought forth the people out of Egypt, you shall serve God upon this mountain" (Exod 3:12); "He touched my mouth and said: 'Behold, this has touched your lips; your guilt is taken away, and your sin forgiven'" (Isa 6:7); "Do not say, 'I am only a youth'; for to all to whom I send you, you shall go, and whatever I command you, you shall speak. Do not be afraid of them, for I am with you to deliver you" (Jer 1:7-8); "Let it be so now; for it is proper for us in this way to fulfill all righteousness" (Matt 3:15); "Joseph, son of David, do not be afraid to take Mary as your wife, for the child conceived in her is from the Holy Spirit" (Matt 1:20).

IN GIVING US A MISSION, the Lord grounds us; he gives us a solid foundation. And he does not do so with the perfunctory attitude of someone giving us an ordinary task to perform, but with the empowering might of his Spirit, so that our identity is sealed by the very way in which we are made to belong to that mission. Identity is tied up with belonging, and for us belonging means participating in what Jesus grounds—and Jesus grounds us in his Church, in his holy and faithful people, for the glory of the Father. Perhaps our fears and insecurities arise from the same feelings that moved Moses, Isaiah, John, and the other great figures to fight shy of their mission when it was first proposed to them. If so, then all we have to do is allow the Lord to speak to us and to help us place our fear, our pusillanimity, and our self-regard in their true perspective.

JESUS ESTABLISHED the kingdom of God. By his words and by his life he founded it once and for all. Belonging to that kingdom is for us a value we cannot refuse. Jesus establishes us as pastors of his people, and that is what he wants us to be. In speaking of our own foundations, we cannot prescind from this pastoral dimension of our lives. I think that for this meditation we may be helped by reviewing a pastoral document that summons us to *allow ourselves* to be established anew as pastors by Christ our Lord. I therefore propose that you read some passages from *Evangelii Nuntiandi*. Let us reflect on ourselves in the light of that teaching in order to draw some profit from it.

JESUS HIMSELF has a mission: "Going from town to town, preaching to the poorest—frequently the most receptive—the joyful news of the fulfillment of the promises and of the Covenant offered by God is the mission for which Jesus declares that he is sent by the Father. And all the aspects of his mystery—the Incarnation itself, his miracles, his teaching, the gathering together of the disciples, the sending out of the Twelve, the cross and the resurrection, the permanence of his presence in the midst of his own—were components of his evangelizing activity" (*Evangelii Nuntiandi*, 6). Through this evangelizing activity Christ "proclaims a kingdom, the kingdom of God; and this is so important that by comparison everything else becomes 'the rest,' that which is 'given in addition' (cf. Matt 6:31-33). Only the kingdom therefore is absolute and it makes everything else relative" (*Evangelii Nuntiandi*, 8). It is the Lord who establishes the kingdom.

Therefore do not worry, saying, "What will we eat?" or "What will we drink?" or "What will we wear?" For it is the Gentiles who strive for all these things; and indeed your heavenly Father knows that you need all these things. But strive first for the kingdom of God and his righteousness, and all these things will be given to you as well. (Matt 6:31-33)

We may continue this meditation by contemplating the different ways in which Jesus describes "the happiness of belonging to this kingdom—a paradoxical happiness that is made up of things that the world rejects (Matt 5:3-12)." We may further consider "the demands of the kingdom and its Magna Carta (Matthew 5–7), the heralds of the kingdom (Matthew 10), its mysteries (Matthew 13), its children (Matthew 18), the vigilance and fidelity demanded of whoever awaits its definitive coming (Matthew 24–25)" (*Evangelii Nuntiandi*, 8). The Lord establishes us in his kingdom. His Spirit makes us experience the delight of belonging to the kingdom, which constitutes the mystery of our identity.

> *"Blessed are the poor in spirit, for theirs is the kingdom of heaven.*
> *"Blessed are those who mourn, for they will be comforted.*
> *"Blessed are the meek, for they will inherit the earth.*
> *"Blessed are those who hunger and thirst for righteousness, for they will be filled.*
> *"Blessed are the merciful, for they will receive mercy.*
> *"Blessed are the pure in heart, for they will see God.*
> *"Blessed are the peacemakers, for they will be called children of God.*
> *"Blessed are those who are persecuted for righteousness' sake, for theirs is the kingdom of heaven.*
> *"Blessed are you when people revile you and persecute you and utter all kinds of evil against you falsely on my account. Rejoice and be glad, for your reward is great in heaven, for in the same way they persecuted the prophets who were before you."* (Matt 5:3-12)

JESUS ESTABLISHES A COMMUNITY that is both evangelized and evangelizing: "Those who sincerely accept the Good News through the power of this acceptance and of shared faith gather together in Jesus' name in order to seek together the kingdom, build it up, and live it. They make up a community that is in turn evangelizing. The command to the Twelve to go out and proclaim the Good News is also valid for all Christians, though in a different way. It is precisely for this reason that Peter calls Christians 'a people set apart to sing the praises of God' (1 Pet 2:9)" (*Evangelii Nuntiandi*, 13). "The task of evangelizing all people constitutes the essential mission of the Church. It is a task and mission which the vast and profound changes of present-day society make all the more urgent. Evangelizing is in fact the grace and vocation proper to the Church, her deepest identity. She exists in order to evangelize, that is to say, in order to preach and teach, to be the channel of the gift of grace, to reconcile sinners with God, and to perpetuate Christ's sacrifice in the Mass, which is the memorial of his death and glorious resurrection" (*Evangelii Nuntiandi*, 14).

By virtue of our vocation and our identity as an evangelizing community, we allow ourselves to be summoned "to proclaim with authority the Word of God, to assemble the scattered People of God, to feed this People with the signs of the action of Christ which are the sacraments, to set this People on the road to salvation, to maintain it in that unity of which we are, at different levels, active and living instruments, and unceasingly to keep this community gathered around Christ faithful to its deepest vocation" (*Evangelii Nuntiandi*, 68).

Our mission, then—the mission that frightens us and makes us offer excuses like the ones we hear from the lips of the reluctant prophets in the scriptures—is to evangelize, to shepherd the faithful people of God. And that mission establishes us in our vocation. In calling us to that mission, Jesus gives us solidity in the depths of our hearts: he establishes us as pastors and makes that our identity. In our visits to the sick, in our administration of the sacraments, in our teaching of the catechism, and in all the rest of our priestly activity, we are collaborating with Christ in establishing Christian hearts. At the same time and by that same means, that is, by the work we do, the Lord is establishing and rooting our hearts in his own.

THIS COMMUNITY that Jesus establishes "places human beings objectively in relation with the plan of God, with his living presence and with his action; the Church thus causes an encounter with the mystery of divine paternity that bends down toward humanity. In other words, our religion effectively establishes with God an authentic and living relationship" (*Evangelii Nuntiandi*, 53). A vital element for our task of establishing Christian hearts is the anointing that comes from direct experience of the faithfulness of the Lord of history. If our theology is to establish hearts and if it is itself to be established by the Lord, then it must be devout, but not with the kind of devotion that results from superficial attitudes born of prior reflection or study. No, the devotion to which I refer is a basic element for understanding our theology and what we teach. It is life. When we feel the presence of God in our daily life, we cannot help but say, "God is here," and when we feel God present, the first thing we must do is get down on our knees. Then the human intellect tries to understand and explain how God is present—that is the meaning of *fides quaerens intellectum,* faith seeking understanding. And consider the stories we've heard of those saints who studied theology on their knees. We may be helped also by the Pope's reasoning when he states that true evangelization includes "the preaching of the mystery of evil and of the active search for good. It likewise includes the preaching—and this is always urgent—of the search for God himself through prayer which is principally that of adoration and thanksgiving, but also through communion with the visible sign of the encounter with God which is the Church of Jesus Christ; and this communion is in turn expressed by the application of those other signs of Christ living and acting in the Church which are the sacraments." In sum, we must not forget either the nature of what we're called to establish or the foundation on which we let ourselves be established by the Lord: "For in its totality, evangelization—over and above the preaching of a message—consists in the implantation of the Church, which does not exist without the driving force which is the sacramental life culminating in the Eucharist" (*Evangelii Nuntiandi*, 28).

IN SPEAKING OF what are called base communities, Paul VI outlines the criteria that Jesus wants for establishing his Church. These criteria can provide us light for our reflection today and help us examine our conscience. The basic foundational attitude involves being formed in the Church. What Jesus wants are people rooted and established in the Church. He wants men and women:

- "who seek their nourishment in the Word of God and do not allow themselves to be ensnared by political polarization or fashionable ideologies, which are ready to exploit their immense human potential";
- "who avoid the ever present temptation of systematic protest and a hypercritical attitude, under the pretext of authenticity and a spirit of collaboration";
- "who remain firmly attached to the local Church in which they are inserted, and to the universal Church, thus avoiding the very real danger of becoming isolated within themselves, then of believing themselves to be the only authentic Church of Christ, and hence of condemning the other ecclesial communities (and persons)";

- "who maintain a sincere communion with the pastors whom the Lord gives to his Church, and with the magisterium which the Spirit of Christ has entrusted to these pastors";
- "who never look on themselves as the sole beneficiaries or sole agents of evangelization—or even the only depositaries of the Gospel—but, being aware that the Church is much more vast and diversified, accept the fact that this Church becomes incarnate in other ways than through themselves";
- "who constantly grow in missionary consciousness, fervor, commitment, and zeal"; and
- "who show themselves to be universal in all things and never sectarian" (*Evangelii Nuntiandi*, 58).

THE LORD WHO ESTABLISHES us evokes in us the image of *Deus semper maior*, God always greater. Let us meditate and pray today on letting ourselves be established by the Lord. Let us meditate also, as the pastors we're going to be, on how God helps us in this mission we have been given of establishing Christian hearts. Let us recover the memory of the many zealous priests we've known who have seen the face of Christ. This memory will "strengthen our hearts" and keep us from being "carried away by all kinds of strange teachings" (Heb 13:9). Those doctrines establish nothing; rather they undermine the solid foundations of a priestly heart and provide no nourishment to God's faithful people. Indeed, they call to mind the reflections of Dante: "Christ did not say, 'Go and preach nonsense to the world,' to his first gathering, but gave them the true foundation. That, and only that, was on their lips so that they made the Gospels lance and shield in their fight to enkindle the faith."[3] Instead of being a shield and a lance, these seductive and disruptive doctrines starve the hearts of God's holy and faithful people, for "the sheep, knowing nothing, return from the pasture fed on air."[4]

For Prayer and Reflection

Let us strengthen our spirits by recalling the many pastors who have preceded us. To this end, it will help us to read again that exhortation from the letter to the Hebrews: "Therefore, since we are surrounded by so great a cloud of witnesses, let us also lay aside every weight and the sin that clings so closely, and let us run with perseverance the race that is set before us, looking to Jesus the pioneer and perfecter of our faith, who for the sake of the joy that was set before him endured the cross, disregarding its shame, and has taken his seat at the right hand of the throne of God. Consider him who endured such hostility against himself from sinners, so that you may not grow weary or lose heart. In your struggle against sin you have not yet resisted to the point of shedding your blood" (Heb 12:1-4).

7. Nurtured by the Church

JESUS ESTABLISHES THE CHURCH, and he establishes us within the Church. The mystery of the Church is closely united to the mystery of Mary, mother of God and mother of the Church. Mary brings us forth and cares for us, and the Church does also. Mary helps us grow, and the Church does also. And at the hour of death, the priest bids us farewell in the name of the Church and leaves us in the arms of Mary. She is "a woman clothed with the sun, with the moon under her feet, and on her head a crown of twelve stars" (Apoc 12:1). That is the Church and that is the modest Virgin that our faithful people venerate. That is why in speaking of the Church we need to feel the same devotion as we feel for the Virgin Mary. A favorite expression of Saint Ignatius was *Santa Madre Iglesia hierarchica*, "our holy Mother the hierarchical Church" (SpEx 353). This expression evokes three concepts that are linked to one another: holiness, fruitfulness, and discipline.

WE WERE BROUGHT FORTH for holiness within the body of our holy Mother the Church. Keeping ourselves firmly inserted in that holy body is the key to our apostolic fruitfulness and our calling to "be holy and immaculate in God's presence." The Church is holy: it is present to the world "as a sign—simultaneously obscure and luminous—of a new presence of Jesus, of his departure and of his permanent presence. She prolongs and continues him" (*Evangelii Nuntiandi*, 15). The Church's holiness is manifest in "the intimate life of this community—the life of listening to the Word and the apostles' teaching, of charity lived in a fraternal way, of sharing of bread (cf. Acts 2:42-46; 4:32-35; 5:12-16). This intimate life acquires its full meaning only when it becomes a witness, when it evokes admiration and conversion, and when it becomes the preaching and proclamation of the Good News" (*Evangelii Nuntiandi*, 15). The Church's holiness is not naïve, for she knows that "she is the People of God immersed in the world and often tempted by idols, and she always needs to hear the proclamation of the 'mighty works of God' (cf. Acts 2:11; 1 Pet 2:9) which converted her to the Lord; she always needs to be called together afresh by him and reunited" (*Evangelii Nuntiandi*, 15). The holy Church Fathers expressed this mystery of the Church's holiness by calling her *casta meretrix*, the "chaste prostitute." The Church's holiness is reflected in the face of Mary, the sinless one, the pure and spotless one, but she does not forget that she gathers in her bosom the children of Eve, mother of all us sinners.

> *They devoted themselves to the apostles' teaching and fellowship, to the breaking of bread and the prayers. Awe came upon everyone, because many wonders and signs were being done by the apostles. All who believed were together and had all things in common; they would sell their possessions and goods and distribute the proceeds to all, as any had need. Day by day, as they spent much time together in the temple, they broke bread at home and ate their food with glad and generous hearts.* (Acts 2:42-46)

There is a wealth of theological literature about holiness. In canonizing saints, the Church, with the unfailing assistance of the Spirit, uses criteria with which we are all familiar. In our clerical lingo, we often jokingly overuse the word "holy," such as when we say with a smile, "this holy house" or "these holy customs." But it is also true that when we are impressed with a person's virtues and want to pay tribute to them, we say, "This person is a saint." In doing so, we renounce our many idols and kneel down before the mystery of God and of his infinite goodness as revealed in a human person. Love and devotion for Holy Mother Church means love and devotion for her faithful children. In our Church, we have many saints with whom we deal on a daily basis: in our parish life, in the confessional, in spiritual direction. Sometimes I wonder about the real reasons for the bitter criticism of the Church, the censure of her many sins, the despondency we feel with respect to her. Are these negative attitudes perhaps not due to our being malnourished because we fail to take delight in the human holiness that surrounds us and reconciles us all? For it is by such holiness that God dwells in his body.

Holiness reveals itself in us through our desire to announce the Good News: "Our evangelizing zeal must spring from true holiness of life, and as the Second Vatican Council suggests, preaching must in turn make the preacher grow in holiness, which is nourished by prayer and above all by love for the Eucharist" (*Evangelii Nuntiandi*, 76). This is the nexus between the Church's holiness and her maternal nature, and it is also the nexus between our holiness as consecrated persons and our effectiveness in forming Christian hearts. Here we may reflect on the questions proposed to us by Paul VI, questions that we are all responsible for answering: "What is the state of the Church ten years after the Council? Is she firmly established in the midst of the world and yet free and independent enough to call for the world's attention? Does she testify to solidarity with people and at the same time to the divine Absolute? Is she more ardent in contemplation and adoration and more zealous in missionary, charitable, and liberating action? Is she ever more committed to the effort to search for the restoration of the complete unity of Christians, a unity that makes more effective the common witness, 'so that the world may believe'?" (*Evangelii Nuntiandi*, 76).

TALKING ABOUT HOLY MOTHER CHURCH makes us think of fertility. Often we become skeptical in hoping for fertility, like Sarah who laughed to herself when she was promised a child (Gen 18:9-15). Other times, in contrast, we become euphoric and set about quantifying and planning our productivity so assiduously that we end up repeating the sin of David, whose vanity impelled him to take a census of his people. The fecundity of the Gospel travels by different paths. It is always aware that the Lord never abandons us and that he fulfills his promise to be with us until the end of the world. This fecundity is paradoxical: it means being fruitful but at the same time never being fully aware of it—and yet not being unaware either! I remember the words of that indefatigable missionary of Patagonia, Father Matthias Crespí, who when he was old used to repeat, "My life has flown past," as if to say that it seemed to him that he had never done anything for the Lord. This is the fecundity of the dew that dampens everything without a sound. It is the fertility that comes from a faith that may ask for proofs but understands that those proofs can never be definitive. The only unfailing proof is to be found in the "passing of the Lord" who consoles us, who strengthens us in faith, and who places us in our mission as stewards who will faithfully await him "until he comes."

They said to him, "Where is your wife Sarah?" And he said, "There, in the tent." Then one said, "I will surely return to you in due season, and your wife Sarah shall have a son." And Sarah was listening at the tent entrance behind him. Now Abraham and Sarah were old, advanced in age; it had ceased to be with Sarah after the manner of women. So Sarah laughed to herself, saying, "After I have grown old, and my husband is old, shall I have plea-sure?" The LORD *said to Abraham, "Why did Sarah laugh, and say, 'Shall I indeed bear a child, now that I am old?' Is anything too wonderful for the* LORD? *At the set time I will return to you, in due season, and Sarah shall have a son." But Sarah denied, saying, "I did not laugh"; for she was afraid. He said, "Oh yes, you did laugh."'*

The Church is Mother; she brings forth children with the strength of the deposit of faith. She "is the depositary of the Good News to be proclaimed. The promises of the New Alli-ance in Jesus Christ, the teaching of the Lord and the apostles, the Word of life, the sources of grace and of God's loving kind-ness, the path of salvation—all these things have been entrusted to her. It is the content of the Gospel, and therefore of evange-lization, that she preserves as a precious living heritage, not in order to keep it hidden but to communicate it" (*Evangelii Nun-tiandi*, 15). The Church's mission, then, is to bring forth chil-dren, to give life. The Church brings forth her children in undy-ing fidelity to her Spouse for "she sends them out to preach: to preach not themselves or their personal ideas (cf. 2 Cor 4:5), but a Gospel of which neither she nor they are the absolute masters and owners, to dispose of it as they wish, but a Gospel of which they are the ministers, in order to pass it on with com-plete fidelity" (*Evangelii Nuntiandi*, 15). By her fidelity to her Spouse, who is supremely faithful, the Church teaches us how to be faithfully fruitful.

Wanting to be fruitful is a legitimate desire, but the Gospel has its own laws for determining the legitimacy of our activities.

It's as if someone were to tell us: you will be fruitful only if you carefully maintain your status as a hired worker, only if you seek to balance your hard work with a sense of your own uselessness, and ultimately only if you convince yourself that, after you till the earth and plant the seed, the watering and the harvest are pure grace—they belong to the Lord.

We should love the mystery of the Church's fertility as we love the mystery of Mary who is Virgin and Mother, and in light of that love we should love the mystery of our own unprofitable servanthood, but always with the hope that the Lord will pronounce over us those words, "Good and faithful servant."

OUR LOVE FOR THE CHURCH is a love that inserts us into a body, and this requires discipline. The same idea may be expressed in the phrase, "discerning charity." For a priest, indiscipline means lack of discernment, which always involves a lack of love. Discerning love will help us grow to be "fully conscious of belonging to a large community which neither space nor time can limit" (*Evangelii Nuntiandi*, 61). Our consciousness of belonging will make us understand that the mission of evangelizing on which we are sent "is for no one an individual and isolated act; it is one that is deeply ecclesial. When the most obscure preacher, catechist, or pastor in the most distant land preaches the Gospel, gathers his little community together, or administers a sacrament, even alone, he is carrying out an ecclesial act, and his action is certainly attached to the evangelizing activity of the whole Church by institutional relationships, but also by profound invisible links in the order of grace. This presupposes that he acts not in virtue of a mission which he attributes to himself or by a personal inspiration, but in union with the mission of the Church and in her name" (*Evangelii Nuntiandi*, 60). Our discipline is rooted in the fact that "no evangelizer is the absolute master of his evangelizing action, with a discretionary power to carry it out in accordance with individualistic criteria and perspectives; he always acts in communion with the Church and her pastors" (*Evangelii Nuntiandi*, 60).

Our belonging to the kingdom "cannot remain abstract and disincarnate; it reveals itself concretely by a visible entry into a community of believers: ... the Church, the visible sacrament of salvation" (*Evangelii Nuntiandi*, 23). We are called to "communion with the visible sign of the encounter with God which is the Church of Jesus Christ; and this communion is in turn expressed by the application of those other signs of Christ living and acting in the Church which are the sacraments" (*Evangelii Nuntiandi*, 28). Our belonging to the kingdom, then, must enter into the side of Christ suspended on the cross, for it is from there that his Spouse is born, the fruitful Mother of a well-disciplined body nourished by the sacraments. "There is thus a profound link between Christ, the Church, and evangelization. During the period of the Church that we are living in, it is she who has the task of evangelizing. This mandate is not accomplished without her, and still less against her" (*Evangelii Nuntiandi*, 16).

Discipline is not something decorative, nor is it an exercise in good manners. An undisciplined heart can end up producing the kind of "disruptive person" Saint Ignatius wrote about, for those who have not controlled their passions are often "disruptive." Persons who are undisciplined may sow division and disunion in the heart of a community or a diocese; using deceitful and pharisaical means, they seek to gain a few followers and create a situation of injustice. In presenting the theme of discipline in this way, I don't mean that we should engage in obsessive self-examination and penance before the Lord regarding our defects as pastors. That would be sterile introspection. Rather, the correct attitude is to place ourselves in prayer before the Lord, asking him insistently to pronounce over us that efficacious word that corrects us and bonds us to him: "Child, give me your heart."

My intention in this meditation has been to speak about love for our holy Mother, the hierarchical Church. We've already talked about the responsibility we have to be sons and daughters of the Church and at the same time to create Church. Our love for the Church should lead us to make manifest to the world her holiness, her loving fruitfulness, and her discipline, all of which flow from her being totally Christ's. The Council states it succinctly with the words, *Dei Verbum religiose audiens et fidenter proclamans*: the Church "religiously hears the Word of God and faithfully proclaims it." May our Lady, the Virgin Mother, obtain for us from the Lord the grace of a love that is holy, fruitful, and disciplined in accord with the Church.

For Prayer and Reflection

Reflecting once again on *Evangelii Nuntiandi* 60, let us end by meditating on our love for and our belonging to our Mother, the Church:

The observation that the Church has been sent out and given a mandate to evangelize the world should awaken in us two convictions.

The first is this: evangelization is for no one an individual and isolated act; it is one that is deeply ecclesial. When the most obscure preacher, catechist, or pastor in the most distant land preaches the Gospel, gathers his little community together, or administers a sacrament, even alone, he is carrying out an ecclesial act, and his action is certainly attached to the evangelizing activity of the whole Church by institutional relationships, but also by profound invisible links in the order of grace. This presupposes that he acts not in virtue of a mission that he attributes to himself or by a personal inspiration, but in union with the mission of the Church and in her name.

From this flows the second conviction: if each individual evangelizes in the name of the Church, who herself does so by virtue of a mandate from the Lord, no evangelizer is the absolute master of his evangelizing action, with a discretionary power to carry it out in accordance with individualistic criteria and perspectives; he acts in communion with the Church and her pastors.

We have remarked that the Church is entirely and completely evangelizing. This means that, in the whole world and in each part of the world where she is present, the Church feels responsible for the task of spreading the Gospel.

8. Cross and Mission

L ET US REFLECT TODAY on the profound solitude of the prophet Elijah (1 Kings 19:4). He had just completed an important mission by gaining victory over the prophets of Baal on Mount Carmel (1 Kings 18:20-40); but, despite his great success, he felt completely alone and was longing to die. In reality, his mission was still not finished, for he was being invited into an intimate encounter with the living God (1 Kings 19:9-14), an encounter that would make him apostolically fruitful (1 Kings 19:19-21). This was an extraordinary event, but it was one marked by an experience of abandonment and the cross. We might also be helped by meditating on the figure of Jonah, recalling the time when he went off selfishly by himself and desired to die because his human plans did not coincide with those of God (Jonah 4:1-11). These two great prophets had a bitter experience of abandonment and loneliness in the midst of the missions they were given. In different ways they resisted their calling, but they were gently impelled by God to keep moving forward. Let us ask for the grace to accept the dimension of the cross that is involved in every mission.

At that place he came to a cave, and spent the night there. Then the word of the LORD came to him, saying, "What are you doing here, Elijah?" He answered, "I have been very zealous for the LORD, the God of hosts; for the Israelites have forsaken your covenant, thrown

down your altars, and killed your prophets with the sword. I alone
am left, and they are seeking my life, to take it away.'"

He said, "Go out and stand on the mountain before the LORD,
for the LORD is about to pass by." Now there was a great wind, so
strong that it was splitting mountains and breaking rocks in pieces
before the LORD, but the LORD was not in the wind; and after the
wind an earthquake, but the LORD was not in the earthquake;
and after the earthquake a fire, but the LORD was not in the fire;
and after the fire a sound of sheer silence. When Elijah heard it,
he wrapped his face in his mantle and went out and stood at the
entrance of the cave. Then there came a voice to him that said,
"What are you doing here, Elijah?" He answered, "I have been
very zealous for the LORD, the God of hosts; for the Israelites have
forsaken your covenant, thrown down your altars, and killed your
prophets with the sword. I alone am left, and they are seeking my
life, to take it away." (1 Kings 19:9-14)

But this was very displeasing to Jonah, and he became angry. He
prayed to the LORD and said, "O LORD! Is not this what I said
while I was still in my own country? That is why I fled to Tarshish
at the beginning; for I knew that you are a gracious God and mer-
ciful, slow to anger, and abounding in steadfast love, and ready to
relent from punishing. And now, O LORD, please take my life from
me, for it is better for me to die than to live." And the LORD said,
"Is it right for you to be angry?" Then Jonah went out of the city
and sat down east of the city, and made a booth for himself there.
He sat under it in the shade, waiting to see what would become of
the city.

The LORD God appointed a bush, and made it come up over
Jonah, to give shade over his head, to save him from his discom-
fort; so Jonah was very happy about the bush. But when dawn
came up the next day, God appointed a worm that attacked the
bush, so that it withered. When the sun rose, God prepared a
sultry east wind, and the sun beat down on the head of Jonah so

*that he was faint and asked that he might die. He said, "It is better
for me to die than to live."*

*But God said to Jonah, "Is it right for you to be angry about the
bush?" And he said, "Yes, angry enough to die." Then the LORD
said, "You are concerned about the bush, for which you did not
labor and which you did not grow; it came into being in a night
and perished in a night. And should I not be concerned about
Nineveh, that great city, in which there are more than a hundred
and twenty thousand people who do not know their right hand
from their left, and also many animals?"* (Jonah 4:1-11)

A SPECIAL RELATION exists between the Lord and the person
he sends on a mission—recall here what we said in the meditation on our vocation. We cited the examples of Moses, Isaiah,
Jeremiah, John the Baptist, Joseph—all of them felt themselves
to be incompetent for the mission the Lord asked of them:
"Who am I that I should go to Pharaoh, and bring the children of Israel out of Egypt" (Exod 3:11); "Woe is me! For I am
lost; for I am a man of unclean lips (Isa 6:5); "Ah, Lord God!
Behold, I do not know how to speak for I am only a youth" (Jer
1:6); "I need to be baptized by you, and do you come to me?"
(Matt 3:14); even Joseph made plans "to dismiss Mary quietly"
(Matt 1:19). Such is the initial confusion and resistance, the
inability to comprehend the magnitude of the call, the fear of
the mission. This is a sign from the good spirit, especially if
it does not remain there but allows the Lord's strength to be
expressed through our weakness so that we are given consistency and a firm foundation: "I will be with you, and this shall
be the sign that I have sent you: when you have brought forth
the people out of Egypt, you shall serve God upon this mountain" (Exod 3:12); "He touched my mouth and said: 'Behold,
this has touched your lips; your guilt is taken away, and your sin
forgiven'" (Isa 6:7); "Do not say, 'I am only a youth'; for to all to

whom I send you, you shall go, and whatever I command you, you shall speak. Do not be afraid of them, for I am with you to deliver you" (Jer 1:7-8); "Let it be so now; for it is proper for us in this way to fulfill all righteousness" (Matt 3:15); "Joseph, son of David, do not be afraid to take Mary as your wife, for the child conceived in her is from the Holy Spirit" (Matt 1:20).

These experiences of our ancestors in the faith should encourage us greatly. When we realize we are chosen, we feel that the weight on us is too great, and we experience fear—in some cases even panic. That is the beginning of the cross. At the same time, we feel deeply drawn by the Lord who by his very summons seduces us to follow him with a fire burning in our heart (cf. Jer 20:7-18). These two feelings are joined together because since the days of the patriarchs they have prefigured the abandonment that Christ felt on the cross as he fulfilled the Father's will to the very end. The mission places us perforce upon the wood of the cross, for the cross is the sign that the mission has been received by the Spirit of God and not according to the flesh. In the solitude of the person sent on a mission, there is an initial divestment—"leaving all, they followed him" (Luke 5:27-28)—a divestment that will be consolidated through all of life, right up to old age: "When you grow old, you will stretch out your hands, and someone else will fasten a belt around you and take you where you do not wish to go" (John 21:18). When we accept a mission, there is a way in which we abandon everything; it is much like the experience of a dying person. Only when we enter into this experience of being "near death" will we understand the full extent of what is being asked of us, and only then will we discover the right road. "I tell you, unless a grain of wheat falls into the earth and dies, it remains just a single grain; but if it dies"—and this happens only when it is totally alone—"it bears much fruit" (John 12:24).

IN THE COUNSELS Jesus gives his disciples as he sends them out on mission, there are two series of warnings woven together. The first series refers to the struggle they'll have to wage and cautions them about the reality of their situation: "See, I am sending you out like sheep into the midst of wolves.... Beware of men, for they will hand you over to councils and flog you in their synagogues; and you will be dragged before governors and kings because of me, as a testimony to them and the Gentiles" (Matt 10:16-18). "Brother will betray brother to death, and a father his child, and children will rise against parents and have them put to death; and you will be hated by all because of my name. But the one who endures to the end will be saved" (Matt 10:21-22). "Do not think that I have come to bring peace to the earth; I have not come to bring peace, but a sword. For I have come to set a man against his father, and a daughter against her mother, and a daughter-in-law against her mother-in-law; and one's foes will be members of one's own household" (Matt 10:34-36). "Indeed, an hour is coming when those who kill you will think that by doing so they are offering worship to God" (John 16:2).

The second series of counsels contains encouragement and offers strength: "When they hand you over, do not worry about how you are to speak or what you are to say; for what you are to say will be given to you at that time; for it is not you who speak but the Spirit of your Father speaking through you" (Matt 10:19-20). "So have no fear of them" (Matt 10:26). "Do not fear those who kill the body but cannot kill the soul; rather fear him who can destroy both soul and body in hell" (Matt 10:28). "So do not be afraid; you are of more value than many sparrows" (Matt 10:31).

These two series of counsels, which capture something of both the fear and the fascination that the ancient patriarchs and prophets experienced when they were called, create the dialectic within which our mission is situated. Many years after this discourse of Jesus, the first Christians described as follows the special status of those who were sent on mission: "Thanks to faith they conquered kingdoms, administered justice, obtained promises, shut the mouths of lions, quenched raging fire, escaped the edge of the sword, won strength out of weakness, became mighty in war, put foreign armies to flight. Women recovered their dead by resurrection. Others were tortured, refusing to accept release, in order to obtain a better resurrection. Others suffered mocking and flogging, and even chains and imprisonment. They were stoned to death, they were sawn in two, they were killed by the sword; they went about in skins of sheep and goats, destitute, persecuted, tormented—of whom the world was not worthy. They wandered in deserts and mountains, and in caves and holes in the ground" (Heb 11:33-38).

All this is true because the mission of the apostle participates totally in the mission of Jesus Christ, the Son of God: "Whoever welcomes you welcomes me, and whoever welcomes me welcomes the one who sent me" (Matt 10:40). Every person who is sent on a mission is caught up in the dialectic between the promise of persecution and death and the promise of consolation because such was the experience of Christ, who was sent by the Father, died on the cross out of obedience, and then—because God "would not allow his chosen one to see corruption"—was constituted Lord. By contemplating the *Kyrios* Jesus, the Lordship of Christ, we can understand the true dimensions of our vocation to mission. What the letter to the Hebrews proclaims so boldly is no anachronism: "By faith Moses, when he was grown up, refused to be called a son of Pharaoh's daughter, choosing rather to share ill-treatment with the people of God than to enjoy the fleeting pleasures of sin. He considered abuse suffered for the Christ to be greater wealth than the treasures of Egypt" (Heb 11:24-26). A person receives a mission for two purposes: to be with the Lord (unto the cross) and to preach. These two aspects of mission are inseparable, as we see clearly from Jesus' calling of his apostles (Mark 3:13-19). Our being with the Lord will be genuine only if it leads to preaching, and our preaching will be authentic only if it derives from our being with Christ on the cross. In choosing disciples, Jesus undertakes a mission, and we are now the caretakers of that mission—but not the owners, so as to be able to shape it to our liking. We undertake this mission according to the *formalitas Christi*, just as Christ would.

> *He went up the mountain and called to him those whom he wanted, and they came to him. And he appointed twelve, whom he also named apostles, to be with him, and to be sent out to proclaim the message, and to have authority to cast out demons. So he appointed the twelve: Simon (to whom he gave the name Peter); James son of Zebedee and John the brother of James (to whom he gave the name Boanerges, that is, Sons of Thunder); and Andrew, and Philip, and Bartholomew, and Matthew, and Thomas, and James son of Alphaeus, and Thaddeus, and Simon the Cananaean, and Judas Iscariot, who betrayed him. Then he went home.* (Mark 3:13-19)

THE MISSION PLACES US in the same place as Christ Jesus, on the cross: "If the world hates you, be aware that it hated me before it hated you" (John 15:18). "Remember the word that I said to you. 'Servants' are not greater than their master. If they persecuted me, they will persecute you.... But they will do all these things to you on account of my name because they do not know him who sent me" (John 15:20-21; cf. Matt 10:24-25). When a follower complains of the difficulty of discipleship, Jesus will not respond by telling him that he was acting freely when he decided: "You followed me because you chose me freely and because you wanted to." While such a statement may be true, it is not a response that imparts strength at the moment of crucifixion. The Lord's actual response will point rather to the undertaking of the mission: "You did not choose me, but I chose you. And I appointed you to bear fruit, fruit that will last" (John 15:16). This referral to what gives us grounding and establishes us as persons "sent on a mission" can be resolved in only one way: by seeking through every means possible not to come down from the cross, by taking on the *formalitas Christi:* "Let the same mind be in you that was in Christ Jesus, who, though he was in the form of God, did not regard equality with God as something to be exploited, but emptied himself, taking the form of a slave, being born in human likeness. And being found in human form, he humbled himself and became obedient to the point of death—even death on a cross" (Phil 2:5-8). This is not a simple counsel, for Paul is speaking here with a depth of conviction that is expressed majestically: "If then there is any encouragement in Christ, any consolation from love, any sharing in the Spirit, any compassion and sympathy ..." (Phil 2:1).

The true apostle is one who has died and been buried with Christ and no longer belongs to himself (Rom 6:3-4, 8; Col 2:12). Any other path means being ashamed of Christ, and for such a person is reserved the eschatological shame of the Lord: "Those who are ashamed of me and of my words in this adulterous and sinful generation, of them the Son of Man will also be ashamed when he comes in the glory of the Father with his holy angels" (Mark 8:38). The cross, then, takes on a dimension of testimony, but it is also the place to which we are led when our testimony is authentic.

Do you not know that all of us who have been baptized into Christ Jesus were baptized into his death? Therefore we have been buried with him by baptism into death, so that, just as Christ was raised from the dead by the glory of the Father, so we too might walk in newness of life.... But if we have died with Christ, we believe that we will also live with him. (Rom 6:3-4, 8)

When you were buried with Christ in baptism, you were also raised with him through faith in the power of God, who raised him from the dead. (Col 2:12)

I WANT TO MENTION now two attitudes that clearly reveal that a person has assumed the Lord's mission on the cross. The two attitudes are apostolic courage and constancy, and they go together. They characterize the person who, having received the mission, seeks to have the same sentiments as the Lord who gives the mission. The defects opposed to these attitudes are presumption and baseless fear. One woman devoted to the Church spoke thus: "Fearful people will never make great progress in virtue, nor will they ever accomplish anything great; those who are presumptuous will not persevere till the end." Both attitudes, courage and constancy (*parrhēsia* and *hypomonē* in Greek) go together and reinforce one another, as the letter to the Hebrews indicates: "Do not, therefore, abandon that confidence [*parrhēsia*] of yours; it brings a great reward. For you need endurance [*hypomonē*], so that when you have done the will of God, you may receive what was promised. For yet 'in a very little while, the one who is coming will come and will not delay; but my righteous one will live by faith. My soul takes no pleasure in anyone who shrinks back.' But we are not among those who shrink back and so are lost, but among those who have faith and so are saved" (Heb 10:35-39). Cowardice means shrinking back toward perdition. When we lack constancy and patience, the very first challenge makes us want to come down from the cross in order to fight our own battle and not the Lord's. Courage (*parrhēsia*) supposes constancy (*hypomonē*); it makes us persons who strive after an ideal. To embrace the cross, we need courage, and, to remain on it, we need constancy. There are Christians who are "strong" in undertaking apostolic works, but when difficulties arise, they fade away: they do not know patience. Suffering with Christ and for his sake is what most bolsters our courage. These two virtues, then, patience and courage, are eminently apostolic. Both are forged on the cross and are the clearest sign that we have taken on our mission with the *formalitas Christi,* just as Christ would.

In the course of these reflections, we have seen the intimate relationship that exists between "receiving the mission" and "being nailed on a cross." The Christian mission we receive from Christ our Lord cannot be conceived outside the ambit of the cross, much less apart from the cross. When we forget this truth, we become triumphalist and fail to remain always open. The triumphalist attitude appears mostly "as an angel of light" in our choice of pastoral methods, but it can always be reduced to an invitation to come down from the cross: "You who would destroy the temple and build it in three days, save yourself! If you are the Son of God, come down from the cross!" (Matt 27:40). In contrast, those who share in the cross have no need to bolster their activities with triumphalism because they know that the cross itself is triumph—and therefore their only hope: *Salve Crux, spes unica!* When they face challenges that may provoke in them unseemly pastoral anxieties, they will respond only with the sign of Jonah. They will not come down from the cross: they will remain there with the same patience and courage that Jesus showed, and they will continue on with the mission that was given them.

For Prayer and Reflection

In light of the passage we have seen from the letter to the Hebrews, 10:35-39, let us take a look at our lives and ask ourselves: What are the crosses that I want to come down from now in my life?

9. The Courage of the Cross

Our belonging to the Church acquires its basic stability in the very place where the Church is born: on the cross. That is where the definitive "Yes" of obedience was pronounced, overcoming the primordial disobedience. That is where the "ancient serpent," instigator of rebellion and sin, was cast into the abyss once and for all. That is where our belonging becomes filial because we are made sons and daughters in the Son. And there at the foot of the cross, participating in Jesus' total dereliction, is the Mother who brings us forth as God's sons and daughters. This is what we experience when we seek to ground our hearts by renewing our sense of belonging to the Church. Because the Church comes to birth and has its foundation in the cross, every other foundation will also share in the cross. In every ecclesial foundation there is a cross, for the very hour of the Church's birth coincides with the hour of Lord's death.

The cross is the "final battle" of Jesus: in the cross is to be found the definitive victory. Considering this war of God that takes place on the cross, we need to speak now of the militant sense our lives take on if we commit them to the Lord. It is impossible to conceive the "essence" of our service to Jesus Christ without this dimension. In our pastoral work, we will always be tempted to avoid the struggle or to hedge our bets; or else we will confuse the whys and wherefores of the struggle, the "how" and the "when." How many men and women have become entangled in their pastoral action because they did not know how to struggle "divinely"? How many have confused the battle with the bustle? And how many, in the midst of the daily dust-ups, have failed to recognize who the enemy really was and have ended up wounding one another? Still others, fearful of any struggle and seeking a counterfeit peace, have consumed their lives in a quietude that is as unfruitful as it is ineffective.

Let us ask the Lord on this day for the grace to appreciate fully the militant aspect of our apostolic lives. Let us seek the grace that frees us from the foolish attitude that makes us "play at peace" as well as "play at war." If we grasp the militant sense of our apostolic lives, then we will recognize that the struggle in our hearts will involve a search for the cross; if we truly want to serve God, then the cross will be seen as the sole theological locus of victory. This struggle will require that we be able to offer and receive criticism and that we offer ourselves generously for the most serious and most grueling work. Walking along this road leads us, as it led the Lord, to Jerusalem.

Jesus himself points out to us the difficulties of the Christian way of life, especially for those who want to follow the Lord more closely: "Whoever loves father or mother more than me is not worthy of me; and whoever loves son or daughter more than me is not worthy of me; and whoever does not take up the cross and follow me is not worthy of me. Those who find their life will lose it, and those who lose their life for my sake will find it" (Matt 10:37-39). Following Jesus means deciding to walk in his footsteps, and that guarantees the cross. Such a path is far removed from the concessions made by those whose divided hearts dream of peaceful harmony between the Lord of glory and the spirit of the world!

THE HOSTILITY EXPERIENCED by those who decide to walk in the footsteps of Christ our Lord becomes manifest in frequent persecution. When authentic, Christian service banishes all reveries about living our lives according to the sweet sentiments of a pastoral poem. Saint Ignatius Loyola offered the following counsel in a letter: "Experiencing difficulty is nothing exceptional; rather, it is what ordinarily happens in matters of much importance for the divine service and glory.... The contradictions we saw before and those we see now are nothing new for us; in view of our experience in other places, the hopes we have that Christ our Lord will be well served in this city are all the greater because of the obstacles put in our way by those who are always attempting to obstruct the service of God. For the enemy moves people who have good intentions but bad information to reject that which they do not understand."

Sometimes the difficulties go beyond simple "obstacles" and take the shape of true persecution. The experience of persecution is normal in our Christian existence, something we should undergo with the humility of the unprofitable servant who has no desire to take on the identity of victim. The early Christians underwent a progressive purification in the way they conceived of persecution. At first, they saw the persecutions as a kind of punishment that the Jews were inflicting on them as messengers of the Lord (Matt 23:29-36; Acts 7:51-52). Later on, the persecutions against the Christians were seen in an eschatological context. They were viewed as a form of judgment on human deeds and so took on an importance they did not possess before. Persecution was understood to be "filling up the measure" (1 Thess 2:15-16) until the moment when the Son of Man would come to judge humankind and to separate the good from the wicked (see Matt 5:10-12). Still later, at a third stage of reflection, those undergoing persecution were seen as being invited to suffer and die "for the sake of the Son of Man" (Luke 6:22; cf. Mark 8:35; 13:8-13; Matt 10:39) and, ultimately, to imitate his passion (see Matt 10:22-23; Mark 10:38). The martyrdom of Stephen corresponds to this last conception (Acts 6:8–7:60); we would do well to reread this passage slowly at some time during the day. Stephen does not die simply for Christ's sake; he dies with him and like him. And this participation in the very mystery of the passion of Jesus Christ is the basis of the martyrs' faith: dying in this way, the martyrs affirm by their own surrender that death did not have the last word in the life of Jesus.

> *For nation will rise against nation, and kingdom against kingdom; there will be earthquakes in various places; there will be famines. This is but the beginning of the birth pangs.*
>
> *As for yourselves, beware; for they will hand you over to councils; and you will be beaten in synagogues; and you will stand before governors and kings because of me, as a testimony to them. And the good news must first be proclaimed to all nations. When they bring you to trial and hand you over, do not worry beforehand about what you are to say; but say whatever is given you at that time, for it is not you who speak, but the Holy Spirit. Brother will betray brother to death, and a father his child, and children will rise against parents and have them put to death; and you will be hated by all because of my name. But the one who endures to the end will be saved.* (Mark 13:8-13)

Similarly, we experience in our own lives these three manners of experiencing difficulties and persecutions. It is when we live according to the third manner that we find ourselves living in closest contact with Christ. That is why the death of Christ is in a way the basic "a priori" of every Christian attitude: "The love of Christ urges us on, because we are convinced that one has died for all; therefore all have died. And he died for all so that those who live might live no longer for themselves but for him who died and was raised for them" (2 Cor 5:14-15). When we contemplate Christ on the cross, we become aware that we owe our lives to him because—and this is the only reason—he handed over his life so that we might live. Our gratitude, if it is genuine, places us on the same plane, for we hand over our lives as Jesus did. Consequently, every attempt to define Christian attitudes completely in terms of "civil behavior" turns out to be pretentious. The response to Christ's generosity should not be simply a courteous, conventional "many thanks." Christ's surrender calls for us to give our lives, and our lives are given by following the way the Lord marked out on the cross. Our gratitude to him should encompass all that we are. This "giving thanks" with our lives becomes real every day in the celebration of the Eucharist, which is the "thanksgiving" par excellence and that at the same time calls to mind the passion of the Lord. The Eucharist grounds the Church, nourishes her, and keeps her alive. "For as often as you eat this bread and drink this cup, you proclaim the Lord's death until he come" (1 Cor 11:26). In celebrating the Eucharist, we make present the very hour of the Church's birth, which coincides with the hour of the Lord's death. Our way of giving thanks is to assume that death and take on its very form. This is what ultimately determines the shape of our belonging to the Church.

AT THE SAME TIME, the death of Christ is the beginning of true glory. "Was it not necessary that the Messiah should suffer these things and then enter into his glory?" (Luke 24:26). This is the glory that Stephen saw before he was killed (Acts 7:55), the glory that is promised to us, the glory with which the tribulations of this life are not worth comparing (Rom 8:18). It is the glory that Jesus longs for and asks the Father to give him: "So now, Father, glorify me in your own presence" (John 17:5). The glory of Jesus is the hour of his cross: "The hour has come for the Son of Man to be glorified.... Unless a grain of wheat falls into the ground and dies, it remains just a single grain; but if it dies, it bears much fruit" (John 12:23-24). So that there will be no doubt about the relation that exists between this glory and the loss of life, the Lord continues: "Those who love their life will lose it, and those who hate their life in this world will keep it for eternal life" (John 12:25). The apostles understood that the glory of Jesus was his cross, but they understood this only later. That is why John says of the disciples: "When Jesus was glorified, then they remembered that these things had been written of him" (John 12:16).

It is Saint Paul who most audaciously assumes this glory of the cross as the glory of his own life: "May I never boast of anything except the cross of our Lord Jesus Christ, by which the world has been crucified to me, and I to the world" (Gal 6:14). Glorying in the cross of Jesus Christ and glorying in the Lord (cf. 2 Cor 10:17) are ways of giving praise, and they constitute the best defense against the worldly-wise enemies of the cross of Christ, those who speak on their own authority and seek their own glory (John 7:18), who glorify one another (John 5:44), and who prefer human glory to the glory of God (John 12:42-43). The Lord himself states that he does not seek human glory: "I do not accept glory from human beings" (John 5:41). It is the radical clinging to the cross that will ultimately become the criterion of truth for any true follower of Jesus. Our Christian boasting, insofar as it passes through the cross and gets its bearings from the cross, is purified of every trace of vanity; it is no longer vainglorious for it focuses on its sublime origin, which it delights in calling the Lord of glory (1 Cor 2:8).

Many, even of the authorities, believed in him. But because of the Pharisees they did not confess it, for fear that they would be put out of the synagogue; for they loved human glory more than the glory that comes from God. (John 12:42-43)

EXULTING IN THE CROSS of the Lord implies a vivid, constant recalling of the cross. "Remember our Lord Jesus Christ" was the oft-repeated counsel to the disciples. The Lord himself prepares his followers for his passion: "I have told you this before it occurs so that when it does occur, you may believe" (John 14:29). Remembering the cross of the Lord brings us consolation, confirmation, and peace in the divine service. By recalling this glory of the Lord and exulting in it, we not only reject vain and frivolous forms of glory but also rely on the consolation of that memory to build up our strength for the time when our own fundamental option for the cross is truly put to the test. The apostles kept alive the memory of the cross as a glorious reality, and they were therefore able to interpret the signs of the times and so prepare believers to deal with them: "Beloved, do not be surprised at the fiery ordeal that is taking place among you to test you, as though something strange were happening to you. But rejoice insofar as you are sharing Christ's sufferings, so that you may also be glad and shout for joy when his glory is revealed. If you are reviled for the name of Christ, you are blessed, because the spirit of glory, which is the Spirit of God, is resting on you. But let none of you suffer as a murderer, a thief, a criminal, or even as a mischief-maker. Yet if any of you suffers as a Christian, do not consider it a disgrace, but glorify God because you bear this name.... Therefore, let those suffering in accordance with God's will entrust themselves to a faithful Creator, while continuing to do good" (1 Pet 4:12-19).

This final phrase brings to our minds the attitude of the

heart of Christ: surrendering oneself into the hands of God, without seeking to control the results of crises and storms. Such surrender is resolute but in no way naïve; it is the surrender that Jesus himself, even before his death, recommended to his disciples: "When they hand you over, do not worry about how you are to speak or what you are to say; for what you are to say will be given to you at that time; for it is not you who speak but the Spirit of your Father speaking through you" (Matt 10:19-20). Such surrender implies confidence in the fatherhood of God, for it does not receive an immediate answer and it does not exempt us from the anguish of suffering. Jesus himself was tested by the silence of God, a silence that can sorely try our faith when we hear the heart-rending cry that is the ultimate test: "Father, why have you forsaken me?" (Matt 27:46).

THE MEMORY OF THE CROSS could be called the domain of Christian existence. Outside this domain, we are unable to determine properly how to practice our ministry or what pastoral means to use. Outside this domain, we run the risk of seeking solutions that prescind from the cross, either because we lead lukewarm lives (neither hot nor cold) or because we use pastoral forms that lack grounding in the human and the divine. In contrast, deciding for the way of Jesus means surrender into the hands of the Father—and readiness to be abandoned by the Father.

Both the experience of surrendering ourselves into the Father's hands and the sense of being abandoned by the Father are part of every cross, and they help us understand the eschatological nature of this "foundation stone" of our Christian life. In the cross, we must lose everything in order to gain everything. The cross means selling everything in order to buy the precious pearl or the field with the buried treasure. It means losing everything: "Those who lose their life for my sake will find it" (Matt 16:25; Mark 8:34-35; Luke 17:33). By losing everything, we seek new life, and our very existence will be a new gift, but at the cost of losing everything. There is no room here for the holding back or the foot-dragging we see in the story of Ananias and Sapphira (Acts 5:1-11). Nobody is forcing us. We are being freely invited, but the invitation is to "all or nothing." We are being invited to have no place to lay our head, even though the foxes have their holes; we are being invited to let the dead bury their dead; we are being invited to become daily more convinced that "no one who puts a hand to the plow and looks back is fit for the kingdom of God" (Luke 9:57-62).

> *He called the crowd with his disciples, and said to them, "If any want to become my followers, let them deny themselves and take up their cross and follow me. For those who want to save their life will lose it, and those who lose their life for my sake, and for the sake of the gospel, will save it." (Mark 8:34-35)*

> *As they were going along the road, someone said to him, "I will follow you wherever you go." And Jesus said to him, "Foxes have holes, and birds of the air have nests; but the Son of Man has nowhere to lay his head." To another he said, "Follow me." But he said, "Lord, first let me go and bury my father." But Jesus said to him, "Let the dead bury their own dead; but as for you, go and proclaim the kingdom of God." Another said, "I will follow you, Lord; but let me first say farewell to those at my home." Jesus said to him, "No one who puts a hand to the plough and looks back is fit for the kingdom of God." (Luke 9:57-62)*

The cross is what marks out the militant dimension of our existence. With the cross it is impossible to negotiate, impossible to dialogue: the cross is either embraced or rejected. If we decide to reject it, our life will remain trapped in our own hands, encased in the petty confines of our short horizons. If we embrace the cross, then by that very decision we lose our life; we leave it in the hands of God, in the time of God, and it will be given back to us in a different form. During our time of prayer, we would do well to reflect on this crossroads that decide our future. Let us humbly ask the Lord of glory that he consider us worthy to share in his destiny and his cross. And let us very humbly and with childlike tenderness ask the mother of the Lord, who is our own mother and mother of the Church, to place us with her Son.

For Prayer and Reflection

To conclude our prayer, let us meditate again on that passage from the first letter of Peter, 4:12-19, and let us apply its message to the crises of our own lives. Let us embrace the cross that is our destiny here and now, placing ourselves in the strong hands of our Lord and having great confidence in his mercy.

10. The Challenge of Sin

"WE ARE SURROUNDED by so great a cloud of witnesses; therefore, let us also lay aside every weight and the sin that ensnares us so easily" (Heb 12:1). Sadly, we find ourselves ensnared in a sinful condition that undermines our identity as persons grounded in and belonging to the Church. The snare is lifelong and astutely laid, for it has been devised by someone with great intelligence: "He shall bruise your head, and you shall bruise his heel" (Gen 3:15). In explaining to us the problem of sin, the apostle John uses certain basic criteria: "If we say that we have no sin, we deceive ourselves, and the truth is not in us" (1 John 1:8; cf. 1 John 1:5–2:2). "Everyone who commits sin is guilty of lawlessness; sin is lawlessness" (1 John 3:4; cf. 1 John 3:4-10). There is no communion with God without transformation of the heart, and there is no transformation of the heart apart from Jesus Christ. An unconverted heart walks in darkness; it loves the darkness more than the light and does not seek to escape from the shadows (John 3:19-20). We can view the whole Gospel message in this perspective of the struggle between light and darkness. "The light shines in the darkness, and the darkness did not overcome it" (John 1:5). "He came to his own people, and they did not receive him" (John 1:11). And so the apostle John exhorts us, "My little children, do not sin" (1 John 2:1). Let us ask for the grace not to take sin lightly (cf. Rom 6:1).

And this is the judgment, that the light has come into the world, and people loved darkness rather than light because their deeds were evil. For all who do evil hate the light and do not come to the light, so that their deeds may not be exposed. (John 3:19-20)

On the one hand, we cannot know God without being totally transformed; on the other hand, we cannot be transformed by our own efforts. Only when we situate ourselves in between these two truths can we begin to have hope. Only then will prayer arise in us—"Out of the depths I cry to you, O Lord!" (Psalm 130:1)—for it arises out of our consciousness of being next to nothing (cf. Psalm 103:15-16). In this cry from the depths we recognize that we are captives, torn apart within ourselves (cf. Rom 7:15). In the degree that we move toward the light, the confession of our sins will resound ever louder.

As for mortals, their days are like grass; they flourish like a flower of the field; for the wind passes over it, and it is gone, and its place knows it no more. (Psalm 103:15-16)

All those who sin also commit "iniquity." This word has an eschatological meaning; it designates the primordial iniquity, the wickedness of the last times when the evil of the world subject to the devil is revealed. The concept of iniquity conveys not so much a sense of sinful weakness as the definitive rejection of the light. The absence of iniquity is clearly related to the presence of Jesus. Now that Jesus has come, "they have no excuse for their sin" (John 15:22), and the world will be convinced of this by the Spirit whom Jesus sends (John 16:8-10). The essence of sin and iniquity is the radical rejection of the freedom solicited by love. Rather than specific acts, iniquity is a deep-seated attitude with respect to life: it is *being* iniquitous.

> *And when he comes, he will prove the world wrong about sin and righteousness and judgment: about sin, because they do not believe in me; about righteousness, because I am going to the Father and you will see me no longer.* (John 16:8-10)

SIN INSTALLS ITSELF stealthily in our hearts by twisting them and hardening them more and more. Behind our disobedience, there is always a turning away from the Lord, an idolatry, a sin of magic: "For rebellion is as the sin of divination, and stubbornness is as iniquity and idolatry" (1 Sam 15:23). The scriptures often remind us of this hardening of the heart by sin and this turning away from God by sinners (cf. Rom 1:18-32). This hardening comes at the end of a long process, when our guilt dominates us, when "our iniquities, like the wind, carry us away" (Isa 64:5-6). Its principal characteristic is our instinctive rejection of love, our dismissal of the Word of God made flesh, who speaks to us of the humble dereliction of the cross. When our hearts are hardened, we spurn every solicitude that comes from the heart of the Lord. Some scriptural texts almost seem to say that it is the word of God itself that further hardens stubborn hearts and makes them more rebellious (Luke 8:9-10; Matt 13:10-13; Mark 4:10-12).

> *Then the disciples came and asked him, "Why do you speak to them in parables?" He answered, "To you it has been given to know the secrets of the kingdom of heaven, but to them it has not been given. For to those who have, more will be given, and they will have an abundance; but from those who have nothing, even what they have will be taken away. The reason I speak to them in parables is that 'seeing they do not perceive, and hearing they do not listen, nor do they understand.'"* (Matt 13:10-13)

Jesus encourages the people to walk in the light while there is time so that they won't stumble (John 11:9-10). This phrase, "while there is time," needs to be applied also to sin. How long will God's patience last? Saint Ignatius urges us to be amazed at how other creatures in the universe "have allowed us to live and have preserved us in life" (SpEx 60). Do I abuse God's patience? Do I play games with his love? Let us not become like Isaac's son, Esau, "who sold his birthright for a single meal. You know that later, when he wanted to inherit the blessing, he was rejected for he found no chance to repent, even though he sought the blessing with tears" (Heb 12:16-17).

We can end our prayer with these anguished words of Isaiah: "Look down from heaven and see, from your holy and glorious habitation. Where are your zeal and your might? The yearning of your heart and your compassion? They are withheld from me. For you are our father, though Abraham does not know us and Israel does not acknowledge us; you, O Lord, are our father; our Redeemer from of old is your name. Why, O Lord, do you make us stray from your ways and harden our heart, so that we do not fear you? Turn back for the sake of your servants, for the sake of the tribes that are your heritage. Your holy people took possession for a little while; but now our adversaries have trampled down your sanctuary. We have long been like those whom you do not rule, like those not called by your name" (Isa 63:15-19).

For Prayer and Reflection

Do we pray to God for the grace of conversion? At what times in our lives have we preferred the darkness to the light?

11. The Hopelessness of Sin

W E NEED TO MEDITATE on what is the fundamental contradiction of our lives: the opposition between God's
desire to integrate us firmly into his Church and the sinfulness that destroys our relationship to the Lord and to our holy
Mother the hierarchical Church. Conscious of our humble
state, let us enter into this meditation by realizing we are "the
People of God immersed in the world, and often tempted by
idols. As God's people we always need to hear the proclamation
of the 'mighty works of God' (Acts 2:11) which first converted
us to the Lord; we always need to be called together afresh by
him and reunited" (*Evangelii Nuntiandi*, 15). Our humility is
born of our consciousness of how seriously and how frequently
we have sinned against the Gospel.

In this meditation, let us ask the Lord for the grace to realize how our sin puts limits on holy Mother Church's power
to reach out to people, for she is "a universal Church without
boundaries or frontiers except, alas, those of the heart and
mind of sinful man" (*Evangelii Nuntiandi*, 61). Our sin is not
ours alone; rather, it affects the whole Church. By our sin we
obscure her holiness; we make the Church less fruitful and less
disciplined. Let us ask for the grace to "experience the emp-
tiness of all idols" (*Evangelii Nuntiandi*, 26), especially those
that are found within "the frequent situations of dechristianiza-
tion in our day" (*Evangelii Nuntiandi*, 52). These situations, in

which we ourselves take part, attack our faith, which "is nearly always exposed today to secularism, even to militant atheism. It is a faith exposed to trials and threats, and even more, a faith besieged and actively opposed. It runs the risk of perishing from suffocation or starvation if it is not fed and sustained each day" (*Evangelii Nuntiandi*, 54).

UNDERSTANDING THIS, let us ask the Lord for the grace of conversion, for his goodness reveals to us that even "the best structures and the most idealized systems soon become inhuman if the inhuman inclinations of our hearts are not made wholesome, if we who live in these structures or who rule them do not undergo a conversion of heart and of outlook" (*Evangelii Nuntiandi*, 36). May God give us the grace to commit our hearts once again totally to the proclamation of the Gospel. The good news of the kingdom is given to us "as grace and mercy, and yet at the same time each individual must gain it with great effort, for 'everyone tries to enter it by force' says the Lord (Luke 16:16)" (*Evangelii Nuntiandi,* 10). That is to say, the gift of God is unmerited, but at the same time it is won. May God give us the strength to persevere in the conversion of our hearts.

Conversion is a grace we should ask for; we should spend much time in such prayer of petition. Our heart becomes enclosed in its sin; it becomes hardened. Even before the God who never tires of forgiving, our impatient heart gradually yields to human ways and grows weary of asking for pardon. We need the word of Jesus to wake us up: "How foolish you are and how slow of heart to believe all that the prophets have declared! Was it not necessary that the Messiah should suffer these things and then enter into his glory?" (Luke 24:25-26). These words of the Risen Lord will help us understand the great good that can come from recognition of our sins and from sincere conversion of heart. We must ask God for this conversion since it is part of the grace of our vocation, a grace to which we must always remain open. As Saint Ignatius suggests, therefore, let us ask repeatedly for the grace of "growing and intense sorrow and tears for our sins" (SpEx 55).

AS THE WORK OF SATAN, sin takes aim directly at what gives us cohesion: our heart, our hope. What disintegrates the human heart is hopelessness. Instead of the bonding virtue of hope, we are confronted with the hollow alternative of hopelessness, coiled up aimlessly and fruitlessly within itself. Let us consider the different forms that hopelessness has taken in the history of salvation, and let us examine our own hearts to see whether they also are breeding grounds of desperation.

WE READ OF the hopelessness of the Israelites who, while wandering in the desert, say "No" to the hopefulness of the living God and prefer to adore an impotent idol (Exod 32:7-10, 15-24). We read of the liberated slaves who say "No" to God's hope-filled plan of salvation and prefer to dream about "the onions and the garlic" of their days of servitude (Num 11:5-6; Exod 16:1-3). We read of the bewildered throngs who say "No" to divinely inspired leadership and take refuge instead in the facile anarchy of grumbling (Exod 16:6-8; 17:1-7). The people of Israel want to know nothing of tests, nothing of difficulty. By succumbing to this temptation, they fail to see that God's grace, even though totally unmerited, is also a gift that must be won: "This kingdom and this salvation ... are available to every human being as grace and mercy, and yet at the same time each individual must gain them by force, ... through toil and suffering, through a life lived according to the Gospel, through abnegation and the cross" (*Evangelii Nuntiandi*, 10).

From the wilderness of Sin the whole congregation of the Israelites journeyed by stages, as the LORD commanded. They camped at Rephidim, but there was no water for the people to drink. The people quarreled with Moses, and said, "Give us water to drink." Moses said to them, "Why do you quarrel with me? Why do you test the LORD?" But the people thirsted there for water; and the people complained against Moses and said, "Why did you bring us out of Egypt, to kill us and our children and livestock with thirst?" So Moses cried out to the LORD, "What shall I do with this people? They are almost ready to stone me." The LORD said to Moses, "Go on ahead of the people, and take some of the elders of Israel with you; take in your hand the staff with which you struck the Nile, and go. I will be standing there in front of you on the rock at Horeb. Strike the rock, and water will come out of it, so that the people may drink." Moses did so, in the sight of the elders of Israel. He called the place Massah and Meribah, because the Israelites quarreled and tested the LORD, saying, "Is the LORD among us or not?" (Exod 17:1-7)

In attempting to skip over stages of growth, the impatient heart ceases to be a creature; it becomes instead a creator of shallow projects of protest that are inherently self-seeking. The eventual punishment of the Israelites is inevitable because impatience brings with it the built-in punishment of sterility. Because they want everything all at once, the impatient are left with nothing. Their projects are like so many seeds that fall on rocky soil: their roots have no depth; their words lack consistency. Impatience and hopelessness can deform the project of a people; they can distort the image of the Father who calls us to be a people; they can undermine our maturity, our ability to struggle, our apostolic stamina; they can turn us into gossiping busybodies. In seeking to obviate time, impatience and hopelessness tempt us to trust in the illusion of magic as a way of controlling or manipulating God. On the cross, Christ assumes all these spurious challenges born of impatience and hopelessness. In him we learn that God is great above all, that sin is ephemeral, and that patience and constancy are born of hope. That is why the kingdom of God does not come about all of a sudden, but "must be patiently carried on during the course of history, in order to be realized fully on the day of the final coming of Christ" (*Evangelii Nuntiandi*, 9).

HOPELESSNESS CAUSES FAMILIES to disintegrate (2 Sam 11 and 12). David was given the mission of uniting the people of God, but his impatience led him to destroy the family, the basic unit of the people. He vitiated his mission; he vitiated the justice that was due to his kin. When such a process takes root in us, we consider it of little importance—it starts insinuating itself as a fleeting desire, but then it grows stronger and enslaves us. Its disintegrating force leads us to betray our mission as pastors of God's people.

IMPATIENCE MAKES our confidence disintegrate. When David decided to carry out the census (2 Sam 24:1-17), he was effectively replacing hopefulness with empirical evidence. For it is one thing to assess one's forces in order to make sensible plans (cf. Luke 14:28-32), but it is something else to measure one's strength in order to boast about it. David was "reducing" salvation to what was within his own power. The Church, in contrast, must not yield to those who would "reduce her mission to the dimensions of a simply temporal project. They would reduce her aims to a human-centered goal; the salvation of which she is the messenger would be reduced to material well-being. Her activity, forgetful of all spiritual and religious preoccupation, would become initiatives of the political or social order"

(*Evangelii Nuntiandi,* 32). King David, entranced by his own power and forgetful of his sins, made a decision to "sacrifice the liberation that God desires for his people to the needs of a particular strategy or practice of short-term efficiency" (*Evangelii Nuntiandi,* 33). In so doing, he destroyed the union of his people with their God and created a new idol, the idol of "my power, our power." How often we have seen such manhandling of the people's union with God! How often our pastoral performance has taken on a princely style or been transformed into a personality cult! That can happen when we play the games of certain sectors or when we take advantage of the weaknesses of others. As creatures of our times, we are capable of causing ruptures and divisions rather than creating communion and communication; we can bring about oppression and domination instead of cultivating respect for individual and collective rights in true solidarity. We also take part in the blindness and the injustice of society.

HOPELESSNESS CAUSES solidarity to disintegrate (1 Sam 18:6-17; 19:8-18). Saul's envy of David betrayed a serious obtuseness on his part. Instead of joining with the people and benefitting from the unification of the whole nation around David, Saul preferred to go his own way, stubbornly refusing to recognize this man anointed by God. Envy always errs in its object and frustrates the struggle. When people desire something good but do so with envy, they end up losing what is truly good, and, in the case of Saul, it was the common project, the corporate institution. When Saul's isolated, disobedient conscience separated him from the Lord, he dragged the whole people down with him, for the people ended up violating what was consecrated to God. In sparing the enemies' livestock and not exterminating them, they disobeyed an express order of God: "Go and exterminate those sinful Amalekites. Destroy everything they have" (cf. 1 Sam 15:1-19).

Saul's sin revealed not only his envy but also his impatience, his presumption, his disobedience, and even his demagogy (cf. 1 Sam 15; 28:3-25). Rather different was the case of the priest Zachary (Luke 1:19-22), who also sinned by doubt and disbelief. Because of Zachary's failure to believe, the dialogue between pastor and flock was cut off (he lost his voice and could not talk to them), but the faith of the people was not affected (they understood that he had had a vision in the sanctuary).

> *The angel replied, "I am Gabriel. I stand in the presence of God, and I have been sent to speak to you and to bring you this good news. But now, because you did not believe my words, which will be fulfilled in their time, you will become mute, unable to speak, until the day these things occur."*
>
> *Meanwhile, the people were waiting for Zechariah, and wondered at his delay in the sanctuary. When he did come out, he could not speak to them, and they realized that he had seen a vision in the sanctuary. He kept motioning to them and remained unable to speak.* (Luke 1:19-22)

HOPELESSNESS DESTABILIZES the constancy of apostolic leadership. Esau lost his birthright for a plate of lentil stew (Gen 25:29-34; 26:34-35; Heb 12:15-18). Desire for immediate pleasure renders us incapable of sacrifice. We are careless about the things of God because we grow listless. I think that sometimes in our clerical world the lentil stew is any adulation that is offered us. It's very hard for us not to have the last word, not to utter the always definitive prophecy. We do not like being fools. We have a hard time saying "I don't know" without feeling disturbed or showing indifference. Leading God's faithful people sometimes requires us to forgo the urgency of answers and to remember that silence is often the best response of the wise. Don't go on the attack or throw up an immediate defense. Refuse the glamor of being the popular priest or saying the trendy word. Reject the kinds of affection or disaffection that arise not from our vocation of belonging to a body but from our interior rigidities or our predetermined stances.

> *Once when Jacob was cooking a stew, Esau came in from the field, and he was famished. Esau said to Jacob, "Let me eat some of that red stuff, for I am famished!" (Therefore he was called Edom.) Jacob said, "First sell me your birthright." Esau said, "I am about to die; of what use is a birthright to me?" Jacob said, "Swear to me first." So he swore to him, and sold his birthright to Jacob. Then Jacob gave Esau bread and lentil stew, and he ate and drank, and rose and went his way. Thus Esau despised his birthright.* (Exod 25:29-34)

We could give other examples, but we have already seen that the word of God offers us many examples of the disintegrating force of hopelessness—and sadly, we have it within our power to become one more example of it. Even after the evil spirit has been driven out, it will go forth and find seven worse than itself in order to renew the assault on our souls (Luke 11:24-26). Humbly recognizing that we are sinners and yet chosen by the Lord, let us end our meditation "with a colloquy of mercy, conversing with God our Lord and thanking him for granting us life until now, and proposing, with his grace, amendment for the future" (SpEx 61).

> *"When the unclean spirit has gone out of a person, it wanders through waterless regions looking for a resting-place, but not finding any, it says, 'I will return to my house from which I came.' When it comes, it finds it swept and put in order. Then it goes and*

brings seven other spirits more evil than itself, and they enter and live there; and the last state of that person is worse than the first." (Luke 11:24-26)

For Prayer and Reflection

Let us reflect now on what it means to allow ourselves to give way to hopelessness. Have we experienced hopelessness in recent days? Do we have confidence at this moment in God's fatherly forgiveness? After answering these questions, let us renew our prayer of petition, asking the Lord for the experience of conversion.

12. Testing and Temptation

O UR FAITHFULNESS to the call of Christ will be tested. Sometimes the temptation will come to us as a hardly audible whisper, and at other times it will challenge us face to face, but the words will always be the same: "He saved others; he cannot save himself. He is the King of Israel, let him come down from the cross, and we will believe in him" (Matt 27:42-43). The blinding force of this temptation is all the stronger when our sinful heart clings to other paths of salvation or other ways of life different from the ones the Lord desires. At times the Lord wants us crucified alongside himself: "Are you not the Messiah? Save yourself and us!" (Luke 23:39)—and we will not always have some companion at hand to tell us the truth: "Do you not fear God, since you are under the same sentence of condemnation? And we indeed have been condemned justly, for we are getting what we deserve for our deeds, but this man has done nothing wrong" (Luke 23:40-41).

The devil is intelligent. He knows how and where to tempt people. Saint Ignatius describes him as "a military commander who is attempting to conquer and plunder his objective. The captain and leader of an army on a campaign sets up his camp, studies the strength and structure of a fortress, and then attacks at its weakest point. In the same way, the enemy of human nature prowls around and from every side probes all our theological, cardinal, and moral virtues. Then at the point where he finds us weakest and most in need in regard to our eternal salvation, there he attacks and tries to take us" (SpEx 327). The evil spirit mounts his assault by use of bravado ("making himself like a woman: weak when faced by firmness but strong in the face of acquiescence" [SpEx 325]).[5] He even tries to charm us, but for that he needs an ambience of secrecy. [6] However he attacks, he is always astute in his planning. He know what he wants. And if he attacks something, it is because he recognizes that it is dangerous. That is why Christian tradition asserts that where there is temptation there is also grace. Temptation is a "difficult time," Cardinal Pironio tells us, and as such "it belongs to the designs of the Father, being essentially a time of grace and salvation."[7]

Temptation is a time of grace not only in our personal lives but also at the level of community living: "the moments of turmoil and testing that sporadically threaten our fraternal communion can become moments of grace that strengthen our loyalty to Christ and make it credible."[8] In our meditation, we should be very attentive both to the exceptional temptations that come to us infrequently and to those that are part of our daily lives. If we confront all of them in the Lord, they will be spaces of grace. We gain nothing when we create a false sense of security by concealing the true face of temptation from ourselves. There is no grace is such a ploy. This is the profound meaning of the Ignatian annotation: "When the one giving the Exercises notices that the exercitant is not experiencing any spiritual motions in his or her soul, such as consolations or desolations, or is not being moved one way or another by different spirits, the director should question the retreatant much about the Exercises" (SpEx 6). Making the Exercises "with great spirit and generosity toward our Creator and Lord" (SpEx 5) presupposes that we have the basic courage to tell ourselves the truth about what usually causes us the greatest shame: sin and temptation.

Temptation has a concrete face, it insinuates itself with concrete words; even the gestures we make when we're tempted are concrete. Temptation has its own "style" even within the Church: it grows, it spreads, and it justifies itself. It grows within one person and gains strength. It grows within the community and spreads like a disease. It always has a word ready to justify its stance. Saint Teresa had this experience in mind when she stated that the nuns who complained about "being treated unreasonably" were traveling the wrong path. When temptation follows the lead of the evil one, it seeks to make us enemies of the cross of Christ (Phil 3:18).

When subjected to temptation, we do well to remember that we are not the first. Our ancestors knew temptation; they experienced this test that reveals the inmost recesses of our human reality. It is temptation that unveils the inner reality that hides behind appearances. We are vain creatures who worship appearances. The truth of our existence is revealed and is "tested" in temptation, just as the potter's clay vessels are tested in the kiln (Sir 27:5). An old formula of canonization that is consecrated by history brings this home to us: "Who has been tested and been found perfect? Let it be for him a ground for boasting. Who has had the power to transgress and did not transgress, and to do evil and did not do it? His prosperity will be established, and the assembly will relate his acts of charity" (Sir 31:10-11).

Our ancestors were tested, and the people to whom we belong have tasted temptation often in their history. Abraham was tempted in his faith: "After these things God tested Abraham" (Gen 22:1). And his faith became obedience (cf. Heb 11:8, 17-19). This feat of our father in the faith later gave rise to spiritual reflection among his people: "Remember what God did with Abraham" (Jdt 8:26; Sir 44:21). The Israelites were tempted during the forty years they wandered in the desert. "You shall remember all the way which the Lord your God has led you these forty years in the wilderness, that he might humble you, testing you to know what was in your heart, whether you would keep his commandments or not" (Deut 8:2). The temptation of the desert was great not only because it revealed the inward sinfulness of the Israelites' stubborn hearts but also because it unveiled for us the fidelity of God and his promise: "the rock was Christ" (1 Cor 10:1-4). (See also Exod 17:7; Psalms 77:20; 94:9; 105:41; 113:7-8; Deut 9:22.) The rod of Moses, which in the desert was a sign of contradiction, would be held fast in the memory of that people, and, over the centuries, it would slowly be transformed into the lance, which, in the hands of a centurion, brought forth life from the Rock: "Truly this man was God's Son" (Matt 27:54; John 19:31-37).

Since it was the day of Preparation, the Jews did not want the bodies left on the cross during the sabbath, especially because that sabbath was a day of great solemnity. So they asked Pilate to have the legs of the crucified men broken and the bodies removed. Then the soldiers came and broke the legs of the first and of the other who had been crucified with him. But when they came to Jesus and saw that he was already dead, they did not break his legs. Instead, one of the soldiers pierced his side with a spear, and at once blood and water came out. (He who saw this has testified so that you also may believe. His testimony is true, and he knows that he tells the truth.) These things occurred so that the scripture might be fulfilled, "None of his bones shall be broken." And again another passage of scripture says, "They will look on the one whom they have pierced." (John 19:31-37)

The people were tested to see what was in their hearts; they were tested in their love and in their fidelity to the covenant. Even while undergoing temptation, the people were able to perceive (immediately or by prophetic hindsight) the presence of their faithful God, the loving Lord who rewards all who seek him (Heb 11:6). The people's hope was put to the test again during the exile, when the messianic hopes of their ancestors appeared to be nothing but illusion. In that difficult trial, it was only the prophetic force of memory that enabled them to remain faithful to the promise. Listen to Judith encouraging her compatriots to take heart: "In spite of everything let us give thanks to the Lord our God, who is putting us to the test as he did our forefathers. Remember what he did with Abraham, and how he tested Isaac, and what happened to Jacob in Mesopotamia in Syria while he was keeping the sheep of Laban, his mother's brother. For he has not tried us with fire, as he did them, to search out their hearts, nor has he taken revenge upon us; but the Lord scourges those who draw near to him, in order to admonish them" (Jdt 8:25-27).

For the people, temptation will always consist in demanding clear signs, in wanting to hold the pledge securely in their hands from the start, but Judith warns: "Do not try to bind the purposes of the Lord our God; for God is not like man, to be threatened, nor like a human being, to be won over by pleading. Therefore, while we wait for his deliverance, let us call upon him to help us, and he will hear our voices, if it pleases him" (Jdt 8:16-17). At the same time, the holiness of the just consists in hoping against all hope (Rom 4:18), in daring to believe in God's promises even before they are made: "All of these died in faith without having received the promises, but from a distance they saw and greeted them" (Heb 11:13). Even when tempted, they persevered as though they already "saw him who is invisible" (Heb 11:27).

Temptation is at times a testing of our human condition, and it should not be compared to punishment. When temptation came upon the innocent man Job, figure of the Servant of Yahweh, it served to prepare his eyes for the ultimate vision: "I had heard of you by the hearing of the ear, but now my eye sees you; therefore I retract what I said, and I repent in dust and ashes" (Job 42:5-6).

Jesus also experienced testing during his life. It began in the desert (Matt 4:1-11) and continued afterward, for the devil only "departed from him until an opportune time" (Luke 4:13). Jesus was tested to the point of agony: "Now my soul is troubled. And what should I say—'Father, save me from this hour'? No, it is for this reason that I have come to this hour" (John 12:27; cf. Luke 22:40-46). Jesus was also tested by his relatives (Mark 3:31-35); by Peter, whom he does not hesitate to call "Satan" (Mark 8:31-33); and by those who would make him a temporal messiah (John 6:15).

> *Then his mother and his brothers came; and standing outside, they sent to him and called him. A crowd was sitting around him; and they said to him, "Your mother and your brothers and sisters are outside, asking for you." And he replied, "Who are my mother and my brothers?" And looking at those who sat around him, he said, "Here are my mother and my brothers! Whoever does the will of God is my brother and sister and mother."* (Mark 3:31-35)

> *Then he began to teach them that the Son of Man must undergo great suffering, and be rejected by the elders, the chief priests, and the scribes, and be killed, and after three days rise again. He said all this quite openly. And Peter took him aside and began to rebuke him. But turning and looking at his disciples, he rebuked Peter and said, "Get behind me, Satan! For you are setting your mind not on divine things but on human things."* (Mark 8:31-33)

The Church must follow the same path as Christ (Mark 10:35-40). Peter vacillated in his perseverance but later on was converted and strengthened his brothers (Luke 22:31-33). All Christians must similarly walk along this road and be examined by God (1 Thess 2:3-5). They will be subjected to testing (1 Tim

3:8-10), but they should be aware that they will experience no temptation that is beyond their strength (1 Cor 10:11-13). We know that we must "suffer various trials so that the genuineness of [our] faith—being more precious than gold that, though perishable, is tested by fire—may be found to result in praise and glory and honor when Jesus Christ is revealed" (1 Pet 1:6-7; cf. Heb 12:11). When the testing seems to go beyond our possibilities, we do well to lift our eyes to "consider him who endured such hostility, ... so that we may not grow weary or lose heart." And we should dare to tell one another with a good dose of humor: "You have not resisted yet to the point of shedding your blood" (Heb 12:3-4).

The core of temptation is in the tension between fidelity and infidelity. God our Lord seeks a fidelity that is renewed with every test. But that is where the devil, the seducer, enters in. Satan provokes infidelity in love by leading people to spiritual adultery (cf. Ezekiel 16); he provokes infidelity in hope by goading people to grumble constantly as they stubbornly demand idols to worship and proofs and guarantees in the form of onions and garlic. All of these infidelities pronounce a "No" to love, to hope, and to the leadership of Yahweh. The world is the broad stage of temptation.

Mary was present in the great battle, the great test, of Jesus: his cross. Nailed to the cross, he left her to us as our mother. She knows how to counsel us during times of temptation.

For Prayer and Reflection

Before the image of Our Lady, let us leave at her feet the temptations that invade our life. Humbly recognizing our weakness, let us ask that in our difficult moments we not forget to raise our sight toward her so that her mother's hand leads and protects us.

13. Humility and Hope

L
ET US ASK the Holy Spirit, who knows how to imprint on our hearts all that is good, to grant us the gift of hope and make us ready to receive it. The hope I speak of is different from optimism. Hope is not boisterous; it has no fear of silence; it sinks deep, as do roots in wintertime. Hope is sure, for it is given by the Father of all truth. It discerns what is good and what is bad. It does not worship what is best (thus not yielding to optimism), nor does it rest content with what is worst (it is not pessimistic). Since hope distinguishes between good and evil, it is militant but not in an anxious or obsessive way; it struggles on steadily, like those who know they are running toward a sure goal, as the scripture tells us: "Let us lay aside every weight and the sin that clings so closely, and let us run with perseverance the race that is set before us" (Heb 12:1). What we propose, then, is precisely a militant hope.

TO UNDERSTAND the process of discernment that such hope requires, we do well to consider the despairing attitudes that every so often take root in our souls. Sometimes we experience them in obvious ways; other times we feel them in the dark corners of our hearts, those recesses where we "store" the odds and ends of our existence, the shoddy baggage with which we soothe ourselves. These despairing attitudes develop in the same way as does the anti-kingdom: they begin with being barely poor, they continue with vain ambitions, and they end up with bloated pride.

"THEY BEGIN with being barely poor...." Here I would like to refer to some of the particular ways we fail in poverty, "under the guise of the angel of light." For example, in our institutions and our diocese we have experienced a considerable decrease in vocations. When we look at our young people, we have at times felt that our legitimate hopes are being threatened, and yet we often refuse to share our pain in this regard; we don't suffer together as a body. We opt rather for the "wealth" of not suffering. As a result, we expend our energies searching for a solution by blaming some scapegoat for the disaster, or we diagnose the problem in abstract terms, all the while defending ourselves as our hearts cling jealously to their precious treasures (Luke 12:32-34). We leave no space for the mystery of freedom and grace, the mystery that makes us docile and anoints us with true poverty.

> *"Do not be afraid, little flock, for it is your Father's good plea-sure to give you the kingdom. Sell your possessions, and give alms. Make purses for yourselves that do not wear out, an unfailing trea-sure in heaven, where no thief comes near and no moth destroys. For where your treasure is, there your heart will be also."* (Luke 12:32-34)

With respect to other painful circumstances in the Church, our institutions, our diocese, and our nation, we disguise the pov-erty of the solutions that are within our reach as wealth, and we often take no notice of how corroded that wealth is, for it is rich only in criticism. We opt to be rich in negativity. Other times we exaggerate the circumstances surrounding a painful fact as if we preferred to have a comfortable seat for watching the tragedy instead of pitching in to solve what is really a family problem. We could go on listing examples, but let these suffice. We should consider in prayer these suggestions of how attached we really are to wealth, and we should ask the Lord to divest us of these attitudes that are rich only insofar as they are despairing. May the Lord remind us that the hope of the kingdom comes with birth pangs.

"THEY CONTINUE WITH vain ambitions ..." When sowed on soil that has not been plowed with pain, seed will be condemned to inconsistent yields (cf. Luke 8:11-15). We are permeated with vanities of every sort, but the most common type of vainglory among us is defeatism. Vainglorious is the person who prefers to be the general of defeated armies rather than a simple soldier in a squadron that continues to fight on even when it has been devastated. How often we dream of expansionist apostolic plans that are really those of defeated generals! Curiously, in such cases, we deny the history of our Church, which is glorious precisely because it is a history of sacrifices, of hopes, of daily struggles. Sometimes we spend endless hours talking and planning about "what needs to be done." Absorbed in that spirit of "what needs to be done," we insulate ourselves from reality instead of taking on with humility and dogged diligence the lowly work that exhausts us—and it exhausts us simply because, as poor humans expelled from paradise, all work is by the "sweat of our brow." In contrast, caught up with ideas of "what needs to be done," our imagination labors feverishly but without making contact with the painful, humble reality of our suffering people. That is vanity, and all vanity is futile.

"AND THEY END UP with bloated pride." This is the pride that so often leads us to despise the humble means of the Gospel; it is the pride that alienates us from the "divine weakness of the Beatitudes." Such pride does not inspire us to put all our hope in God and to seek him in simple supplication, in continuous prayer, and in the laborious penance of every day. Rather it leads us away from all this and makes us fall short in our pastoral leadership. We manage conflicts badly, or we keep our distance from them in order not to "get our hands dirty," like the Levite and the priest in the parable of Luke (10:29-37). Maybe we get entangled in conflicts hoping for personal triumph or sectarian advantage, or, conversely, we avoid conflicts and play the role of simple referees of history. But when we avoid conflicts, we run the risk of treating everything with a bland neutrality: all values are equalized, and the supreme goal becomes pluralistic coexistence at the expense of truth and justice. Our vocation to evangelize requires that we cultivate the humility that comes with being stewards, not masters, and we develop this humility by taking on the opprobrium and the contempt of the cross of Christ in our daily labors and in the unraveling of our lives in the service of Jesus Christ who precedes us on the road.

But wanting to justify himself, he asked Jesus, "And who is my neighbor?" Jesus replied, "A man was going down from Jerusalem to Jericho, and fell into the hands of robbers, who stripped him, beat him, and went away, leaving him half dead. Now by chance a priest was going down that road; and when he saw him, he passed by on the other side. So likewise a Levite, when he came to the place and saw him, passed by on the other side. But a Samaritan while travelling came near him; and when he saw him, he was moved with pity. He went to him and bandaged his wounds, having poured oil and wine on them. Then he put him on his own animal, brought him to an inn, and took care of him. The next day he took out two denarii, gave them to the innkeeper, and said, 'Take care of him; and when I come back, I will repay

you whatever more you spend.' Which of these three, do you think,
was a neighbor to the man who fell into the hands of the robbers?"
He said, "The one who showed him mercy." Jesus said to him, "Go
and do likewise." (Luke 10:29-37)

I THINK THAT we all feel consternation when we realize that the
only way for us to escape our despairing attitudes is by accepting the opprobrium and contempt suffered by Jesus crucified.
They are the true road toward hope. We know from experience
that spiritual directors have to work hard to free from various
forms of vanity our decision to follow Jesus Christ crucified.
Perhaps the example of the wise virgins will help us here, for
it teaches us something we need to learn as evangelizers and
also as an institution. As you'll recall, the wise virgins refuse
to share their oil with the foolish ones (Matt 25:1-12). Some
who read the parable rapidly and carelessly condemn the wise
virgins, criticizing them as miserly and selfish. A deeper reading
shows us the greatness of their attitude, for they could not share
what was unsharable, they could not risk what was unriskable:
the encounter with their Lord and the import of that encounter. Possibly in our own evangelizing work we will meet up with
opprobrium and contempt if, in our desire to follow the Lord,
we fail to examine the oxen or buy the field or get married (cf.
Luke 14:16-21).

Someone gave a great dinner and invited many. At the time for
the dinner he sent his slave to say to those who had been invited,
"Come; for everything is ready now." But they all alike began to
make excuses. The first said to him, "I have bought a piece of land,
and I must go out and see it; please accept my regrets." Another
said, "I have bought five yoke of oxen, and I am going to try them
out; please accept my regrets." Another said, "I have just been

married, and therefore I cannot come." So the slave returned and reported this to his master. (Luke 14:16-21)

AS WE FOLLOW the Lord, our humility will give evidence of our poverty, and it will help us know what is "essential," what is proper, and what is not, without getting lost in the deceits of wealth. The life of God in us is not a luxury but our daily bread; we must nourish it with our prayer and penance. This spirit of prayer and penance, even in moments of great adversity, will help us keep hopeful watch for the ways of God. When we allow space for hope, along with the humble prayer and penance of our (sometimes boring) work, then we free ourselves from those mundane attitudes that are riddled with "spiritual worldliness" (as DeLubac likes to call it). Such attitudes are despairing because they sink their roots in wealth, vanity, and pride.

For Prayer and Reflection

To conclude our prayer, I suggest that we contemplate Mary, the "humble Daughter of Zion," who can soothe our insatiable longings for wealth, vanity, and pride. It might help us here to recite slowly this simple hymn from the breviary[9]:

> Let me see, simply see;
> Let my sight be turned only to you,
> to behold you wholly and wordlessly,
> to tell you all with reverent silence.
>
> Not disturbing the breeze on your forehead,
> but cradling my breached solitude
> in your eyes as loving Mother,
> I rest in your nest of transparent earth.

The hours collapse; death and
the trash of life, with all their noise,
nip at the heels of the thoughtless.

Let me barely hold you, Mother, in my gaze,
as my heart is silenced in your tenderness,
in the chaste hush of white lilies. Amen.

14. United by the Grace of Memory

W HEN SAINT IGNATIUS asks us to "call back into our memory the gifts we have received—creation, redemption, and other particular gifts—so as to ponder with deep affection how much God has done for us," he wants us to go beyond simple gratitude for all we have received. He wants to teach us to be more loving; he wants to confirm in us the commitment we have made, and this is what our memory does, for memory is a grace of the Lord's presence in our apostolic lives. The memory of the past accompanies us not as a dead weight but as a reality interpreted in the light of our present consciousness. Let us ask for the grace to recover memory: memory of our own personal journeys, memory of how the Lord sought us out, memory of our families, memory of our people. Looking back helps us to be more alert in perceiving the force of God's word: "Recall those earlier days when, after you had been enlightened, you endured a hard struggle with sufferings" (Heb 10:32). "Remember your leaders, those who spoke the word of God to you; consider the outcome of their way of life, and imitate their faith" (Heb 13:7). This memory saves us from being "led away by all kinds of strange teachings," and it strengthens our hearts (Heb 13:9).

MEMORY OF THE PEOPLES. Peoples have memory, just as persons do. Humankind also has a common memory. In the face of the Mataco Indian is the living memory of a suffering race. In the voice of the poor folk of La Rioja is Saint Nicholas. Bishop Tavella used to recount that in a town of his diocese he once found a simple man praying with tremendous concentration. After the man had remained in intense prayer a long while, the bishop was impressed and asked him what he was praying. The man answered, "The catechism." It was the catechism of Saint Toribio of Mogrovejo. The memory of the peoples is not a computer but a living heart. Like Mary, the people "treasure all these things" in their hearts. The covenant of the people of Salta with the Lord of the Miracle, the Tincunaco, and all the other religious manifestations of the faithful are a spontaneous blossoming of their collective memory. It's all there: Spaniard and Indian, missionary and conquistador, Spanish colonization and racial assimilation. The same thing happens here in Buenos Aires. The people who have come from the interior seeking work go to Luján, as do the immigrants coming to work on the América—but the unifying element is always the same: *la Virgencita*, the dear Virgin, symbol of our nation's spiritual unity, deeply rooted in the memory of our people.

The reason for this is that memory has the power to unite and integrate. Just as intellect, given over to its own forces, partitions reality, so memory becomes the vital unifying force of a family or a people. A family without memory hardly deserves to be called such. A family that doesn't respect and care for its grandparents, who are its living memory, is a family in disintegration, but the families and the peoples that remember their past are families and peoples with a future.

The whole of humankind has its own common memory. There is the memory of the ancestral struggle between good and evil, the ongoing combat between Michael and "the ancient serpent" who, though decisively defeated, still rises up as the "enemy of human nature" (cf. Apoc 12:7-9). "How you are fallen from heaven, O Day Star, son of Dawn!" (Isa 14:12). "But you are brought down to Sheol, to the depths of the Pit!" (Isa 14:15). This is the memory of humankind, the common heritage of all peoples, and the revelation of the God of Israel. Human history is a long struggle between grace and sin, and memory of that shared history is seen concretely in the faces of our peoples. Most of them are anonymous individuals whose names will not be recorded in the history books. Their faces show signs of suffering and deprivation, but their dignity, inexpressible with words, speaks to us of a people with a history, a people with a common memory. They are the faithful people of God.

THE MEMORY OF THE CHURCH is the passion of the Lord, and we are reminded of this by an antiphon for Corpus Christi composed by Aquinas: *Recolitur memoria passionis eius,* "the memory of his passion is recalled." The Eucharist is the recalling of the Lord's passion. There in the passion is the victory. Forgetfulness of this truth has sometimes made the Church appear triumphalist, but the resurrection cannot be understood without the cross. In the cross is the history of the world: grace and sin, mercy and repentance, good and evil, time and eternity. The voice of God resounds in the ears of the Church through the words of the prophet: "Fear not, for I have redeemed you, … and I will redeem you again" (Isa 43:1-21). "Be strong and of good courage, do not fear or be in dread of them: for it is the Lord your God who goes before you; he will not fail you or forsake you" (Deut 31:6-8). The memory of God's salvation, of the path already traveled, gives us strength for the future. By memory, the Church testifies to God's salvation. "You shall not be afraid of them, but you shall remember what the Lord your God did to Pharaoh and to all Egypt … and how with mighty hand and outstretched arm he brought you out of Egypt. So will the Lord your God do to all the peoples of whom you are afraid" (Deut 7:18-20).

> But now thus says the LORD,
>   he who created you, O Jacob,
>   he who formed you, O Israel:
> Do not fear, for I have redeemed you;
>   I have called you by name, you are mine.
> When you pass through the waters, I will be with you;
>   and through the rivers, they shall not overwhelm you;
> when you walk through fire you shall not be burned,
>   and the flame shall not consume you.
> For I am the LORD your God,
>   the Holy One of Israel, your Savior. (Isa 43:1-3)

The people of God were tested as they traveled through the desert. In the wilderness they were guided by God as children by their parents. The counsel given by Deuteronomy is the same as that is found in all the scriptures: "You shall remember all the way which the Lord your God has led you these forty years in the wilderness" (Deut 8:2-6). We are incapable of understanding anything if we are incapable of remembering well, if our memory fails us. "Only take heed, and keep your soul diligently, lest you forget the things your soul has seen, and lest they depart from your heart all the days of your life; make them known to your children and your children's children" (Deut 4:9). Our God is eager for us to be mindful of him, so much so that at the least sign of repentance he pours out his mercy: "Do not forget the covenant he swore with our ancestors" (Deut 4:23).

> Remember the long way that the LORD your God has led you these
> forty years in the wilderness, in order to humble you, testing you to

know what was in your heart, whether or not you would keep his commandments. He humbled you by letting you hunger, then by feeding you with manna, with which neither you nor your ances-tors were acquainted, in order to make you understand that one does not live by bread alone, but by every word that comes from the mouth of the LORD. The clothes on your back did not wear out and your feet did not swell these forty years. Know then in your heart that as a parent disciplines a child so the LORD your God disci-plines you. Therefore keep the commandments of the LORD your God, by walking in his ways and by fearing him. (Deut 8:2-6)

In contrast, those who have no memory are satisfied with idols, and servitude comes upon them: "Because you did not serve the Lord your God joyfully and with gladness of heart for the abundance of everything, therefore you shall serve your enemies" (Deut 28:47-48). Only memory allows us to discover God in our midst; only memory makes us understand that every saving solution apart from God is an idol (Deut 6:14-15; 7:17-26). Worship of idols is the fitting punishment for those who forget (Deut 4:25-31).

The Church recalls God's merciful acts and therefore tries to be faithful to the law. The Ten Commandments that we teach our children are the other side of the covenant; they are the legal mandates that put a human stamp on God's mercy. When the people were liberated from Egypt, they received grace then and there, and the law was the complement of the grace received, the reverse side of the coin. The commandments are fruits of memory (Deut 6:1-12) and are therefore to be passed on from generation to generation: "When your children ask you in time to come, 'What is the meaning of the decrees and the statutes and the ordinances that the Lord our God has commanded you?' then you shall say to your children, 'We were Pharaoh's slaves in Egypt, but the Lord brought us out of Egypt with a mighty hand. The Lord displayed before our eyes great and awesome signs and wonders against Egypt, against Pharaoh and all his household. He brought us out from there in order to bring us in, to give us the land that he promised on oath to our ancestors. Then the Lord commanded us to observe all these statutes, to fear the Lord our God, for our lasting good, so as to keep us alive, as is now the case" (Deut 6:20-24). Memory binds us to a tradition, to a norm, to a living law inscribed in our hearts. "You shall therefore lay up these words of mine in your heart and in your soul; and you shall bind them as a sign upon your hand" (cf. Deut 11:1-32). In like manner, God has his "gift"—or "project"—of salvation bound to his own heart and his whole being. The action of the Church and of each one of us is grounded in memory, in the certainty that we are remembered by the Lord, that God has us bound up in his love.

> *Hear, O Israel: The L*ORD *is our God, the L*ORD *alone. You shall love the L*ORD *your God with all your heart, and with all your soul, and with all your might. Keep these words that I am commanding you today in your heart. Recite them to your children and talk about them when you are at home and when you are away, when you lie down and when you rise. Bind them as a sign on your hand, fix them as an emblem on your forehead, and write them on the doorposts of your house and on your gates.* (Deut 6:4-9)

That is why our prayer should be redolent with memory. The prayer of the Church keeps us ever mindful of the salvation of God the Father brought by the Son in the Holy Spirit. In the creed we find not only the compendium of Christian truths but also the history of our salvation: "he was born of the Virgin Mary," "he suffered under Pontius Pilate," "he was crucified," "he rose." Our creed is thus the persistence in history of the faith of that Israelite who, when about to make an offering to the Lord, prayed thus: "A wandering Aramaean was my father; and he went down into Egypt and sojourned there.... The Egyptians treated us harshly.... Then we cried to the Lord the God of our fathers, and the Lord heard our voice.... The Lord brought us out of Egypt ... and gave us this land, a land flowing with milk and honey" (cf. Deut 26:1-11).

Memory is a grace we should ask for. It is so easy to forget, especially when we feel satisfied. "When the Lord your God has brought you into the land that he swore to your ancestors, to Abraham, to Isaac, and to Jacob, to give you—a land with fine, large cities that you did not build, houses filled with all sorts of goods that you did not fill, hewn cisterns that you did not hew, vineyards and olive groves that you did not plant—and when you have eaten your fill, take care that you do not forget the Lord, who brought you out of the land of Egypt, out of the house of slavery" (Deut 6:10-12). "Take care that you do not forget the Lord your God, by failing to keep his commandments, his ordinances, and his statutes.... When you have eaten your fill and have built fine houses and live in them, and when your herds and flocks have multiplied, and your silver and gold is multiplied, and all that you have is multiplied, then do not exalt yourself, forgetting the Lord your God, who brought you out of the land of Egypt, out of the house of slavery" (Deut 8:11-14).

Let us ask for the grace of memory so that we will know how to choose wisely between life and death: "I have set before you this day life and good, death and evil" (Deut 30:15-20; cf. also Deut 11:26-28 and all of Deut 28). This is the choice we must make every day between the Lord and the idols. Remembering these things will also help us to be merciful because we will hear in our heart that great truth: "You shall remember that you were a slave in the land of Egypt" (Deut 15:15).

Let us hope that the Lord will grant his Church the same grace he bestowed on Moses, that great champion of memory whose "eye was not dim" (Deut 34:7). Let us pray that the idols, which have no memory but are only "present," may never remove memory from our mind's eye. In memory is found the "devotion of our youth" (Jer 2:1-13). May we never have to hear the word spoken by the Lord to the Church of Ephesus: "I have this against you, that you have abandoned the love you had at first" (Apoc 2:4).

Our Virgin Mother, who treasured all these things in her heart, will teach us the grace of memory if we know how to request it of her humbly. Like the brave mother of the Maccabees, she will speak to us in her "maternal tongue" (2 Macc 7:21, 26-27), in the language of our ancestors, the one we learned to speak in earlier times (Heb 10:32-33). May we never fail to experience the affection and tenderness of Mary, who whispers in our ears the word of God in familiar language. Hearing that, we will have the strength to resist the sweet-talk of the Evil One and disdain his enticements.

For Prayer and Reflection

After reflecting on these things, let us look back. Let us take a moment to recall gratefully all the graces God has worked in us throughout the course of our lives.

Part II

Manifestations of Light

15. The Light of Jesus

T HE FIRST ENTRY of Jesus into the temple is proclaimed to us in Luke 2:22-40. The first reading of today's liturgy tells us, "Suddenly he will enter his temple" (Mal 3:1-4). The one who enters the temple is a human being with flesh like ours: having our same blood and our same flesh, he shares in our condition (cf. Heb 2:14-18). This is the first time since that fateful afternoon in Eden that our human flesh enters justified into the Father's house. Centuries have passed, and now the promise is fulfilled.

> *Now there was a man in Jerusalem whose name was Simeon; this man was righteous and devout, looking forward to the consolation of Israel, and the Holy Spirit rested on him. It had been revealed to him by the Holy Spirit that he would not see death before he had seen the Lord's Messiah. Guided by the Spirit, Simeon came into the temple; and when the parents brought in the child Jesus, to do for him what was customary under the law, Simeon took him in his arms and praised God, saying,*
> *"Master, now you are dismissing your servant in peace,*
>   *according to your word;*
> *for my eyes have seen your salvation,*
>   *which you have prepared in the presence of all peoples,*
> *a light for revelation to the Gentiles*
>   *and for glory to your people Israel."*
> . . .

There was also a prophet, Anna the daughter of Phanuel, of the tribe of Asher. She was of a great age, having lived with her husband for seven years after her marriage, then as a widow to the age of eighty-four. She never left the temple but worshipped there with fasting and prayer night and day. At that moment she came, and began to praise God and to speak about the child to all who were looking for the redemption of Jerusalem. (Luke 2:25-32, 36-38)

JESUS IS WELCOMED into the temple by the older folk, signified in Simeon and Anna. They perceive that this child is something more than perfectly human: he is "the Savior," God. Behind that human flesh they are able to discover divinity, and so they give praise and glory. These two venerable souls express patience and hope, fidelity and proclamation.

FOR CENTURIES, the Father has been waiting for his son Adam to return. He has been waiting anxiously, like the father in the parable (Luke 15:20). And he goes forth to meet him in the person of the Spirit who inspires the elderly worshipers to speak out and give glory: "She began to praise God and to speak about the child to all who were looking for the redemption of Jerusalem" (Luke 2:38). There and then is accomplished all that was once hidden but now will be proclaimed from the rooftops (Mark 4:22; Luke 8:17; 12:2).

So he set off and went to his father. But while he was still far off, his father saw him and was filled with compassion; he ran and put his arms around him and kissed him. (Luke 15:20)

THERE IS RADIANCE in the temple because the Light is entering into it: "a light for revelation to the Gentiles and for glory to your people Israel" (Luke 2:32). It is Candlemas day, the day of the candles that will become the paschal candle on the night of Passover and a dazzling sun at the end of history. A hymn for the feast of Epiphany tells us that the Magi are the just ones "who seek the Light with the help of light": *lumen requirunt lumine.* Today in the temple, the final epiphany is foreshadowed.

THE SPIRITUAL EXERCISES of Saint Ignatius have a definite forward movement. Some of the key meditations provide the overall structure of the Ignatian method. Having made them several times before, we are quite familiar with that structure. The Principle and Foundation lays the foundation by affirming the wisdom of indifference and explaining how "we ought to desire and choose only that which is more conducive to the end for which we are created" (SpEx 23). The First Week impresses with us two fundamental realities: we recognize and abhor our sins and their roots in a worldly spirit, and we converse about all this with Jesus "suspended on the cross." There is only one sure way to enter into the labyrinth of our sins: by holding on to the wounded hand of Jesus. In the Second Week, we hear the summons to work for the kingdom; we come to understand the meaning of the struggle and how much is at stake; we begin to comprehend that the only weapon by which we can win the battle is humility; and we make our election. In the Third and the Fourth Weeks, we meditate on the paschal mystery and how we are integrated by means of it into the community and the Church. In the light of this mystery, we also confirm the election we have made.

ALL OF THESE ELEMENTS are in the meditations I will be proposing to you in the coming days. Each of you should discover them personally by following the inspiration of the Spirit. The connecting thread of the meditations will be the Epiphany. As we go through the Spiritual Exercises and consider the mysteries of the Lord's revelation, we should focus our meditations in accord with what we personally feel in the Lord.

Prayer

Whom do you hold in your hands,
tell us, old Simeon;
why do you feel such delight?

"Because I have seen the Savior.
This child will be a banner
and a sign of contradiction;
by his death he will bring life;
by his cross, resurrection.

Jesus the son of Mary
is the eternal Son of God,
the light that will show the nations
the ways of salvation."
Amen.

16. Staying Alert

Saint Ephrem the deacon, in his *Commentary on the Diatesseron* (18:15-17), tells us: "The Lord concealed (the time of his coming) so that we would be watchful and so that each of us might think that it could happen in our own time. ... With the last coming will happen something similar to what happened in the first coming.... But how can the time be unknown to the one who has determined this day from all eternity and has described in detail the signs that will precede it? Nevertheless, by speaking thus, he has invited us to consider these signs so that the generations of every century will now and always think that his coming might happen in their own time ... and so that they will stay awake, because when the body sleeps, it is human nature that rules it; in such a state, we are guided not by our will but by the impulses of our nature. And when a profound stupor born of pusillanimity or sadness pervades the soul, then the soul is ruled by the enemy, and, under the effects of that stupor, the soul does what it does not wish to do. Impulses dominate our nature, and the enemy rules our soul.... That is why the Lord recommends that we remain vigilant in the whole of our being: in the body so as to avoid drowsiness and in the soul so as to avoid indolence and pusillanimity."

The Lord is "he who comes," and so we must be watchful and remain vigilant. We must await his revelation. He will manifest himself. Revelation means uncovering something that is veiled, bringing it out of hiding. Manifestation implies a type of transfiguration: it is epiphany. We can begin this meditation by considering chapter 60 of Isaiah.

THE LORD SAID that he would come like a thief in the night, and so we must keep watch even as we attend to all our duties. "Keep awake for you do not know on what day your Lord is coming" (Matt 24:42). Perhaps we will be helped by meditating on the parable of the maidens: they are allowed to doze off, but in such a way that they are ready at the slightest signal (Matt 25:1-12). For his part, Mark warns us to be watchful doorkeepers (Mark 13:33-37).

> *Beware, keep alert; for you do not know when the time will come. It is like a man going on a journey, when he leaves home and puts his slaves in charge, each with his work, and commands the doorkeeper to be on the watch. Therefore, keep awake—for you do not know when the master of the house will come, in the evening, or at midnight, or at cockcrow, or at dawn, or else he may find you asleep when he comes suddenly. And what I say to you I say to all: Keep awake.* (Mark 13:33-37)

There is an active type of vigilance, such as when we are asked to do some things and not others. From this active vigilance is born fidelity. The unfaithful servants are those who take selfish advantage of what was entrusted to their care, either using it for their own profit (Matt 21:33-46) or administering it irresponsibly (Matt 25:14-30). "Who then is the faithful and wise servant," Jesus asks (Matt 24:45), and who is not?

INFIDELITY AND LACK OF VIGILANCE go hand in hand. They nourish one another mutually. We refuse the Lord's invitation when our hearts are attached to our own judgment, our own interior space, our own business. Even though invited to the wedding feast, some of us prefer our own celebration. And then there are those unfaithful guests who attend but play it safe: they go to the party but remain aloof; they dress informally, as if ready to leave at any moment (Matt 22:1-4).

There is a special kind of vigilance that is more than just paying close attention: it is vigilance that anticipates. In the scriptures we read that among God's faithful people there were many just men and devout women who hoped with great longing. There was John the Baptist, who sent to ask Jesus if he was the one they were hoping for (Matt 11:2-3), and there was Joseph of Arimathea, who was keenly awaiting the kingdom (Mark 15:43). Eagerly waiting as well were Simeon (Luke 2:25-33) and Anna (Luke 2:36-38). Indeed, "all the people were filled with expectation" (Luke 3:15). We would do well to ask ourselves whether our own vigilance has this same element of impatient hopefulness, the kind Paul writes about: "It is my eager expectation and hope that I will not be put to shame in any way, for the creation waits with eager longing for the revealing of the children of God" (Rom 8:19). "And not only the creation, but we ourselves ... groan inwardly while we wait for adoption, the redemption of our bodies" (Rom 8:23), "but we wait for it with patience" (Rom 8:25). This attitude of expectation has the virtue of hastening the coming of God's kingdom, for, as Saint Peter tells us, we ought to be "waiting for and hastening the coming of the day of God." And he later counsels us: "While you are waiting for these things, strive to be found by him at peace, without spot or blemish" (2 Pet 3:12-14).

When John heard in prison what the Messiah was doing, he sent word by his disciples and said to him, "Are you the one who is to come, or are we to wait for another?" (Matt 11:2-3)

Joseph of Arimathea, a respected member of the council, who was also himself waiting expectantly for the kingdom of God, went boldly to Pilate and asked for the body of Jesus. (Mark 15:43)

THE SCRIPTURES DESCRIBE God himself as earnestly hoping for our redemption (2 Pet 3:8-9). Longing for God's manifestation is our way of responding in kind to this paternal longing on God's part. Our watchfulness should be eager but also patient, careful, and faithful; its instruments are prayer and daily examination of conscience. Such longing means waiting patiently for God's manifestation (Jas 5:7-9), yearning for his coming (2 Tim 4:8), and anticipating "the glory of our great God and Savior Jesus Christ" (Titus 2:12-13). It means expecting Christ, the revelation of the Christ, and nothing else.

Do not ignore this one fact, beloved, that with the Lord one day is like a thousand years, and a thousand years are like one day. The Lord is not slow about his promise, as some think of slowness, but is patient with you, not wanting any to perish, but all to come to repentance. (2 Pet 3:8-9)

Be patient, therefore, beloved, until the coming of the Lord. The farmer waits for the precious crop from the earth, being patient with it until it receives the early and the late rains. You also must be patient. Strengthen your hearts, for the coming of the Lord is near. Beloved, do not grumble against one another, so that you may not be judged. See, the Judge is standing at the doors! (James 5:7-9)

That is why the community prays that God reveal himself (Num 6:24-25; 1 Cor 16:22; Apoc 22:20). Let us ask God to reveal to us the one who revealed himself once and for all as both humiliated and glorified for our sake. This petition commits us to hope.

Staying Alert

Prayer

This is the time when you arrive,
Beloved Spouse, so suddenly
that you invite those who are awake
and disregard those who are sleeping.

Behold, we stay alert,
Beloved Spouse, in case you come;
our hearts remain awake
while our eyes take their rest.

Give us a place at your table,
O Love who arrives in darkness,
before the night is over
and the door is finally shut. Amen.

17. The Hardening of Hearts

THE MANIFESTATION OF Jesus Christ makes evident the presence of the spirit of evil, the spirit of sin. Jesus says it clearly: "The world cannot hate you, but it hates me because I testify against it that its works are evil" (John 7:7). No one can know the true reality of sin except by the grace of God, that is, by the manifestation of Jesus Christ: "The Son of God was revealed for this purpose, to destroy the works of the devil" (1 John 3:8). Jesus is the cornerstone of contradiction. Through his incarnation and his sacrifice "the inner thoughts of many are revealed" (Luke 2:35). The epiphany of Jesus Christ is most definitely judgment: "And this is the judgment, that the light has come into the world, and people loved darkness rather than light because their deeds were evil" (John 3:19). In his presence, "nothing is covered up that will not be uncovered, and nothing secret that will not become known" (Luke 12:2; cf. Matt 10:26; Mark 4:22; Matt 5:5).

IN OUR SINFUL HUMAN HEART, as well as in our mysterious clinging to the realm that Paul calls "the law" (cf. Rom 7:13), there exists a secret sector that we guard with special zeal. It is our hidden shame; it is the wound with which we torture ourselves; it is the fear that makes us adhere to law's domain; it is our attachment to death as a way to ward off the life that threatens us; it is so many other things. Each of us knows where in our hearts that zone is located, and often we find ourselves seeking refuge there. We see that space as our private domain, and we believe that only we need see it. Nevertheless, the vision we have of our inner heart is tenuous and myopic. Only the brightness of Jesus' judgment can provide the light we need to correct the distortions of our vision and judgment: "I came into the world for judgment so that those who do not see may see, and those who do see may become blind" (John 9:39). We are blind, and by ourselves we are incapable of envisioning salvation. By holding on to our impotence, we try to keep hidden that shadowy sector of our hearts; not wanting to be saved, we end up becoming ever blinder until our hearts are hopelessly hardened.

THIS HARDNESS OF our hearts takes diverse forms according to our situation, but its origin is always the same sinfulness. It is sin as a veil that beclouds our intelligence (cf. 2 Cor 3:14-16); it is sin as our abandonment of God out of obstinate refusal to open ourselves to his saving grace (recall the tragic text of Rom 1:18-23); it is our self-reliant deceit when we have not just opted for sin but have stubbornly refused to stop sinning despite the strongest evidence (Matt 28:11-15). When hearts grow accustomed to living in darkness, their vision becomes like that of a mole, and all light blinds them. This hardness of heart, which Jesus challenges, was long ago prophesied by Isaiah: "Go and tell these people: 'You keep listening, but do not comprehend; you keep looking, but do not understand.' Make the mind of these people dull, and stop their ears, and shut their eyes, so that they may not look with their eyes, and listen with their ears, and comprehend with their minds, and turn and be healed" (Isa 6:9-11; cf. Matt 13:14-15; Acts 28:26-27; John 12:40). Often the heart's fears lead it to become hardened, and every means available is used to keep it so: that was the drama of Herod. He knew about Israel's great hopes, and he received the guidance needed so that at least a spark of light might enter his heart. But he shut himself off, resorting to hypocrisy and mendacity, and finally to crime. Saint Quodvultdeus notes this very astutely in his second sermon on symbols: *necas parvulos corpore quia te necat timor in corde* ("you slay the bodies of the little ones because the fear in your heart is slaying you"). This terrible drama would reach a climax decades later when the corrupt and feeble heart of Herod's heir yielded to the ire of a lustful woman, the swaying of a flirtatious dancer, and a whimsical request—and was served a severed head.

> *The wrath of God is revealed from heaven against all ungodliness and wickedness of those who by their wickedness suppress the truth. For what can be known about God is plain to them, because God has shown it to them. Ever since the creation of the world his eternal power and divine nature, invisible though they are, have been understood and seen through the things he has made. So they are without excuse; for though they knew God, they did not honor him as God or give thanks to him, but they became futile in their thinking, and their senseless minds were darkened. Claiming to be wise, they became fools; and they exchanged the glory of the immortal God for images resembling a mortal human being or birds or four-footed animals or reptiles.* (Rom 1:18-23)

Often the hearts of men and women who accept Christ are no more than partially hardened. They have not quite crystallized into the sin of obstinacy, the sin against the Holy Spirit. Jesus had to reprehend the apostles for their incomprehension and disbelief with regard to the resurrection (Luke 24:5-11), and such was the case also with many others, like the disciples of Emmaus (Luke 24:25). Peter's hardness of heart left him perplexed even after he had seen the empty tomb; the disciples in the upper chamber were terrified when confronted with what they thought was a ghost; and even after the others believed, Thomas remained the skeptical empiricist. Behind their hesitant hardness of heart, there was also an unnerving fear: the fear of disillusion. So overwhelming was the joy and astonishment of the disciples that they could hardly believe their eyes (Luke 24:41). They were afraid that the joy and delight that each appearance of the Lord brought them might end up being only an ephemeral illusion. Such also is the situation of those who are languid and lukewarm in the service of God: they turn out to be poor, frightened souls who have placed their confidence in a ghost. As a result, they suffer from the kind of rigidity that inhibits their joy, clouds their vision, and obscures the light of Jesus' epiphany.

> *The women were terrified and bowed their faces to the ground, but the men said to them, "Why do you look for the living among the dead? He is not here, but has risen. Remember how he told you, while he was still in Galilee, that the Son of Man must be handed over to sinners, and be crucified, and on the third day rise again." Then they remembered his words, and returning from the tomb, they told all this to the eleven and to all the rest. Now it was Mary Magdalene, Joanna, Mary the mother of James, and the other women with them who told this to the apostles. But these words seemed to them an idle tale, and they did not believe them.* (Luke 24:5-11)

Then there are those persons, similarly lukewarm and mediocre in spirit, who cultivate appearances as a camouflage for true revelation. They take on all the appearances of being good, and they make sure they are seen by others (cf. Matt 6:5, 16-18; 23:27-36; 2 Cor 13:7). But only the Lord is good (Mark 10:18), and only he can set straight the confusion of their infirm hearts. This is the drama of vanity with its artificial light of vainglory: it often fascinates but does not really enlighten us because it fades as quickly as the flower that lasts a day. The radiance of the Lord's epiphany is the only light capable of illuminating the sinful recesses of our hearts with the soft glow of the manger, for this is what produces the only true joy: the joy of feeling saved.

> *And whenever you pray, do not be like the hypocrites; for they love to stand and pray in the synagogues and at the street corners, so that they may be seen by others. Truly I tell you, they have received their reward.* (Matt 6:5)

> *And whenever you fast, do not look dismal, like the hypocrites, for they disfigure their faces so as to show others that they are fasting. Truly I tell you, they have received their reward. But when you fast, put oil on your head and wash your face, so that your fasting may be seen not by others but by your Father who is in secret; and your Father who sees in secret will reward you.* (Matt 6:16-18)

THE REVELATION OF SIN also has its history, not only in human hearts but also in institutions, in peoples, in the entire world. The weeds that grow alongside the tiny shoots of wheat increase in size until the day of the Lord, that day of Christ that will be preceded by the power of the anti-Christ (2 Thess 2:2, 3, 6, 8). It will be the day of the revelation of God's wrath over sinful humankind (Rom 1:18), the day of punishment when God's just judgment will be manifest (Rom 2:5), the day of fire (1 Cor 3:13). At that time, all obstinacy and tepidity will be confounded in fulfillment of the scriptural prophecy, for it will be a day of darkness: "The light of the lamp will shine in you no more; and the voice of the bridegroom and bride will be heard in you no more; for the merchants were the magnates of the earth, and all nations were deceived by your sorcery" (Apoc 18:23). It will be a day of wrath, bitter beyond belief, a day when darkness will suffice fully unto itself, a day when hardened hearts will recognize how irreversible their deluded expectations are. It will be a decisive day in which every human heart will remain fixed in the attitude it adopted during life.

Prayer

Transfigure me, Lord, transfigure me,
but not only me.
Purify also
all the children of your Father
who pray to you with me or who have prayed to you
or who perhaps did not even have a mother
who helped them babble an Our Father.

Transfigure us, Lord, transfigure us.

If perhaps they know you not or have their doubts
or even blaspheme you, wipe their face clean
as Veronica wiped yours;
draw back the thick cataracts of their eyes
so that they see you, Lord, as I see you.

Transfigure them, Lord, transfigure them.

18. God's Plan Unveiled

WE WILL NEVER be able to explain to our complete satisfaction the mysterious designs of God, who has wanted to reveal himself in the course of history. Over a long stretch of time we humans have been learning, like little children from their father, how to recognize and respond to the face of God. None of the Lord's past revelations was partial; they all mysteriously contained the totality of the mystery of his saving plan. But we humans, because of the hardness of our hearts, were unable to grasp the entirety of the mystery of God in Christ; we perceived it only slowly, in bits and pieces. It is the same with our personal histories: the Lord reveals himself "historically" in the unfathomable mystery of those who seek God and allow themselves to be sought by God, but he reveals himself also in those who reject God and flee from him. That is to say, God reveals himself in the historical mystery of our movement through grace and sin.

ON MANY OCCASIONS and in diverse manners (Heb 1:1), the Lord has revealed himself to human beings: he has revealed his name (Exod 6:3), his intentions (Exod 33:12), his ways (1 Kings 8:36; 2 Chron 6:27), his mysteries or secrets (Psalm 50:8; Deut 2:28-30), his covenant (Psalm 24:8), his power (Jer 16:21), and his glory (2 Macc 2:8). Throughout the whole of history, the Lord has unceasingly manifested himself (1 Sam 3:21) and revealed his salvation. "Concerning this salvation, the prophets who prophesied of the grace that was to be ours made careful search and inquiry, inquiring about the person or time that the Spirit of Christ within them indicated when it testified in advance to the suffering destined for Christ and the subsequent glory" (1 Pet 1:10-12). This same salvation history is still a driving force for our Christian living today, for our sad-but-ever-so-great history: "So we have the prophetic message more fully confirmed. You will do well to be attentive to this as to a lamp shining in a dark place, until the day dawns and the morning star rises in your hearts" (2 Pet 1:19). Learning to reinterpret our lives according to the great events of salvation history will help us to understand the revelation contained in the Gospel proclamation we have received: "The righteousness of God is revealed through faith for faith" (Rom 1:17). It was by faith upon faith and by grace upon grace (John 1:16) that the manifestation to which the law and the prophets bore witness was transmitted to us (Rom 3:21). The history of the revelation of God to the chosen people offers us, then, guidelines for observing and orienting our own progress in the faith, for we have been preceded by a "great cloud of witnesses" (Heb 12:1, 11). These witnesses foresaw what was promised and hailed it from afar because they placed their hope in the salvation that was to come, the deliverance "which he promised beforehand through his prophets in the holy scriptures" (Rom 1:2). Every manifestation of God points, therefore, to the epiphany of his Son, our Lord Jesus Christ.

> *I appeared to Abraham, Isaac, and Jacob as God Almighty, but by my name "The Lord" I did not make myself known to them.* (Exod 6:3)

Moses said to God, "Who am I that I should go to Pharaoh, and bring the Israelites out of Egypt?" And God said, "I will be with you; and this shall be the sign for you that it is I who sent you: when you have brought the people out of Egypt, you shall worship God on this mountain." (Exod 3:11-12)

Then hear in heaven, and forgive the sin of your servants, your people Israel, when you teach them the good way in which they should walk; and grant rain on your land, which you have given to your people as an inheritance. (1 Kings 8:36)

May you hear in heaven, forgive the sin of your servants, your people Israel, when you teach them the good way in which they should walk; and send down rain upon your land, which you have given to your people as an inheritance. (2 Chron 6:27)

Not for your sacrifices do I rebuke you;
your burnt-offerings are continually before me. (Psalm 50:8)

Who is the King of glory?
The LORD, *strong and mighty,*
the LORD, *mighty in battle.* (Psalm 24:8)

"Therefore I am surely going to teach them, this time I am going to teach them my power and my might, and they shall know that my name is the LORD." (Jer 16:21)

Then the Lord will disclose these things, and the glory of the Lord and the cloud will appear, as they were shown in the case of Moses, and as Solomon asked that the place should be specially consecrated. (2 Macc 2:8)

The God of our ancestors has manifested himself not only through words and prophecies but also through his works, his prodigies, his wondrous deeds. The word of God explained the meaning of these works, and these in turn confirmed the word.

Thus, it is that the God of the Old Testament presents himself to us as the "God of great deeds": "He is your praise; he is your God who has done for you these great and terrible things that your eyes have seen" (Deut 10:21). As the people behold these amazing works, they sing out in praise: "One generation shall laud your works to another, and shall declare your mighty acts. On the glorious splendor of your majesty, and on your wondrous works, I will meditate. The might of your awesome deeds shall be proclaimed, and I will declare your greatness. They shall celebrate the fame of your abundant goodness, and shall sing aloud of your righteousness" (Psalm 145: 4-7; cf. also Isa 64:1-2; Psalm 106:21-22; 2 Macc 3:24; 14:15; 15:27; Num 6:24-25). By using words, deeds, and laws, therefore, God carefully led his people toward the manifestation of the only word, the only deed, the only law: "Now before faith came, we were imprisoned and guarded under the law until faith would be revealed. Therefore, the law was our disciplinarian until Christ came, so that we might be justified by faith" (Gal 3:23-24). If we were to consider salvation history as something over and done with, revealing the *history* God's deeds, words, and laws but without reaching the fullness of Christ, then we would be incapable of receiving the definitive manifestation that justifies us, and so we would not be free. God speaks and reveals himself to his people; he orients them and guides them on the way, but always toward the definitive, once-and-for-all manifestation of Christ, who truly sets us free (John 8:36).

The Lord bless you and keep you;
the Lord make his face to shine upon you,
and be gracious to you. (Num 6:24-25)

If the Son makes you free, you will be free indeed. (John 8:36)

As I said before, if we want our lives to become part of God's manifestation, they must be inserted into human history. What is more, they must be reinterpreted in light of the great events of this history. Only in this way will our lives attain their full explanation and supreme significance, for while it is true that all things are ours, "we are Christ's, and Christ is God's" (cf. 1 Cor 3:23). Our lordship over all things is always oriented to the lordship of Christ and of God. If we were to understand our own lives or the life of the institution to which we belong outside this perspective, then we would be expressing merely human attitudes. Our judgments would be based on worldly criteria, which inevitably fall outside the shadow of the mystery of the cross. In the Gospel narratives of Jesus' birth, we find him revealing himself to the simple folk, the shepherds, the humble sages (the Magi). The preferences of God do not incline toward social elites or the worldly wise, but only toward the lowly, simple folk who insert themselves into history as servants of the only "Servant," the one who gives meaning to the whole of our journey.

SAINT IGNATIUS, at the end of the Spiritual Exercises, proposes that we "call back into our memory the gifts we have received—creation, redemption, and other particular gifts—so as to ponder with deep affection how much God has done for us, and how much he has given us of what he possesses, and consequently how he, the same Lord, desires to give us his very self, according to his divine design" (SpEx 234). Doing this means searching out in our own lives the traces of God, the God who desires to will himself to us as our final and definitive destiny. Following Ignatius's lead, let us end our prayer by contemplating Jesus Christ, the Lord to whom every revealed promise points. Beneath his gentle gaze, let us look back over our lives and the life of this institution with its ups and downs, its pains and joys. Deuteronomy can help us: "Remember the long way that the Lord your God has led you these forty years in the wilderness, in order to humble you, testing you to know what was in your heart, whether or not you would keep his commandments. He humbled you by letting you hunger.... The clothes on your back did not wear out and your feet did not swell these forty years. Know then in your heart that as a parent disciplines a child so the Lord your God disciplines you. Therefore keep the commandments of the Lord your God, by walking in his ways and by fearing him" (Deut 8:2-6).

Prayer

Because I have seen you, Lord,
and desire to see you again,
I want to believe.
I saw you, yes, when as a child
I was baptized in water.
Then, cleansed of ancient blame,
I could see you unveiled...

Now my eyes are tired from seeing
so much light without really seeing;
stumbling through the darkness of the world,
I proceed like one who's blind yet sees.
You who gave sight to the blind
and to Nicodemus as well,
infuse into my arid pupils
two drops fresh with faith.

19. Passing On the Faith

THE EPIPHANY OF GOD in Christ did not end with the earthly existence of Jesus. The revelation of God's gift has been transmitted "from faith in faith" throughout history by all those who assumed it into their own lives by becoming disciples of Jesus and apostles for others. Paul speaks of this transmission from generation to generation when writing to Timothy: "I am reminded of your sincere faith, a faith that dwelt first in your grandmother Lois and your mother Eunice and now, I am sure, dwells in you" (2 Tim 1:5). Similarly, in our own day, we can speak of the faith of our ancestors, recalling the men and women who were the instruments God used to manifest his grace toward us. We can also look into the future and envision our own spiritual descendants, those who will receive our mission and our testimony about this revelation.

EACH ONE OF US can say with Paul, "God was pleased to reveal his Son to me" (Gal 1:15-16), for we have received the revelation of God's glory in Christ (cf. John 21:1). Speaking mystically, we can also say that we have seen the risen Lord in our lives (cf. 1 Cor 9:1; 15:8, 11). We are blessed because we have believed even without seeing him physically. As disciples, we are made participants in the mystery of Christ, who was not made known to earlier generations but "has now been revealed to his holy apostles and prophets by the Spirit" (Eph 3:4-5).

Saint Paul bids us give glory "to God who is able to strengthen us according to the gospel and the proclamation of Jesus Christ, according to the revelation of the mystery that was kept secret for long ages but is now disclosed, and through the prophetic writings is made known to all the Gentiles, according to the command of the eternal God, to bring about the obedience of faith" (Rom 16:25-27).

WE RECEIVE OUR MISSION as apostles from Christ himself when he reveals himself to us (cf. Rom 1:5), and it is by means of us that Christ now speaks and acts (Rom 15:18). He is not weak but powerful in the preaching of those who accept his revelation (2 Cor 13:2-3). We are heirs to the mission of the disciples: making public what has been revealed to us and what Jesus has told us (Matt 10:26-33). Whoever hears the disciples hears Jesus himself (Luke 10:16). Thus, the revelation, the epiphany, the "dis-covering" of God, is carried on through those who are constituted disciples. As disciples, we are promised the Spirit of truth who will bear witness, who will teach us all things, and who will lead us to the fullness of truth (John 14:26; 15:26; 16:13). In our docility to the Holy Spirit, the source of all revelation (cf. 1 Cor 2:10), we have the assurance of receiving and transmitting the revelation of Christ rather than a merely human message (1 Thess 2:13).

"So have no fear of them; for nothing is covered up that will not be uncovered, and nothing secret that will not become known. What I say to you in the dark, tell in the light; and what you hear whispered, proclaim from the housetops. Do not fear those who kill the body but cannot kill the soul; rather fear him who can destroy both soul and body in hell. Are not two sparrows sold for a penny? Yet not one of them will fall to the ground unperceived by your

Father. And even the hairs of your head are all counted. So do not be afraid; you are of more value than many sparrows.

"Everyone therefore who acknowledges me before others, I also will acknowledge before my Father in heaven; but whoever denies me before others, I also will deny before my Father in heaven."
(Matt 10:26-33)

When we accept God's epiphany, we are constituted disciples and set out on a journey, as did Abraham. We become bearers of the epiphany, which may take the form of the Magi's star (Matt 2:2, 7, 9-12), or Joseph's doubts (Matt 1:20), or the angel's warning in a dream to save the child (Matt 2:13, 19, 22), or the news Mary receives about her cousin's pregnancy (Luke 2:26-38). Whatever form it takes, our task as bearers of the epiphany always goes beyond the simple acts of transmitting a message, relating a verifiable history, or proving some truth. When fully accepted, the epiphany of God becomes flesh in the life of the disciple in such a way that it can be transmitted only from this "incarnation." That is to say, it can be transmitted to others not by words of flesh and blood, not by human wisdom, but only by the scandalous inevitability of the cross; it can be transmitted only by *martyrion*, by bearing witness. The disciple is first and foremost a witness: "I myself did not know him; but I came baptizing with water for this reason, that he might be revealed to Israel.... I myself have seen and have testified that this is the Son of God" (John 1:31, 34).

Jesus asks us to let the light of our truth, our testimony to the truth, shine before others so that they may see our good works and give glory to the Father in heaven (Matt 5:14-16). As disciples, we replicate in some way the very mystery of Christ's epiphany. By bearing witness, we produce light that provokes joy, and from the joy flows glory. This is the essence of bearing testimony: stirring praise and adoration of the Father through the joy that invades the hearts of those who see and hear the message. The true disciple is light, as Jesus declares about the Baptist: "He was a burning and shining lamp, and you were willing to rejoice for a while in his light" (John 5:35). The life of the disciples must be irreproachable so that their light reaches into the darkest shadows: "Do all things without murmuring and arguing, so that you may be blameless and innocent, children of God without blemish in the midst of a crooked and perverse generation, in which you shine like stars in the world" (Phil 2:14-15).

> *"You are the light of the world. A city built on a hill cannot be hidden. No one after lighting a lamp puts it under the bushel basket, but on the lampstand, and it gives light to all in the house. In the same way, let your light shine before others, so that they may see your good works and give glory to your Father in heaven."* (Matt 5:14-16)

The testimony the disciples give is the very reason why they must be continually divested of self-interest. They are to proclaim and confirm the faith of their brothers and sisters. They must strive to awaken profuse joy in the hearts of the faithful so that they give glory to their Father in heaven. The disciples are to decrease so that Christ increases. If they remain faithful to their vocation of discipleship, their final destiny is already marked out: "Very truly, I tell you, when you were younger, you used to fasten your own belt and to go wherever you wished. But when you grow old, you will stretch out your hands, and someone else will fasten a belt around you and take you where you do not wish to go" (John 21:18). There is nothing improvised in this following of Jesus—it requires the preparation of a lifetime.

Prayer

Seeing God in creatures,
seeing God made mortal,
seeing celestial beauty
in humble human attire,

Seeing joy weep tears,
seeing wealth so poor,
seeing greatness brought low,
and seeing that so was God's desire.
Great was the mercy we received
on that most blessed day!
Whoever sees it, may it be I!

Making peace amid so much war,
bringing warmth to such great cold,
letting what is mine belong to all,
planting heaven here on earth.
What a magnificent mission
God has entrusted to our hands!
Whoever does it, may it be I! Amen.

20. The Son Reveals the Father

THE WHOLE HISTORY of God's revelation, which for us is salvation history, reaches its culmination in Christ, who is the "revealer" of the Father. Christ is the one who comes in the fullness of time; all earlier revelation was pointing to him as the ultimate secret that the Father wants to reveal to us. When Christ appears among us, the Father is revealing himself in his mysterious entirety.

JESUS CHRIST is the definitive revealer of the mystery of God. He announces the Father and makes him known (cf. John 1:18). What he has heard from the Father, he announces to the world (John 3:3, 32; 8:26; 15:15). Jesus is the Father's only-begotten Son who comes into the world keenly aware of his mission of revealing the Father and fully empowered to carry it out. He has authority and he makes it felt: "They were astounded at his teaching, for he taught them as one having authority, and not as the scribes.... They were all amazed, and they kept on asking one another, 'What is this? A new teaching—with authority! He commands even the unclean spirits, and they obey him.' At once his fame began to spread throughout the surrounding region of Galilee" (Mark 1:22, 27-28). Jesus produces amazement among those who hear his words and behold his deeds. This capacity to cause astonishment comes from who he is: the one to whom all power in heaven and on earth has been given (Matt 28:18). That is why, when he reveals the mystery of God, he reveals also the conflicting desires of people's hearts (cf. Luke 1:35-36). By reflecting God's authority as the only-begotten Son, he becomes a cornerstone of contradiction among his own people (cf. Matt 21:42; Acts 4:14). As revealer of the triune mystery, Jesus Christ enters into people's lives with unprecedented authority, but he also suffers in his own flesh the rejection brought on by this very revelation.

> *I do not call you servants any longer, because the servant does not know what the master is doing; but I have called you friends, because I have made known to you everything that I have heard from my Father.* (John 15:15)

As REVEALER OF GOD, Jesus Christ brings light to every human being (John 1:9) because he himself is the light of humankind (John 1:4-5; 8:12).

> *Again Jesus spoke to them, saying, "I am the light of the world. Whoever follows me will never walk in darkness but will have the light of life."* (John 8:12)

When Jesus Christ is present, the true light shines and all shadows disappear (1 John 2:8). But then begins the drama of the rejection of the light. This light, which brings the law and the prophets to fulfillment, is spurned because its luminosity is different from what was expected; its brilliance illumines places other than those imagined; it provokes opposition as challenging as it is perplexing. That is why the announcement of the fullness of God's revelation in God's good time is addressed precisely to those most deprived of fullness from a human perspective: the simple folk, the poor fishermen (cf. Matt 5:3), those who humbly keep God's commandments (John 14:21).

To these Jesus imparts knowledge of the Father that only the Son can give (Matt 11:27): "Whoever has seen me has seen the Father" (see John 14:7-9). What is more, this privilege granted the poor brings forth praise from Jesus: "I thank you, Father, Lord of heaven and earth, because you have hidden these things from the wise and the intelligent and have revealed them to infants; yes, Father, for such was your gracious will. All things have been handed over to me by my Father; and no one knows who the Son is except the Father, or who the Father is except the Son and anyone to whom the Son chooses to reveal him" (Luke 10:21-22).

In reporting these words of praise, the Gospel tells us that Jesus, inspired with the Holy Spirit, was filled with joy (Luke 10:21). This outburst of Jesus reveals the joy that exists deep within the Trinity. The revelation of this divine joy stirs human hearts to rejoicing, as we see in the joy of Elizabeth and Mary during the visitation (Luke 2:39-45) and in the joy of the shepherds in Bethlehem (Luke 2:10-20). It is the joy of all those who draw close to Jesus with good will and receive from him the revelation of the Father, who is life (1 John 1:2). It is an almost compulsive joy that emboldens those who experience it for they cannot help but speak of what they have seen and heard (Acts 4:19-20). Such joy is maintained even in the midst of persecution and punishment: "The disciples left the presence of the council, rejoicing that they were counted worthy to suffer dishonor for the name of Jesus" (Acts 5:41). It is a joy that goes beyond all practical outcomes, whether human or superhuman, even those that are miraculous; it finds its culmination in rejoicing that our names stand written in the heavens (cf. Luke 10:20).

But the angel said to them, "Do not be afraid; for see—I am bringing you good news of great joy for all the people: to you is born this

day in the city of David a Savior, who is the Messiah, the Lord.
This will be a sign for you: you will find a child wrapped in bands
of cloth and lying in a manger." And suddenly there was with the
angel a multitude of the heavenly host, praising God and saying,
"Glory to God in the highest heaven,
*   and on earth peace among those whom he favors!"*

(Luke 2:10-14)

Saint Ignatius calls this joy "spiritual consolation": "By consolation I mean that which occurs when some interior motion
is caused within the soul through which it comes to be inflamed
with love of its Creator and Lord. As a result it can love no
created thing on the face of the earth in itself, but only in the
Creator of them all. Similarly, this consolation is experienced
when the soul sheds tears which move it to love for its Lord—
whether they are tears of grief for its own sin, or about the Passion of Christ our Lord, or about other matters directly ordered
to his service and praise. Finally, under the word consolation
I include every increase in hope, faith, and charity, and every
interior joy which calls and attracts one toward heavenly things
and to the salvation of one's soul, by bringing it tranquility and
peace in its Creator and Lord" (SpEx 316). This should be the
habitual state of those who receive the revelation of Jesus Christ
with eagerness and sincerity of heart.

Even in the midst of tribulation (such as when the apostles
were scourged), spiritual consolation is preserved in some
form. Even when suspended on the cross, the person who faithfully receives the word of revelation will not be lacking that
profound peace that is part of consolation.

THOSE WHO HEAR the voice of Jesus are filled with joy (cf.
John 10:3, 27). But this joy is oriented toward a definite goal,
as was the case with Abraham (John 8:56). Just as Jesus "was

filled with joy in the Holy Spirit," so also our joy, under the influence of the same Spirit, learns to raise its sights beyond time and space. It is through joy that our salvation history gains access to the glory of God, and it is Jesus who reveals to us the glory of the Father (John 1:14) because the Father is glorified in the Son (cf. John 14:13). This is how we should understand the affectionate way in which Jesus reproaches Martha: "Did I not tell you that if you would believe, you would see the glory of God?" (John 11:40). The glory of God poured out in Christ, almost as if it were escaping through a crack (cf. John 2:11), is the glorious fullness of light that gives us the hope of beholding it everlastingly: "In his right hand he held seven stars, and from his mouth came a sharp, two-edged sword, and his face was like the sun shining with full force" (Apoc 1:16). When time comes to an end, God will be manifested as the fullness of light; he will be the ultimate light not only for each one of us but also for the world: "The heavenly city has no need of sun or moon to shine upon it, for the glory of God is its light, and its lamp is the Lamb" (Apoc 21:23).

> *The gatekeeper opens the gate for him, and the sheep hear his voice. He calls his own sheep by name and leads them out.* (John 10:3)

> *My sheep hear my voice. I know them, and they follow me.* (John 10:27)

WE HAVE STRESSED that Jesus Christ is not only the revealer but also the supreme revelation of the Father. God's efforts to open human eyes and ears (cf. Num 22:31; 1 Sam 9:15-16) have a long and diverse history that tends toward Christ and culminates in him: "Long ago God spoke to our ancestors in many and various ways by the prophets, but in these last days he has spoken to us by a Son, whom he appointed heir of all things, through whom he also created the worlds. He is the reflection of God's glory and the exact imprint of God's very being, and he sustains all things by his powerful word. When he had made purification for sins, he sat down at the right hand of the Majesty on high" (Heb 1:1-3). God makes Christ manifest to us. God "saved us and called us with a holy calling, not according to our works but according to his own purpose and grace. This grace was given to us in Christ Jesus before the ages began, but it has now been revealed through the appearing of our Savior Christ Jesus, who abolished death and brought life and immortality to light through the gospel" (2 Tim 1:9-10). God's grace, which is the source of salvation for all human beings, was revealed in Christ (Titus 2:11), and in him was made manifest the goodness and loving kindness of God our Savior (Titus 3:4-5).

Jesus is the Word made flesh, the word of life that the first apostles and disciples saw and heard and touched with their hands (John 1:4; 1 John 1:1). They were blessed because they saw and heard what many ancient prophets had desired to experience (cf. Matt 13:16; 1 Pet 1:12). But they were blessed not so much because they could see Christ in the flesh but because it was the Father who revealed him to them (Matt 16:17). That is why Jesus himself clearly proclaimed what might have seemed contradictory: "Blessed are those who have not seen and yet have come to believe!" (John 20:29). Into this blessed state will enter all of us if we trust not in the revelation of flesh and blood (cf. Matt 16:17) but rather open our hearts to the Father's supreme revelation, his great gift to us. By doing this, we are inserted into the history of all those who hope against all hope (Rom 4:18); we are counted among those who allow themselves to be led by God toward the promised land and who persevere as though seeing the one who is invisible (cf. Heb 11:27).

THE GIFT OF CHRIST we receive from the Father is a manifestation of love: "God's love was revealed among us in this way: God sent his only Son into the world so that we might live through him" (1 John 4:9). This is true for all of us who have not seen or heard in the flesh and yet believe, for the revelation of Christ is the gift of the Father and the work of the Spirit; it is communicated to all who allow the Spirit to act in their souls (cf. 1 Cor 14:26, 30; Phil 3:15). The Spirit leads us to the truth (John 16:13). Christ Jesus, made manifest in the flesh, has come for all times "to give light to those who sit in darkness and in the shadow of death and to guide our feet into the way of peace" (Luke 1:79). That is why the definitive revelation of Jesus Christ will surpass all history and reach its fullness beyond our present time and space. It will be "the revelation of Jesus Christ which God gave him to show to his servants about what must soon take place" (Apoc 1:1).

What should be done then, my friends? When you come together, each one has a hymn, a lesson, a revelation, a tongue, or an interpretation. Let all things be done for building up. (1 Cor 14:26)

If a revelation is made to someone else sitting nearby, let the first person be silent. (1 Cor 14:30)

When the Spirit of truth comes, he will guide you into all the truth; for he will not speak on his own, but will speak whatever he hears, and he will declare to you the things that are to come. (John 16:13)

Prayer

Word of God, eternal light divine,
eternal source of all pure truth,
glory of God that illumines the cosmos,
bright burning torch in darkest night.

Word eternally pronounced
in the Father's mind, what joy
that in our history he was born a child
from the bosom of the Virgin.

Do not cease to shine, heavenly beacons,
with the rays of light that God sends forth;
faithfully guide our friends, our peoples;
proclaim the truth on every path. Amen.

21. The Vision of the Wedding Feast

T HE ANTIPHON FOR VESPERS in the liturgy of the Lord's Epiphany unites three signs: "Three mysteries mark this holy day: on this day, the star leads the Magi to the infant Christ; on this day, water is changed into wine for the wedding feast; and on this day, Christ desires to be baptized by John in the river Jordan to bring us salvation. Alleluia." These mysteries represent three manifestations of the Messiah, the Son of God: to the nations (the Magi), to the people of Israel (the baptism of Jesus), and to his disciples (the wedding at Cana). Not only does the liturgy bring the three mysteries together, but it draws out the relations among them, as the antiphon of lauds explains: "Today the Bridegroom claims his bride, the Church, since Christ has washed her sins away in Jordan's water; the Magi hasten with their gifts to the royal wedding; and the wedding guests rejoice, for Christ has changed water into wine. Alleluia."

The three mysteries are united in the vision of a wedding feast: the bridegroom is Christ the Messiah, who loves the Church as his bride, who entrusts himself to her (cf. Eph 5:25), and who purifies her in the waters of baptism, making her his own. The language is not just of engagement but of marriage: it tells about a wedding feast attended by many guests who bring gifts and grow merry on fine wine. It is the epiphany of Christ, but not only that; it is the wedding of the king's son, the Son of

God, who takes this people as his own and becomes one with them as husband does with wife. It is the epiphany of a wedding that is also the epiphany of the bride, the saintly and sinful Mother Church.

Husbands, love your wives, just as Christ loved the church and gave himself up for her. (Eph 5:25)

IN THE COURSE of salvation history, matrimony has been conceived in terms of family descent and a people's history. It is based on a command of God (Gen 1:27-28; 2:24) that is repeated frequently in the New Testament (cf. Mark 10:6; Matt 19:4; Eph 5:31). Those who marry are to leave mother and father and be united as one flesh. It is a commitment that involves uprooting for the sake of fusion, but it does not just end there. When man and woman are joined together, they share a common life with its ups and downs, which do not exclude rupture (adultery) or separation (widowhood), but through it all they seek fulfillment. Everything is conceived in stages: the betrothal (Adam dreams of Eve before knowing her), the wedding (time of joy and celebration), and slow growth toward fullness ("that you may see the children of your children till the third and the fourth generation"). All this has become a symbol of salvation history: before Christ there is the time of waiting, the betrothal; the earthly presence of the Messiah represents the time of the wedding; then there is the time of separation, of widowhood; and finally there is the time of moving toward the consummation, the expectation of the final, eschatological wedding.

So God created humankind in his image,
   in the image of God he created them;
   male and female he created them.

> *God blessed them, and God said to them, "Be fruitful and multiply, and fill the earth and subdue it; and have dominion over the fish of the sea and over the birds of the air and over every living thing that moves upon the earth."* (Gen 1:27-28)

> *Therefore a man leaves his father and his mother and clings to his wife, and they become one flesh.* (Gen 2:24)

Though matrimony is usually conceived in terms of family descent and a people's history, it can also be seen as providing symbols that help us define the history of God's people. Thus, the New Testament concepts regarding both matrimony and salvation history relate directly to the "Now" of Jesus' presence among us as we move eschatologically toward the definitive "Now" of the final consummation.

IN THE OLD TESTAMENT, the relation between man and woman was seen as a symbol of the relation between Yahweh and the people, but now it has come to symbolize the relation between Jesus and the Church. Saint Paul cites the Old Testament prophet Hosea (Rom 9:25), who declares that the people will be called "my beloved," the spouse of Yahweh, his companion and helpmate (Gen 1:27; 2:18, 23). Other prophets also announce that Israel is the spouse of Yahweh (Jer 2:2; Isa 62:5), a bride richly adorned and restored, the beautiful one to whom the nations will be drawn from all the earth: "Lift up your eyes round about and see; they all gather, they come to you. As I live, says the Lord, you shall put them all on as an ornament, you shall bind them on as a bride does" (Isa 49:18). "Lift up your eyes round about, and see"—with these words, the prophet addresses Jerusalem as God's bride, and he foretells God's revelation in that city (Isa 60:4). The people of Israel are revealed as the bride of Yahweh, and all nations will be drawn to her to celebrate her wedding. She is "the beloved" of the Song of Songs; she is the one in whom the prophet Hosea takes great delight. The same image relates the Church to Jesus, as Paul tells the Corinthians: "I feel a divine jealousy for you, for I promised you in marriage to one husband, to present you as a chaste virgin to Christ" (2 Cor 11:2). For Christ is to the Church as a husband is to his wife: "Christ is the head of the Church, the body of which he is the savior.... No one ever hates his own body, but nourishes and tenderly cares for it, just as Christ does for the Church, because we are members of his body" (Eph 5:22-23, 29-30). "This is a great mystery, and I am applying it to Christ and the Church" (Eph 5:32).

IT WAS THE CUSTOM in Israel to celebrate weddings with a banquet, and Jesus chose a wedding feast to begin his mission even though his hour had not yet come (cf. John 2:4-5). "Jesus did this, the first of his signs, in Cana of Galilee and revealed his glory; and his disciples believed in him" (John 2:11). Just as Jesus wanted to begin his mission with a banquet, so also the mission will end with a banquet, the wedding feast of the Lamb that will celebrate the definitive bonding of the victorious Christ with his people: "Let us rejoice and exult and give him the glory, for the marriage of the Lamb has come, and his bride has made herself ready; to her it has been granted to be clothed with fine linen, bright and pure—for the fine linen is the righteous deeds of the saints" (Apoc 19:7-8). This wedding banquet is in fulfillment of the ancient prophecy of Isaiah: "On this mountain the Lord of hosts will make for all peoples a feast of rich food, a feast of well-matured wines, of rich food filled with marrow, of well-matured wines strained clear. And he will destroy on this mountain the shroud that is cast over all peoples, the sheet that is spread over all nations; he will swallow up death for ever. Then the Lord God will wipe away the tears from all faces, and the disgrace of his people he will take away from all the earth, for the Lord has spoken" (Isa 25:6-9).

> *And Jesus said to her, "Woman, what concern is that to you and to me? My hour has not yet come." His mother said to the servants, "Do whatever he tells you." (John 2:4-5)*

In the narratives of the Last Supper, Jesus relates his imminent death for his people to the eschatological banquet of the Messiah, saying that he will not drink wine again "until that day when I drink it new with you in my Father's kingdom" (Matt 26:29). "You are those who have stood by me in my trials; and I confer on you, just as my Father has conferred on me, a kingdom, so that you may eat and drink at my table in my kingdom, and you will sit on thrones judging the twelve tribes of Israel" (Luke 22:28-30). Taking part in the wedding banquet of the glorious Lord will be something decisive (cf. Matt 25:10-13). It will be Jesus himself who gloriously serves his people, his bride, his Church. The one who was constituted Lord over all precisely because he took on the form of a servant (cf. Phil 2:6-10) will, even in the fullness of his glory, delight in being the servant of his servants, the footman of his bride (cf. Luke 12:35-38). This is what is decisive in the final banquet: Christ will give himself over to serving his Church, but he will do so now not out of concern for sin and death (cf. Heb 10:18); rather, he will care for her and rejoice in her as only a lover can.

> *Christ, though he was in the form of God,*
> *did not regard equality with God*
> *as something to be exploited,*
> *but emptied himself,*
> *taking the form of a slave,*
> *being born in human likeness.*

And being found in human form,
he humbled himself
and became obedient to the point of death—
even death on a cross.
Therefore God also highly exalted him
and gave him the name
that is above every name,
so that at the name of Jesus
every knee should bend,
in heaven and on earth and under the earth. (Phil 2:6-10)

Be dressed for action and have your lamps lit; be like those who
are waiting for their master to return from the wedding banquet,
so that they may open the door for him as soon as he comes and
knocks. Blessed are those slaves whom the master finds alert when
he comes; truly I tell you, he will fasten his belt and have them sit
down to eat, and he will come and serve them. If he comes during
the middle of the night, or near dawn, and finds them so, blessed
are those slaves. (Luke 12:35-38)

THE BANQUET IS OPEN not just to anybody but to those who are invited, and they indeed are fortunate: "Blessed are those who will break bread in the kingdom of God!" (Luke 14:15). The invitation goes out to many (cf. Matt 22:1-10; Luke 14:15-8; Matt 20:16). The guests arrive for the wedding banquet, and there is an ambience of joy: "He who has the bride is the bridegroom. The friend of the bridegroom, who stands and hears him, rejoices greatly at the bridegroom's voice. For this reason my joy has been fulfilled" (John 3:29). The exuberance of this wedding has been announced from ancient times: "I will greatly rejoice in the Lord, my whole being shall exult in my God; for he has clothed me with the garments of salvation, he has covered me with the robe of righteousness, as a bridegroom decks himself with a garland, and as a bride adorns herself with her jewels" (Isa 61:10). "As a young man marries a young woman, so shall your builder marry you, and as the bridegroom rejoices over the bride, so shall your God rejoice over you" (Isa 62:5; cf. also Psalm 45).

The joy that prevails at the banquet takes on the form of worship in the heavenly Jerusalem and also in our own time of hopeful expectation. It is not fitting that the wedding guests fast while the bridegroom is still with them (Mark 2:19). Our act of worship is a celebration in which the bridegroom becomes truly present: "Jesus said to them, 'The wedding-guests cannot mourn as long as the bridegroom is with them, can they? The days will come when the bridegroom is taken away from them, and then they will fast'" (Matt 9:15). Joy reigns among the disciples because Jesus is with them; there is no fasting, only feasting.

It is worth noting that in the Gospel text the person who speaks of Jesus as the bridegroom is John, who baptized him in the Jordan (cf. John 3:29-30). It is John the Baptist who bears witness to Jesus, calling him the Lamb of God (John 1:32-36), and it is also John who calls him "bridegroom." John bears witness to the fulfillment of what he was told by the one who sent him to baptize (John 1:33-34). He sees the Spirit descend upon Jesus; he hears the voice of the Father affirming that this is indeed his Son. As a faithful Jew, John's heart has longed for the day when his people would be wedded with the Messiah, and now in the baptism of Jesus in the Jordan he is witnessing the revelation of that long-awaited celebration: the bridegroom is purifying the bride of her sins.

> *"He who has the bride is the bridegroom. The friend of the bridegroom, who stands and hears him, rejoices greatly at the bridegroom's voice. For this reason my joy has been fulfilled. He must increase, but I must decrease."* (John 3:29-30)

And John testified, "I saw the Spirit descending from heaven like a dove, and it remained on him. I myself did not know him, but the one who sent me to baptize with water said to me, 'He on whom you see the Spirit descend and remain is the one who baptizes with the Holy Spirit.' And I myself have seen and have testified that this is the Son of God." (John 1:32-36)

I HAVE MENTIONED already the text in which Jesus prophesied that the bridegroom would be taken away from the bride and the wedding guests: "The days will come when the bridegroom is taken away from them, and then they will fast on that day" (Mark 2:20)—or "in those days," in the version of Luke (Luke 5:35). When the bridegroom is taken away, the bride weeps and is left alone as a widow. Thus is revealed the widowhood of the Church as she awaits the definitive coming of the Bridegroom. The widowed Church is pursued by predators (cf. Matt 23:14; Mark 12:40; Luke 20:47); she serves the Lord with prayer and fasting and importunately beseeches God for her needs and those of her children (Luke 18:3). Like the poor widow in the temple, the widowed Church contributes all her livelihood (Mark 12:42-44; Luke 21:1-3) so that her labors will bring honor to the Bridegroom for whom her heart longs. For the widowed Church, every one of her children is an "only child," and they are known by the name with which she gave birth to them in baptism. Even when one of her children is "dead" to the kingdom, he remains her "only child," and she weeps for that child (Luke 7:12).

He looked up and saw rich people putting their gifts into the treasury; he also saw a poor widow put in two small copper coins. He said, "Truly I tell you, this poor widow has put in more than all of them." (Luke 21:1-3)

As he approached the gate of the town, a man who had died was being carried out. He was his mother's only son, and she was a widow; and with her was a large crowd from the town. (Luke 7:12)

The grief-stricken silence of the widowed Church impresses itself on us as we behold Mary at the foot of the cross. She who was by his side in Cana of Galilee (John 2:1) is also standing firm on Calvary (John 19:25). During the wedding at Cana, she interceded with Jesus so that he might hasten his hour. Here on Golgotha, as she silently surrenders her Child, she receives her children. While the Church is born from the open side of her Son, she brings forth the children of the Church, who from this moment on will be her children. It is the hour of the "baptism" with which Jesus has longed to be baptized; it is the hour of his anguish until it be accomplished (Luke 12:50); it is the hour of the Church's epiphany.

THE WIDOWED CHURCH is constant in prayer (Acts 1:14); she preaches the Gospel and cares for the poor (Acts 6:2-4). She looks to the Spirit, who constantly enriches her with new children, and she longs for her Spouse, who will return for the ultimate union. She has in a way accepted the separation from her Spouse, but she earnestly yearns for him: "Come, Lord Jesus!" (Apoc 22:20). She has accepted the first invitation to the wedding.

All these were constantly devoting themselves to prayer, together with certain women, including Mary the mother of Jesus, as well as his brothers. (Acts 1:14)

And the twelve called together the whole community of the disciples and said, "It is not right that we should neglect the word of God in order to wait at tables. Therefore, friends, select from among yourselves seven men of good standing, full of the Spirit and of wisdom, whom we may appoint to this task, while we, for our part, will devote ourselves to prayer and to serving the word." (Acts 6:2-4)

But not all those invited to the wedding feast have accepted the call. Some have even rejected the invitation and have opted instead for their own celebration, if not for an anti-celebration. They talk about business and about fields they've bought, or they cruelly mistreat those who announce the wedding, even killing them. "The wedding is ready, but those invited are not worthy" (Matt 22:2-14). Since their hearts cannot recognize the importance of the feast, they are disinclined to attend and so never find their way there. They place more value on their newly purchased fields, their five yoke of oxen, or their own marriage (wedded as they are with themselves, their plans, their own interests) (Luke 14:15-24). Over them is suspended the judgment: "I tell you, none of those who were invited will taste my dinner" (Luke 14:24). They are not friends of the bridegroom, and they form no part of the people-bride-Church that loves the Lord.

These men and women do not live in a world apart. They form their own generation and have their own offspring. They are the wicked and adulterous generation that asks for revelatory signs that conform to human plans; they seek esoteric revelations (cf. Matt 12:39; 16:4). The Son of Man will be ashamed of this adulterous generation when he returns for the supreme wedding feast (Mark 8:38). This wicked generation not only rejects the invitation to the banquet and demands signs to suit its fancy, but it perversely organizes its own anti-banquet, such as the one celebrated by Herodias, the anti-bride who hated John precisely because of her adulterous behavior (Mark

6:17). This rejection of God's invitation finds its most diabolical expression in a carnal banquet attended by the followers of Jezebel (Apoc 2:20-23) or the great prostitute (Apoc 17:1-2), all of whom will be judged and condemned on the great day of the definitive wedding feast. Following the lead of false and fanatical teachers, these reprobates reject what God has united (cf. 1 Tim 4:3) and end up prostituting their bodies by bedding down with infidelity and willful venality. "The body is meant not for fornication but for the Lord, and the Lord for the body. And God raised the Lord and will also raise us by his power. Do you not know that your bodies are members of Christ? Should I therefore take the members of Christ and make them members of a prostitute? Never! Do you not know that whoever is united to a prostitute becomes one body with her? For it is said, 'The two shall be one flesh.' But anyone united to the Lord becomes one spirit with him. Shun fornication! Every sin that a person commits is outside the body; but the fornicator sins against the body itself" (1 Cor 6:13-18). These words of Paul contain something more than the obvious warning against fornication. Paul understands this sin and "the foulness and evil which [it] contains in itself" (SpEx 57) as symbolic: those who are not faithful to the invitation to the banquet are not faithful to the Bridegroom. They will therefore not be members of the body of the spouse, the Church, but will instead be members of the prostitute, the "anti-Church"—they will belong to the body of the anti-Christ.

ADULTERY HAS ALWAYS been considered a grave sin, even if only desired (Matt 5:27-28). It has been punished severely (Deut 22:22) because it was seen as comparable to violating the covenant (cf. Gen 20:3-7). Thus, Israel differed from other cultures and religions in giving adultery a public dimension; it was seen as offending not only against the private institution of matrimony but also against divine law (Exod 20:14). It threatened the very foundation of the people of Israel, their covenant with God, and so it was the duty of the whole community to inflict the punishment for adultery. For Christians as well, adultery is incompatible with hope for God's kingdom (1 Cor 6:9-11) and will be especially judged by God (cf. Heb 13:4). That is why skepticism about Christ's return in judgment leads to an increase in libertinism (2 Pet 3:3-10), of which adultery forms a part and is also a symbol. The ancient Desert Fathers used to say, "God punishes hidden pride with manifest lust," and Paul lists among the "works of the flesh" the pride of those who keep their distance from the wedding feast (cf. Gal 5:19-21; Eph 5:3-4).

> *"You have heard that it was said, 'You shall not commit adultery.' But I say to you that everyone who looks at a woman with lust has already committed adultery with her in his heart."* (Matt 5:27-28)

What the community must clearly avoid is worship of the flesh, that is, idolatry and paganism (1 Cor 6:12-20; 5:9-12). We are led to such worship through "friendship with the world" (Jas 4:4), as was the case with Solomon. Because adultery symbolizes idolatry, it is seen as an offense against God's union with his people and against Christ's union with his Church (Hosea 1-3; Jer 3:3-9; Ezekiel 16; Isa 50:1). The fleeting delight of our private celebrations and the fascination of our personal plans of salvation end up devoid of eschatological joy; they are evidence of a widowhood without hope, without children, without a spouse who will return—an utterly sterile state (Jer 7:34; 16:9; Apoc 18:23).

I wrote to you in my letter not to associate with sexually immoral persons—not at all meaning the immoral of this world, or the greedy and robbers, or idolaters, since you would then need to go out of the world. But now I am writing to you not to associate with anyone who bears the name of brother or sister who is sexually immoral or greedy, or is an idolater, reviler, drunkard, or robber. Do not even eat with such a one. For what have I to do with judging those outside? Is it not those who are inside that you are to judge? (1 Cor 5:9-12)

IN THE CHURCH, we have both wheat and weeds, both wise maidens and foolish ones (Matt 25:1-13). That is how history proceeds. In the midst of human history, Christ reveals his spouse, his Church, and invites us to share in his wedding feast. He asks us to remain vigilant as we await his coming, and he calls others from afar. He prepares for us fine wine and demands only that we dress suitably, that is, that we be purified by the baptism with which he sanctifies his bride. These three great mysteries are woven together to help us understand the meaning of the Church's epiphany. And presiding over these three mysteries is the singular, admirable presence of Mary, mother and figure of the Church: she was present at Cana (John 2:1-11); she was present in Bethlehem to receive the Magi (Matt 2:1-12); and she was present at the "baptism" on the cross (John 19:25-27) for which Jesus had longed (Luke 12:50). Here on the cross, water and wine flowed together: the water of baptism and the wine of blood flowed from the side of this new Adam (John 19:34) to create the new Eve, dreamed of by him as flesh of his flesh (Gen 2:21-24).

And that is what the soldiers did. Meanwhile, standing near the cross of Jesus were his mother, and his mother's sister, Mary the wife of Clopas, and Mary Magdalene. When Jesus saw his mother and the disciple whom he loved standing beside her, he said to his mother, "Woman, here is your son." Then he said to the disciple, "Here is your mother." And from that hour the disciple took her into his own home. (John 19:25-27)

So the LORD God caused a deep sleep to fall upon the man, and he slept; then he took one of his ribs and closed up its place with flesh. And the rib that the LORD God had taken from the man he made into a woman and brought her to the man. Then the man said,
"This at last is bone of my bones
  and flesh of my flesh;
this one shall be called Woman,
  for out of Man this one was taken.'
Therefore a man leaves his father and his mother and clings to his wife, and they become one flesh. (Gen 2:21-24)

That is how Jesus wanted it, and that is what he will behold when "his hopes" are realized. For if we may speak in these terms, Jesus also has hopes, as did the father in the parable (Luke 15:20). Jesus is constantly hoping to see his bride arrive in all her beauty, prepared to receive him as her spouse (Apoc 21:2). She will possess "the glory of God and a radiance like a very rare jewel, like jasper, clear as crystal" (Apoc 21:11). Trying to hide from sight in hopeful modesty, the bride will seek shelter, but she will not find it because her "temple is the Lord God the Almighty and the Lamb. And the city will have no need of sun or moon to shine on it, for the glory of God is its light, and its lamp is the Lamb. The nations will walk by its light, and the kings of the earth will bring their glory into it. Its gates will never be shut by day—and there will be no night there. People will bring into it the glory and the honor of the nations. But nothing unclean will enter it, nor anyone who practices abomination or falsehood, but only those who are written in the Lamb's book of life" (Apoc 21:22-27). This is what Isaiah foresaw (Isa 60); this was the hidden secret of the star of the Magi. This is what became manifest when the heavens opened up at Jesus' baptism and when his nuptial side spilled blood and wine.

"Blessed are those who wash their robes" (Apoc 22:14) for the wedding feast. "The Spirit and the bride say, 'Come.' And let everyone who hears say, 'Come.' And let everyone who is thirsty come. Let anyone who wishes take the water of life as a gift" (Apoc 22:17). "Come, Lord Jesus!" (Apoc 22:20).

Prayer

Holy Church, beautiful spouse,
go forth to meet the Lord;
clean and adorn your dwelling,
and receive your Savior.

Open your arms to Mary,
Virgin Mother of the Redeemer,
the ever-open Gate of Heaven
by which God entered our world.

Honor and glory to the eternal Father
and to the eternal only-begotten Son,
who through the Spirit's labor
was born of the Virgin Mother. Amen.

22. Faith beyond Space and Time

THE HISTORY OF SALVATION continues to develop in the midst of humanity. The Church—as spouse and widow, virgin and mother, saint and sinner—advances toward the heavenly banquet (cf. Apoc 21:2) while giving away all her livelihood in order to have more abundant life (Mark 12:42; Luke 21:2). The Lord reveals himself in our history to every man and woman; he reveals himself to the Church amid the vicissitudes of life, where grace and sin are always intermingled. The strong stalks heavy with wheat grow tall beside the weaker shoots, and also beside the rugged weed. No one of us is spared doubts about the Lord's appearance, when it will take place or whether it will at all. Bewilderment besets both disciple and adversary, but despite our perplexed state there is always a call from God to keep moving forward, to let ourselves be touched by the revelation of grace that makes possible the "dis-covering" of the Lord.

THE PATHETIC, suspicious Herod Antipas felt a perplexing unease in his heart: "Now Herod the ruler heard about all that had taken place, and he was perplexed because it was said by some that John had been raised from the dead, by some that Elijah had appeared, and by others that one of the ancient prophets had arisen. Herod said, 'John I beheaded; but who is this about whom I hear such things?'" (Luke 9:7-9). Similar consternation will be seen at the end of time when conflicting voices will point to the nearness of the glorious Lord in diverse times and places (cf. Matt 24:26-30). In his heart, John the Baptist, the greatest of those born of women, felt isolated in his bafflement; he feared he was mistaken. The clarity of the revelation he received on the day of Jesus' baptism (cf. John 1:32-34) was now beclouded as he wasted away in prison, and doubt gnawed at his soul: "Are you the one who is to come, or are we to wait for another?" (Luke 7:18-23). He passed through the crucible of doubt, uncertain about his mission, uncertain about his whole life. Humbling himself, John voiced his questions and received his reply. Then he bowed his head—to the point of having it severed.

> So, if they say to you, "Look! He is in the wilderness," do not go out. If they say, "Look! He is in the inner rooms," do not believe it. For as the lightning comes from the east and flashes as far as the west, so will be the coming of the Son of Man. Wherever the corpse is, there the vultures will gather.
> "Immediately after the suffering of those days the sun will be darkened,
>   and the moon will not give its light;
> the stars will fall from heaven,
>   and the powers of heaven will be shaken.
> Then the sign of the Son of Man will appear in heaven, and then all the tribes of the earth will mourn, and they will see 'the Son of Man coming on the clouds of heaven' with power and great glory." (Matt 24:26-30)

In the Old Testament, bewilderment is often evident in those the Lord chooses to proclaim his salvation. After triumphing over the priests of Balaam, Elijah was fearful of a woman's threats; his anguish impelled him to seek escape, even by death (cf. 1 Kings 19). Desperately in need of God's help to continue on his way, Elijah was not spared doubt even as he sought to recognize the Lord in the storm, in the fire, in the earthquake, and in the gentle breeze. Another bewildered prophet is the hard-headed Jonah, who also longed to die out of sheer frustration. He could not understand why his own expectations (arising from God's command to him) were in the end not the realities God wanted. So great was his bewilderment that it eventually turned into bitterness (cf. Jonah 4:3).

We should not confuse bewilderment with the doubt provoked by the devilish curiosity that seeks to know the identity of Jesus in order to take measures against him. Such is the strategy of those who want to know whether or not Jesus is the Son of God (like Satan in the desert, see Matt 4:1-11), or those who call upon him to come down from the cross (Matt 27:39-44), or those who ask him for signs (cf. Luke 11:29-30). It is also the tactic used by those who try to trap him with difficult questions about paying tribute to Caesar or punishing an adulterous woman or marriage arrangements in heaven. Jesus keeps his messianic mission secret, and when asked about it, he replies at most by quoting God's word as found in his people's scriptures, or he shows the contradictions in people's ideas. Our honest perplexity always remains open to God's salvation, but our idle curiosity does not. In our hearts, we experience the contradictions inherent in our search for truth: on the one hand, we may truly desire to find the truth (or at least desire to desire); on the other hand, we may seek the truth in order to control it. In one case, we inquire; in the other, we argue.

Those who passed by derided him, shaking their heads and saying, "You who would destroy the temple and build it in three days, save

yourself! If you are the Son of God, come down from the cross."
In the same way the chief priests also, along with the scribes and
elders, were mocking him, saying, "He saved others; he cannot
save himself. He is the King of Israel; let him come down from the
cross now, and we will believe in him. He trusts in God; let God
deliver him now, if he wants to; for he said, 'I am God's Son.'" The
bandits who were crucified with him also taunted him in the same
way. (Matt 27:39-44)

Honest perplexity and satanic curiosity confronted one
another also in the encounter between Herod the Great and the
Magi (Matt 2:1-12). The travelers from the East were guided by
a star, but when it disappeared, they found themselves entangled in the intrigues of the royal court. Being honest men, they
wanted no involvement in any conspiracy of the king, but they
felt bewildered because they could not see the star and kept
searching for it. Finally, after they left Jerusalem, their hearts
were filled with joy as they caught sight of the star again. Freed
from perplexity by their elation, they realized they were being
tested and so decided to turn the tables on the tyrant. When
Herod understood that he had been fooled by the Magi, his
consternation turned into a terrible rage. Such is the fury of the
spirit of evil that will last throughout history until the second
coming of the Lord.

Then Herod secretly called for the wise men and learned from them
the exact time when the star had appeared. Then he sent them to
Bethlehem, saying, "Go and search diligently for the child; and
when you have found him, bring me word so that I may also go
and pay him homage." When they had heard the king, they set
out; and there, ahead of them, went the star that they had seen
at its rising, until it stopped over the place where the child was.
When they saw that the star had stopped, they were overwhelmed

with joy. On entering the house, they saw the child with Mary his mother; and they knelt down and paid him homage. Then, opening their treasure chests, they offered him gifts of gold, frankincense, and myrrh. And having been warned in a dream not to return to Herod, they left for their own country by another road. (Matt 2:7-12)

Though Herod claimed he wanted to go to worship the newborn king, he sought only to destroy him, just as Satan in the desert inquired about the messianic secret in order to annihilate the anointed one of God. Herod could not carry out his desire, but Satan succeeded in plotting the nearly certain death of Jesus. Satan hungrily bit into the flesh of the Son of Man, but failed to realize that he swallowed the hook along with the bait (as one Church Father put it); unwittingly, he devoured the poison of divinity that would render him utterly powerless (see Saint Maximus the Confessor and Abbot, *Patrologiae Graeca* 90:1182-86).

THE DAY OF THE LORD'S second coming, a great and terrible day (Joel 2:11; 3:4; Mal 3:1-2; Acts 2:20), will be the end of the journey, and, on that day, there will no longer be any place for bewilderment. Satan, the ancient serpent and anti-Christ, will be contained and then destroyed by the Lord of glorious strength (2 Thess 1:9). The struggle for the faith, waged every day by sinful but good-willed men and women, will give them assurance for that day (cf. 1 Tim 6:12-14). The day of the parousia will be the day of Christ's definitive revelation. He will appear in the fullness of his power (1 Cor 1:7; 2 Thess 1:5-7). Here on earth also, the heavenly glory (*doxa*) will appear as epiphany and discovering and will make us forget our present sufferings (Rom 8:18-19). It will be the day of the final revelation (cf. 1 Pet 1:5-

6, 13; 4:13; 5:1), the climactic revelation of the glory we have already contemplated, if only partially, in the transfiguration of Jesus, in Cana of Galilee, in the morning of the resurrection.

> *I consider that the sufferings of this present time are not worth comparing with the glory about to be revealed to us. For the creation waits with eager longing for the revealing of the children of God.* (Rom 8:18-19)

When we experience moments of bewilderment, we will be strengthened by thinking of "the day of the Lord." Perhaps the gospel passage that will help us most is that found in John 21. There we find the "second calling" of the disciples by Jesus. Once we are confirmed in faith, we are asked to continue on our way. There on the shores of the Sea of Galilee (evoking the first calling of the disciples), we witness the miraculous catch of fish (like the one before the resurrection) and the eucharistic setting (recalling the multiplication of the loaves). The disciples, even though still somewhat bewildered, recognize the Lord. It is there that Peter receives the grace of remembering his threefold denial of Jesus, there that he makes his threefold confession (recalling that of Matthew 16), and there that he receives his mission and the promise of ultimate compliance. When we feel bewildered, we should always remember this moment and repeat to ourselves the saving words of the Lord: "What is that to you? Follow me!" (John 21:19-22). Our following of Jesus reaches far beyond time and space and our own bewilderment; it becomes humble entreaty as, with head bent low in simple obedience, we pray with the Church: "Come, Lord Jesus!" (Apoc 22:20). Amen.

> *When they had finished breakfast, Jesus said to Simon Peter, "Simon son of John, do you love me more than these?" He said*

to him, "Yes, Lord; you know that I love you." Jesus said to him, "Feed my lambs." A second time he said to him, "Simon son of John, do you love me?" He said to him, "Yes, Lord; you know that I love you." Jesus said to him, "Tend my sheep." He said to him the third time, "Simon son of John, do you love me?" Peter felt hurt because he said to him the third time, "Do you love me?" And he said to him, "Lord, you know everything; you know that I love you." Jesus said to him, "Feed my sheep. Very truly, I tell you, when you were younger, you used to fasten your own belt and to go wherever you wished. But when you grow old, you will stretch out your hands, and someone else will fasten a belt around you and take you where you do not wish to go." (He said this to indicate the kind of death by which he would glorify God.) After this he said to him, "Follow me." (John 21:15-19)

Prayer

O kings who search for stars,
seek them no longer
for when the sun is shining,
the stars have lost their light.

Follow not your own bright star
nor seek the beauty of other lights
for when the sun is shining,
the stars have lost their light.

Stop your search, for here before you
is the One who lights up all the sky:
God is the surest haven;
if you have found shelter here,
search no more for distant stars.

PART III

The Letters to the Seven Churches

23. Reading the Apocalypse

As we begin our reflection, let us put ourselves in the presence of the Lord who beholds us and loves us. For these meditations, as we read through the first few chapters of the Apocalypse, we should let our eyes be filled with the marvelous vision of John and let the Lord's voice penetrate to the most intimate recesses of our hearts.

As Romano Guardini says, "The Apocalypse is a book of consolation. It is not a theology of history or of the last times but rather contains words of comfort that God wanted to place in the Church's hands as the apostolic times were ending. The Church needed such comfort since it was passing through tribulation."[10] How does God console his people? He does not console them by saying, "The tribulation is really not as terrible as it appears." God beholds the persecution in all its horror, but he also shows us the heavenly reality that lies beyond our troubled earth. He makes it clear to us that Jesus Christ is patiently waiting. "He sees all, he ponders everything, from the first beats of the heart to the final effects of historical events, and he sets it all down in his book of infallible knowledge.... Christ consoles by pronouncing the word that reveals human works for what they are truly worth, and that will be their value forever."[11]

Hans Urs von Balthasar also helps us understand how to read the Apocalypse: "The Lord's consolation does not appear in the form of counsels or theological disquisitions, but in the form of images and symbolic events that must be interpreted correctly. John transposes all of revelation into figures and symbols in accord with the esthetic law of Sacred Scripture. According to that law, every saving event assumes a visible form and every word becomes flesh. Without this dialectic between event and vision, our faith would not be truly human; it would be spiritualistic and irrational."[12]

We cannot enter into these "figures" just by interpreting them allegorically or by representing them conceptually. They are visions, the kind of visions we have in dreams. When we dream, we are mysteriously and forcefully moved by images and feelings that arouse in us powerful figures and forms. As Guardini says: "In dreams life puts imagination at the service of life's own occult drive; in visions it is the Spirit of God who holds sway and who endows the world's images with new forms that reveal divine meaning."[13]

Guardini uses this perspective of dreams to provide a key for reading the Apocalypse. Take the image of John weeping before the sealed book: "I began to weep bitterly because no one was found worthy to open the scroll or to look into it" (Apoc 5:4). "Why is this man so moved to the depths of his being that he sheds tears of grief?" Guardini writes. "We might answer by giving some reason, ... but this would not explain the reality.... Everyone has dreamed of something of this sort: there was something we saw, standing up or lying down, perhaps a book on a table, but it was sealed. A presentiment leads us to believe that everything, absolutely everything, depends on opening that book. But it is not opened, and we despair. If friends were to ask us why we are weeping, we would show them the book and tell them, 'But don't you see? The book is not open!'" The same thing happens in visions. But what is flowing here is not just natural life with all its impulses, anxieties, and hopes; what is flowing here is the new and holy life of God. "It is that life speaking and expressing itself in the images that arise."[14]

Consequently, the proper way to read the Apocalypse is by "becoming a docile listener attentive to the Spirit, grasping the images as they are presented, penetrating into them by subtle probing, and reaching agreement with them at the level of the heart. Then, to the extent that God allows, we will understand."[15]

If we read what the Lord ordered John to write, we find there the image of the priest whom we have been commissioned to represent on earth: "Then I turned to see whose voice it was that spoke to me, and on turning I saw seven golden lampstands, and in the midst of the lampstands I saw one like the Son of Man, clothed with a long robe and with a golden sash across his chest. His head and his hair were white as white wool, white as snow; his eyes were like a flame of fire, his feet were like burnished bronze, refined as in a furnace, and his voice was like the sound of many waters. In his right hand he held seven stars, and from his mouth came a sharp two-edged sword, and his face was like the sun shining with full force" (Apoc 1:12-16).

The image of the Lord is that of the priest (tunic and cincture), at once both old (white hair) and young (feet of burnished bronze), standing in the middle of his Church and carrying out his priestly mission. The Lord takes the firm stand of a judge; his gaze purifies and attracts as does the sun when it shines at its brightest; his voice is heard by all and discerns like a two-edged sword.

This hieratic image of the Lord frightens us. Who can claim to represent it? Which of us has such an image of himself when celebrating Mass or hearing confessions? But this majestic, inaccessible image of the Lord breaks all molds when he finally speaks. For that awesome voice that is like the sound of many waters utters no dreaded oracle, but rather a sweet imperative: "Fear not." The "heavenly priest" with spectral aspect becomes Jesus, the one who sleeps in the back of our boat, the one who walks on the waters, the one who shares with us the eucharistic bread, the one who tells the man of little faith, "Why did you doubt?"

As *divine*, the Word takes on the form of a sacred storm, as in the ancient theophanies when Yahweh revealed himself as mystery, at once fascinating and frightening—*fascinans et tremendum*. As *human*, the Word becomes sweet and gentle to the point of turning into drops of blood that fall silently from the pierced heart of the crucified Lord. Therefore, to his command, "Do not be afraid," the Lord adds, "I am the First and the Last, and the Living One. I was dead, and see, I am alive forever and ever." And he goes further: "Do not be afraid for ... I have the keys of Death and of Hades" (Apoc 1:17-18). He holds the keys of death, of your death, of the death of each of us.

As we behold this Lord and allow his message to emerge for us out of that tension between images and words, let us ask ourselves about the joy we feel in ministry, about our zeal, our sadness, our worries. As symbol, the figure of the Lord makes us holy; as word, he draws close and humanizes us. Let us ask about the ways we sanctify ourselves: With what attitude do we pardon sins? How do we draw close to people in their everyday lives? Does a special love inspire all our gestures? The Lord does away with all the old ritual mechanisms and makes sacred only love, revealed as a quiet word and a gesture of solidarity in the command "Fear not." All sadness in ministry, all fatigue, all drying up of the fountains of fervor result from losing contact with this living Lord. The faithful will experience our ritual gestures as empty and abstract if we cannot tell them, "I am one who lives with you. I rejoice when you laugh, and I suffer when you cry." The people will see us as superfluous if we do not transform our friendship into good liturgy, if we are incapable of making holy their daily bread. People somehow can recognize sterility, and when they do, their joy slowly departs. We find the source of joy in our encounter with the Lord, who makes himself seen and who speaks to us. This is the joy that makes those of us who are "presbyters" (elders) young again, and it also makes young people "elders." ("Let no one despise your youth," Paul tells the "presbyter-bishop" Timothy [1 Tim 4:12].) If we are joined with the Lord, we need not worry about our death for he has it in his hands, protected and insured. It will be neither too soon nor too late, nor will it be untoward. Is it not the case that worrying about our death, whether in its daily forms or at the end of life, makes us "feel old" in ways that militate against our joy?

Let no one despise your youth, but set the believers an example in speech and conduct, in love, in faith, in purity. (1 Tim 4:12)

24. Ephesus—Recapturing the First Love

To the angel of the church in Ephesus write: These are the words of him who holds the seven stars in his right hand, who walks among the seven golden lampstands:

"I know your works, your toil, and your patient endurance. I know that you cannot tolerate evildoers; you have tested those who claim to be apostles but are not, and have found them to be false. I also know that you are enduring patiently and bearing up for the sake of my name, and that you have not grown weary. But I have this against you, that you have abandoned the love you had at first. Remember then from what you have fallen; repent, and do the works you did at first. If not, I will come to you and remove your lampstand from its place, unless you repent. Yet this is to your credit: you hate the works of the Nicolaitans, which I also hate. Let anyone who has an ear listen to what the Spirit is saying to the churches. To everyone who conquers, I will give permission to eat from the tree of life that is in the paradise of God."

WHAT IS THE DISTRESS of the Church of Ephesus that the Lord wants to cure? It may be a bitter dispute among the faithful, who, after "struggling with evildoers" and "uncovering deceits," have lost the love they had at first. Ephesus has been consumed in useless conflicts, and the Lord wants to feed the people there with fruit from the tree of life, which is his cross, sweet and easy to bear. Once we have lost our first love, we recover it in maturity not by "falling in love" but only as the sweetness of the cross.

Symbols of the Lord's Infinite Majesty: Stars and Lampstands

Christ consoles the Church of Ephesus by appearing with seven stars in his right hand as he walks amid the seven lampstands. The Lord holds not only the keys of our death but also the seven stars, which are the angels of the seven churches. The angels signify the bishops and priests, those responsible for the communities, those whose mission it is to protect, guide, and enlighten the communities. These "stars" or "angels" not only signify the priests: they actually *are* the priests. The same may be said of the golden lampstands, those tall candelabras among which the Son of Man walks: they represent our churches and their luminous reality. Let us place ourselves now in the presence of our own ecclesial community, asking the Lord to "take a stroll" among our flock and to grant us the grace of conversion so that our lampstand will not be removed from its place.

The Interior Knowledge That the Lord Has of Us

The Apocalypse contains a moving text about the early fervor of a church community that has been extinguished: "I know your works.... But I have this against you, that you have abandoned the love you had at first" (Apoc 2:2, 4). Perhaps this text can be of some use to us.

As the years go by, the character of people, like that of wines, either matures or sours. The delightful elderly woman whose wise counsel is respectfully sought by her children has not become who she is by improvisation. The old man whose grandchildren eagerly visit him to hear his stories does not simply "happen." Likewise, the old grouch, the tiresome talker, the childish oldster—these don't just appear overnight. The preparation for what we will be as senior citizens begins now, with the question about our first love.

The Church of Ephesus has much to commend it: it has behaved well; it has been patient in its exertions and sufferings; it has resisted evildoers; and it has taught solid doctrine and rejected the deceits of the false apostles. But the Lord, seeking to probe deeper, finally reproaches the Church for its signal failure: "I have this against you, that you have abandoned the love you had at first" (Apoc 2:4).

Later on, the Lord makes a similar complaint regarding the Church of Laodicea, which is quite the opposite of the Church of Ephesus. Laodicea is neither hot nor cold, and because it is lukewarm, the Lord declares that he will "spit" it out of his mouth. Vain and self-satisfied, Laodicea boasts proudly: "I am rich, I have prospered, and I need nothing" (Apoc 3:15-17). The Lord tries to make this Church see how blind she is with regard to what is most important: "Be earnest, therefore, and repent!" But even this reproach is uttered with love: "I reprove and discipline those whom I love" (Apoc 3:19). Both these Churches, Ephesus and Laodicea, must experience conversion and recover their initial fervor, the love they had in the beginning.

> *"I know your works; you are neither cold nor hot. I wish that you were either cold or hot. So, because you are lukewarm, and neither cold nor hot, I am about to spit you out of my mouth. For you say, 'I am rich, I have prospered, and I need nothing.' You do not realize that you are wretched, pitiable, poor, blind, and naked."* (Apoc 3:15-17)

What is at issue here is the ultimate, definitive judgment, the judgment that asks about the reality of our lives. In this judgment, all our secondary virtues and defects fade in importance. It considers not so much our sins as our attitude before the Lord, who is coming, who is even now knocking at the door of our "last supper."

What does it mean "to recover the love that was lost"? Is it a question of returning to early passions? Is this not perhaps a bit ingenuous? The first love must be recovered, but not through the heroic "infatuations" of our youth; the mature heart falls in love only when it is struck by a singular blow.

When people realize that they have lost the energy of their earlier passions, they respond in different ways. Some try to perform "plastic surgery of the soul": they seek to be like young people, adopting their styles of dress and speech. Leaving aside the unfortunate cases, this is at best only a superficial solution, one that conceals the true challenge. Other people, as they age, become fixed in external practices; they harden into a rigid posture that smacks of pharisaical negativity. Questions of dress— for example, cassocks vs. jeans—may reflect inner attitudes, but what is at stake is something much deeper; it can be seen especially in our attitude toward work.

The loss of our initial fervor may lead some of us into enthusiasm about what might be called "secondary tasks" or "busy work." Whereas our mid-life crisis is an invitation from the Lord to become more practiced in the theological virtues, we often prefer to practice the "secondary virtues," which are more suited to "busy work." Some of us become socially involved with such eagerness that we depart from conventional liturgical forms. Others, in contrast, become exceedingly fussy in all that has to do with ritual. In neither case is the real challenge being honestly confronted. Our first love must undergo conversion, which means "concentrating on Jesus Christ alone."

It is a question of fixing our sight on Jesus Christ. "Remember Jesus Christ," Paul told Timothy (2 Tim 2:8). This is the Jesus Christ who sets his face toward Jerusalem (Luke 9:51). This is the Jesus Christ who walks resolutely toward his exaltation, his being lifted up upon the cross as well as in the heavens. For "if we have died with him, we will live with him" (2 Tim 2:11). When we look hard at our own death and resurrection, our life takes on a new center of gravity. The focus is now not on "what we might do" but on what the Lord has already *done with us* and what he will yet *do with us* if we abandon all for his sake.

When the days drew near for him to be taken up, he set his face to go to Jerusalem. (Luke 9:51)

There is a Gospel passage that may illustrate what we want to say better than any reflections of mine: it is the passage in which Mary of Bethany, sensing that the Lord will soon die, anoints him with aromatic nard and wipes his feet dry with her hair. When Judas sees this, he is irritated and voices a bitter reproach, using the needs of the poor as a pretext (John 12:1-8). What for Mary is a joyous expression of her love for Jesus causes in Judas sadness mixed with anger and frustration. No longer sharing friendship with Jesus, Judas is unable to comprehend the feelings of those who love Jesus. Worse still, he has the contrary feelings of spiritual bitterness. His bitterness toward Mary reveals the shabby condition of a heart that does not know how to interpret well the times of the Lord. His attitude reveals the essence of all spiritual bitterness. Judas has an "idea" about what must be done, an idea that detaches itself from the living Jesus he has before him. Even though Jesus' time is near its end, he continues to teach his disciples by the way he lives and by the way he resolutely advances toward the cross. Judas's disoriented state stands in stark contrast to the centeredness of Mary, the one who loves the Lord. Mary's love orients her correctly; she is the soul who adores on her knees and prays with her tears.

Six days before the Passover Jesus came to Bethany, the home of Lazarus, whom he had raised from the dead. There they gave a dinner for him. Martha served, and Lazarus was one of those at the table with him. Mary took a pound of costly perfume made of pure nard, anointed Jesus' feet, and wiped them with her hair. The house was filled with the fragrance of the perfume. But Judas Iscariot, one of his disciples (the one who was about to betray him), said, "Why was this perfume not sold for three hundred denarii and the money given to the poor?" (He said this not because he cared about the poor, but because he was a thief; he kept the common purse and used to steal what was put into it.) Jesus said, "Leave her alone. She bought it so that she might keep it for the day of my burial. You always have the poor with you, but you do not always have me." (John 12:1-8)

Proclamation and Promise of Final Fulfillment: Eating of the Tree of Life

"Let anyone who has an ear listen to what the Spirit is saying to the churches. To everyone who conquers, I will give permission to eat from the tree of life that is in the paradise of God" (Apoc 2:7). "Then the angel showed me the river of the water of life, bright as crystal, flowing from the throne of God and of the Lamb through the middle of the street of the city. On either side of the river is the tree of life with its twelve kinds of fruit, producing its fruit each month; and the leaves of the tree are for the healing of the nations" (Apoc 22:1-2).

The promise of life expands our hearts; it is the best remedy against spiritual indolence, sadness, and anger, all of which shrink the heart. In his rules for the discernment of spirits, Saint Ignatius observes that the devil uses intellectual weapons in his battle against spiritual joy and consolation. To induce distress in the soul, the devil employs "specious reasonings, subtleties, and persistent deceits" (SpEx 329)—and the more truth these contain, the more dangerous they are. In the spiritual life, we must defend our joy against those who use fallacious arguments and try to engage us in futile discussions and vain polemics. "From these come envy, dissension, slander, base suspicions, and wrangling" (1 Tim 6:4-5). The best remedy against these "ideas" that confuse and strangle our hearts is the solid doctrine that expands our emotions and calls to mind the compassion of Jesus. Paul tells us to rely on "the sound words of our Lord Jesus Christ and the teaching that is in accord with godliness" (1 Tim 6:3). This teaching is none other than that of the sweetness of the cross, the only reality that Paul desires to "know": "I decided to know nothing among you except Jesus Christ, and him crucified" (1 Cor 2:2).

For each of us, expanding our heart means reflectively accepting our own personality, with all its sinfulness, in order to be bonded entirely with the heart of the Lord. Truly mature persons do not allow the "latest" ideas, whether their own or others', to lead their emotions blindly astray. While they are eager to feel intensely everything that moves their hearts, they confront external tensions serenely; they discern with care the movement in their souls, and they are always ready to share in the sufferings of Christ.

25. Smyrna—Overcoming Fatigue and Bitterness

And to the angel of the church in Smyrna write: These are the words of the first and the last, who was dead and came to life:

"I know your affliction and your poverty, even though you are rich. I know the slander on the part of those who say that they are Jews and are not, but are a synagogue of Satan. Do not fear what you are about to suffer. Beware, the devil is about to throw some of you into prison so that you may be tested, and for ten days you will have affliction. Be faithful until death, and I will give you the crown of life. Let anyone who has an ear listen to what the Spirit is saying to the churches. Whoever conquers will not be harmed by the second death." (Apoc 2:8-11)

WHAT IS THE DISTRESS of the Church of Smyrna? This Church has not become as bitter as the one in Ephesus: she knows how to bear with suffering, but the devil has infected her with fear, a fear like that of Peter as he walked on the water. The people of Smyrna are afraid that their suffering will last a long time. That is why the Lord consoles them by assuring them that he is close at hand and their suffering will be short ("ten days"). He declares that in him are joined the first and the last, life and death, so that all time between them passes like a sigh. "The Lord your God is a compassionate God. He will not abandon you nor destroy you."

Symbol of the Lord's Infinite Majesty:
"the first and the last,
the one who was dead and came to life"

The Church is undergoing trials, and the Lord consoles her by revealing himself as the one who truly possesses life and disposes of it as uniquely his own. The Lord's self-possessed life prevails over all sufferings; it shortens them and renders them "nothing" compared to the eternity of promised glory.

All persons and all events come into existence ultimately through a word, and the Lord is *Logos*, Word: "In the beginning was the Word, and the Word was with God.... All things came into being through him, and without him not one thing came into being. What has come into being with him was life" (John 1:1, 3-4). The *Logos*, as creative word, is the most inward nucleus of every event, even the most terrible ones. Without the Word, they would not exist. That is why trials and tribulations should not frighten Christians, nor should they be seen as something meaningless. Jesus is "the Son who gives life to whomever he wishes" (John 5:21). As Alpha and Omega, the Lord gives meaning to all things from eternity, but he wants also to give them meaning from within our finite world. That is why he takes on our human history: he is the one "who was dead and came to life." He is the faithful and compassionate high priest who "in the days of his flesh offered up prayers and supplications, with loud cries and tears, to the one who was able to save him from death, and he was heard because of his reverent submission. Although he was a Son, he learned obedience through what he suffered; and having been made perfect, he became the source of eternal salvation for all who obey him (Heb 5:7-9).

The Lord's Knowledge and Judgment of Those Who Are Faithful

This faithful and compassionate high priest consoles the people of Smyrna by making them realize that he is aware of their tribulation and their poverty and that he counts these misfortunes as part of their wealth ("even though you are rich," he tells them). He knows that what is being said about his Church is slander and that those who call themselves Jews are in reality a "synagogue of Satan." He shows his Church that he has taken the measure of their sufferings: the trials to which the devil will submit some of them, including imprisonment, will last only ten days, not too long a time. From a human viewpoint, the situation in Smyrna is disastrous: poverty, slander, the establishment of a synagogue of Satan, and prison for those who remain faithful. But from the viewpoint of the Lord, the Church is immensely rich; she remains true to herself despite the slander, and she becomes purified and consolidated by resisting all temptations and trials.

The Invitation to Persevere and the Promise of Infinite Fulfillment

"Be faithful until death, and I will give you the crown of life" (Apoc 2:10). This is the crown of which Paul writes: "Athletes exercise self-control in all things; they do it to receive a perishable garland, but we an imperishable one. So I do not run aimlessly, nor do I box as though beating the air; but I punish my body and enslave it, so that after proclaiming to others I myself should not be disqualified" (1 Cor 9:25-27).

For those experiencing tribulation, the great temptation is fatigue. The constant exposure to evil makes us lose a proper notion of time so that we end up "running aimlessly" or "beating the air." When persecution is long and drawn out, we frequently begin to imitate the tactics of the enemy. The arena of war—God's war—gets reduced to minor skirmishes where we are at the enemy's mercy. We lose sight of the goal, and our strategy gets muddled. We see only the occasional sniper that the enemy sends our way to wear us down in a difficult stretch. One sign of our disorientation is our tendency to lash out against people who are really only minor enemies, and we often do so with a force that should be reserved only for our true foes.

When the master delays his arrival home, we become like the head servant who beats his fellow servants and who eats and drinks with drunkards. But our true vocation is to be faithful and wise stewards whom the Lord has put in charge of his household to give others the nourishment they need at the proper time (cf. Matt 24:45-50). If we resist this temptation of fatigue, the Lord promises us the crown of life, a crown like the ones the elders throw unceasingly before the throne of the Lamb (Apoc 4:10). Those crowns symbolize the governance of the world, which originates from God and must return to him. The prince of this world, however, usurps that power to govern and wages his own war. If there are any souls he cannot recruit or overcome, he seeks to win the battle by making them fight in his own arena and with his own crude arms.

"Who then is the faithful and wise slave, whom his master has put in charge of his household, to give the other slaves their allowance of food at the proper time? Blessed is that slave whom his master will find at work when he arrives. Truly I tell you, he will put that one in charge of all his possessions. But if that wicked slave says to himself, 'My master is delayed,' and he begins to beat his fellow slaves, and eats and drinks with drunkards, the master of that

slave will come on a day when he does not expect him and at an hour that he does not know." (Matt 24:45-50)

We earnestly desire to win the crown of victory so that one day we also may place it at the feet of the enthroned Lamb, but sometimes the battle seems to go on too long. When it does, we may succumb to ambitious attitudes that reveal in us an infidelity that is transient but pernicious. We chatter idly about the enemy instead of praying and seeking God's will for our own lives; we vie for position with friends instead of confronting the enemy; we argue about who is greatest in the battalion instead of uniting around the head of the army and serving as equals; we worry about the weeds during coffee breaks instead of bending over and caring for the wheat in our own plot of land; we adopt during truces the enemy's style of being indolent but "dedicated to a great cause"; we engage in battle in order to advance our own interests—and these are just some of the signs of our fickleness. The Lord urges us to be faithful unto death in great matters and in small.

26. Pergamum—Holding On to the Truth

And to the angel of the church in Pergamum write: These are the words of him who has the sharp two-edged sword:

"I know where you are living, where Satan's throne is. Yet you are holding fast to my name, and you did not deny your faith in me even in the days of Antipas my witness, my faithful one, who was killed among you, where Satan lives. But I have a few things against you: you have some there who hold to the teaching of Balaam, who taught Balak to put a stumbling block before the people of Israel, so that they would eat food sacrificed to idols and practice fornication. So you also have some who hold to the teaching of the Nicolaitans. Repent then. If not, I will come to you soon and make war against them with the sword of my mouth. Let anyone who has an ear listen to what the Spirit is saying to the churches. To everyone who conquers I will give some of the hidden manna, and I will give a white stone, and on the white stone is written a new name that no one knows except the one who receives it. (Apoc 2:12-17)

THE DESOLATION of the Church of Pergamum originates in a sort of dissolute spiritual gluttony that leads her to feast on strange teachings. The Church is divided: on one side there are martyrs who have been utterly faithful, and on the other there are people who profess false doctrines. The Lord consoles the Church by threatening her with words of truth, which are likened to a sword that comes forth from his mouth. He invites the community of Pergamum to consume the hidden manna, to seek their nourishment solely in the bread of truth, to savor the exclusive and intimate relationship they enjoy with the Lord, and to avoid falling into spiritual worldliness. Since maintaining the community's faith is the work of superiors, the letter to Pergamum is addressed to the Church leaders and attempts to show them the scandal they cause among the faithful when they fail to oppose decisively those who use the Church for their own interests.

Symbol of the Lord's Infinite Majesty:
The Sharp, Two-Edged Sword

Christ reveals himself to the Church of Pergamum as the one who hold the sharp, two-edged sword. A later chapter of the Apocalypse also speaks of the Lord in this way: "Then I saw heaven opened, and there was a white horse! Its rider is called Faithful and True, and in righteousness he judges and makes war.... He has a name inscribed that no one knows but himself. He is clothed in a robe dipped in blood, and his name is called The Word of God.... From his mouth comes a sharp sword with which to strike down the nations, and he will rule them with a rod of iron; he will tread the wine press of the fury of the wrath of God the Almighty. On his robe and on his thigh he has a name inscribed, 'King of kings and Lord of lords'" (Apoc 19:11-16).

The Lord does battle with the two-edged sword, which is the truth of his word. Truth is characterized by fidelity (in Hebrew, *emeth*), and the fate of the Church of Pergamum hinges on her fidelity. She has been faithful to the name of the Lord, and she is fortunate to have had the martyr Antipas as a model member of the community. But now she is being tempted to infidelity by followers of the doctrine of Balaam and by a group known as the Nicolaitans. The Lord desires complete fidelity, but some in the Church seek to introduce innovative doctrines, just as in ancient times, the Israelites were seduced into idolatry by the daughters of Moab (Num 31:16). Satan attacks the Church on her weakest side (food sacrificed to idols and sexual immorality), but the basic question is whether she will maintain the integrity of her faith and remain loyal to the fullness of truth.

> *These women here, on Balaam's advice, made the Israelites act treacherously against the Lord in the affair of Peor, so that the plague came among the congregation of the Lord.* (Num 31:16)

The Lord is faithful and true, but his word seems to lack power among the people, for they let their ears be tickled by other doctrines. Truth, as Romano Guardini tells us, is the spiritual bread that nourishes our existence, but, in the course of human history, truth has been separated from power. Truth has great value, but it lacks immediate clout, whereas power coerces. Paradoxically, the more noble the truth is, the less power it has. Even simple truths have some power because they confirm certain needs and tendencies—think, for example, of the truths that relate to our immediate vital needs. But the more elevated the truth, the less coercive force it possesses; the spirit must grow in freedom simply in order to grasp it. The nobler a truth, the easier it is for cruder realities to discount it or even ridicule it; it must rely even more on nobility of spirit.

All this is valid for truth in general, but it is especially so for holy truth, which always runs the risk of seeming scandalous. Upon entering the world, such truth leaves its omnipotence on the doorstep in order to present itself in the "form of a slave."

This is partly explained by the law we have just enunciated: being of such exalted status, divine truth has the least coercive force. But there is another reason as well, namely, that this holy truth comes from God's grace and love and invites sinners to conversion. Inevitably, this truth will be strongly resisted, but the day will come when truth and power are reunited so that truth once again has power corresponding to its value and its merit. The higher a truth is in the sphere of the intelligible, the more powerful will be its reign. At the present time, mendacity can survive because truth is weak. Similarly, sin can exist because God provides our wills a near-limitless space within which to rebel against him. However, when truth gains power, untruth will no longer be able to exist because all reality will be permeated by truth. Untruth will be banished from the domain of being and will subsist only in the inexpressible form of condemnation. What a great liberation this will be for those who love the truth and for that part of our being that tends toward truth! The experience on that day will be like that of a person who is about to be asphyxiated and then suddenly can breathe again without restraint. All our being will flourish freely and with beauty, for beauty is the splendor of truth become reality. This is the victory that Christ will achieve by "the sword of his mouth."

The Promise of Plenitude in Full Communion with the Lord: Hidden Manna and the White Stone with a New Name

"To everyone who conquers I will give some of the hidden manna, and I will give a white stone, and on that stone is written a new name that no one knows except the one who receives it" (Apoc 2:17).

The hidden manna is Jesus himself, who entrusts himself to us in the Eucharist, thus making us blessed. The truth of God is the bread of the soul. In the form of this bread, the Lord gives himself mysteriously and totally, creating a relation of intimate communion with those who are faithful. Another sign of our personal relationship with the Lord is the new name we receive. The Apocalypse often speaks of great multitudes, of uncountable masses of persons, of saints, of angels: "I heard the voice of many angels surrounding the throne and the living creatures and the elders; they numbered myriads of myriads and thousands of thousands" (Apoc 5:11). But these huge assemblies should not obscure the vision of us as individuals. The seven letters are addressed each to a particular Church, and the individuality of each is respected. When the Lord speaks of "the one who overcomes," and when he counsels, "Keep yourself faithful" or "Repent and be converted," it is always in the singular.

The passage about the white stone with the new name written on it implies great intimacy, for the new name is known only to God and to the person who receives it. Among us, it is often the case that a person in love gives a special name to the beloved; the name expresses what is most delightful and lovable in the other person. Naturally, the lovers don't want that special name to become public; it exists only between them as lover and beloved. The white stone is inscribed with the name by which God the Creator expresses the sublimely personal uniqueness of the person he loves. In this apocalyptic intimacy, every single member of the innumerable multitudes has a special personal relationship with the Lord.

Fidelity is always personal: it has special names, codes, and gestures for every person. Persons are the highest value; above them, there is no higher realm of values. Therefore, if we are not faithful to concrete persons, even under the pretext of serving "ideals," then we are ultimately not being faithful to ourselves. The only remedy for the infidelity of idolatry is our personal relationship with the Lord, and this finds expression both in the Eucharist, where he personally gives himself to us, and in our prayer, above all the prayer in which we allow ourselves to be called by the name God has given us, the name that is indissolubly linked to our mission in life.

27. Thyatira—Loyalty to Our Inheritance

And to the angel of the church in Thyatira write: These are the words of the Son of God, who has eyes like a flame of fire, and whose feet are like burnished bronze:

"I know your works—your love, faith, service, and patient endurance. I know that your last works are greater than the first. But I have this against you: you tolerate that woman Jezebel, who calls herself a prophet and is teaching and beguiling my servants to practice fornication and to eat food sacrificed to idols. I gave her time to repent, but she refuses to repent of her fornication. Beware, I am throwing her on a bed, and those who commit adultery with her I am throwing into great distress, unless they repent of her doings; and I will strike her children dead. And all the churches will know that I am the one who searches minds and hearts, and I will give to each of you as your works deserve. But to the rest of you in Thyatira, who do not hold this teaching, who have not learned what some call 'the deep things of Satan,' to you I say, I do not lay on you any other burden; only hold fast to what you have until I come. To everyone who conquers and continues to do my works to the end,

I will give authority over the nations;
to rule them with an iron rod,

> *as when clay pots are shattered—*
> *even as I also received authority from my Father.*
> *To the one who conquers I will also give the morning star."* (Apoc
> 2:18-28)

The distress of the Church of Thyatira is caused by those who "tolerate" the false prophetess Jezebel and even "adopt" her ways. The figure of Jezebel recalls the story of Naboth, who died as a martyr because he refused to sell to the king the vineyard that was his ancestral inheritance. The Lord consoles the people of Thyatira by showing them that true power is given not to those who negotiate with the reigning potentates, but to those who "continue to do God's work to the end" (Apoc 2:25-26).

Jezebel is the great prostitute who seduces us and teaches us to fornicate adoringly with idols. She is the one who becomes drunk with the blood of the saints and the witnesses of Jesus (Apoc 17:1-6), just as the historical Jezebel did with the martyrdom of Naboth, the faithful farmer who refused to sell his vineyard (1 Kings 21:1-16). In the book of the Apocalypse, two women exist in opposition: the bride and the prostitute, the one who bore the child and the one who becomes inebriated with human blood, the one who serves the Lord and the one who serves the beast. These women are reflected in the two opposed cities, Jerusalem and Babylon, one coming down from heaven like a bride and the other reduced to ashes and cast into the sea.

> *Then one of the seven angels who had the seven bowls came and*
> *said to me, "Come, I will show you the judgment of the great whore*
> *who is seated on many waters, with whom the kings of the earth*

have committed fornication, and with the wine of whose fornica-
tion the inhabitants of the earth have become drunk." So he carried
me away in the spirit into a wilderness, and I saw a woman sitting
on a scarlet beast that was full of blasphemous names, and it had
seven heads and ten horns. The woman was clothed in purple and
scarlet, and adorned with gold and jewels and pearls, holding in
her hand a golden cup full of abominations and the impurities of
her fornication; and on her forehead was written a name, a mys-
tery: "Babylon the great, mother of whores and of earth's abomi-
nations." And I saw that the woman was drunk with the blood of
the saints and the blood of the witnesses to Jesus. When I saw her,
I was greatly amazed. (Apoc 17:1-6)

Symbol of the Lord's Infinite Majesty: The Son of God with Eyes like Flames of Fire and Feet like Burnished Bronze

"These are the words of the Son of God, who has eyes like flames of fire, and whose feet are like burnished bronze" (Apoc 2:18).

We cannot look directly at a person who has eyes like flames of fire; we can only adore such a person. Let us place ourselves in the gaze of the one who "searches minds and hearts ... and will give to each of [us] as [our] works deserve" (Apoc 2:23). The Lord is the All-seeing: all things lie open to his sight; they are observed and judged by him.

The burnished bronze feet of the Son of God recall the statue of Nebuchadnezzar's dream, its feet made partly of clay and partly of iron, a sign of fragility and division (Dan 2:41-43). Unlike the statue's alloyed feet, the "works of the Lord" must be kept undivided, and to those who faithfully keep them so the Lord "will give authority over the nations, to rule them with an iron rod, as when clay pots are shattered" (Apoc 2:27).

As you saw the feet and toes partly of potter's clay and partly of iron, it shall be a divided kingdom; but some of the strength of iron shall be in it, as you saw the iron mixed with the clay. As the toes of the feet were part iron and part clay, so the kingdom shall be partly strong and partly brittle. As you saw the iron mixed with clay, so will they mix with one another in marriage, but they will not hold together, just as iron does not mix with clay. (Dan 2:41-43)

These symbols show us that the Lord is speaking to the people of Thyatira about the kingdom he has received from the Father, which allows no divisions or sectarian conflicts. The Lord observes his realm with his eyes like flames of fire and keeps it integrated in solidarity. That is why he places no additional burden on the people but asks them simply to hold on to what they have until he comes.

28. Sardis—Restoring Self-Respect

And to the angel of the church in Sardis write: These are the words of him who has the seven spirits of God and the seven stars:

"I know your works; you have a name of being alive, but you are dead. Wake up, and strengthen what remains and is on the point of death, for I have not found your works perfect in the sight of my God. Remember then what you received and heard; obey it, and repent. If you do not wake up, I will come like a thief, and you will not know at what hour I will come to you. Yet you have still a few persons in Sardis who have not soiled their clothes; they will walk with me, dressed in white, for they are worthy. If you conquer, you will be clothed like them in white robes, and I will not blot your name out of the book of life; I will confess your name before my Father and before his angels. Let anyone who has an ear listen to what the Spirit is saying to the churches." (Apoc 3:1-6)

THE DISTRESS in the Church of Sardis is that of a community that has sinned grievously by negotiating the faith. She has kept "the name of being alive," but inwardly she is dead.

Symbols of the Lord's Majesty:
The Seven Spirits and the Seven Stars

The Lord consoles Sardis by revealing himself as the one who holds the seven spirits and the seven stars. These spirits and stars are the churches themselves, whose luminous spiritual reality is in the hands of the Lord. Appealing to their sense of belonging, the Lord reminds them of the hour of death and judgment and of the word that was preached to them. He asks them to follow in the footsteps of those who have remained faithful, and he promises to remain faithful himself. The Lord discerns the embers beneath the ashes in the Christian heart, and he does not quench the smoldering coals.

Reviving the Sense of Belonging: Being Aware of Our Death

"Wake up, and strengthen what remains and is on the point of death ... [for] I will come like a thief" (Apoc 3:2-3). These words remind us of the eschatological parables of Jesus. "Be dressed for action and have your lamps lit; be like those who are waiting for their master to return from the wedding banquet.... If the owner of the house had known at what hour the thief was coming, he would not have let his house be broken into. You also must be ready, for the Son of Man is coming at an unexpected hour" (Luke 12:35-36, 39-40; cf. Matt 24:42-44).

Making Judgment a Present Reality

The Lord urges us to examine our works in reality and not just by appearances ("You have a name of being alive, but you are dead.... I have not found your works perfect in the sight of my God" (Apoc 3:1-2). The Lord is our advocate before the Father and will take our part, but he needs to be able to point to works of charity that weigh in our favor: "For I was hungry, and you gave me food" (Matt 25:35).

Remembering the Word

"Remember what you received and heard" (Apoc 3:3). This command recalls Paul's letter to Timothy: "I remind you to rekindle the gift of God that is within you through the laying on of my hands.... Hold to the standard of sound teaching that you have heard from me, in the faith and love that are in Christ Jesus. Guard the good treasure entrusted to you.... Remember Jesus Christ, raised from the dead" (2 Tim 1:6, 13-14; 2:8).

Returning to the Faithful

When we are unfaithful, we usually betray not just ideas but concrete persons. We take leave of those who taught us the faith, those who trained us well, those who remain faithful to the Lord. Sometimes we not only take leave of them but fight fiercely against them, discharging onto them the guilt we have no heart to bear ourselves. The Lord declares that there are in Sardis a few who have kept the coals of faith alive and have not stained their baptismal garments; they continue to walk with him, dressed in white (Apoc 3:4). This is the same immaculate raiment that is destined also for the "remnant of Israel," God's faithful people as a whole and their holy representatives. "One of the elders addressed me, saying, 'Who are these, robed in white, and where have they come from?' I said to him, 'Sir, you are the one that knows.' Then he said to me, 'These are they who have come out of the great ordeal; they have washed their robes and made them white in the blood of the Lamb. For this reason they are before the throne of God, and worship him day and night within his temple, and the one who is seated on the throne will shelter them. They will hunger no more, and thirst no more; the sun will not strike them, nor any scorching heat;

for the Lamb at the center of the throne will be their shepherd, and he will guide them to springs of the water of life, and God will wipe away every tear from their eyes'" (Apoc 7:13-17).

Restoring Respect

Recovering a sense of belonging and of our own history means restoring respect. Sardis has lost its self-respect and is the most unworthy of the seven churches. Perhaps meditating a while on the meaning of respect can help us understand how we as priests can mature wisely and become "presbyters"—that is, elders—without losing our youthfulness or our joy in ministering. The word "respect" comes from the Latin *re-spicere*, meaning to "look back" or "take a second look." It can describe the attitude that the faithful have toward the priest when they take a second look at him, that is, when they take note of his presence, when they seek him out for counsel, when they imitate him. It can also describe the priest's attitude toward himself, toward others, toward things, and toward God.

"Respectful" persons take a second look before speaking and acting; they deliberate, they persevere, they are not carried away by emotion. Respect is the opposite of the attitude that would belittle older folk as "senile" or as caught up in their own little world, completely at the mercy of their changing moods. But respect is also contrary to some attitudes we see in older people that bring respect itself into disrepute. I am thinking of the attitudes of those who continue to get involved in power struggles, of those who speak ill of everybody, and of those who take risks only for their own benefit. And there are many people who adopt a pose of respectability but interiorly have succumbed to the spiritual temptations of vainglory and pride; they are still at the mercy of primordial temptations. Of all such persons, the Lord declares, "You have a name of being alive, but you are dead" (Apoc 3:1).

Let us focus now on respect for others, looking especially at our attitude toward the young, since it is the parent–child or grandparent–grandchild relation that best reveals whether the older person has mastered a crisis or has fled from it.

It is easy to fool others regarding the relation we have with God. A pious bearing, a liturgy celebrated with devout charm, a breviary open in our hands when someone enters our room— these are acquired postures, masks that we have worn so convincingly that even we come to believe that we are pious and worthy of respect.

We may have a dignified air about us as we manage our affairs. We moderate our appetites often not out of virtue but because of fear of illness or hypochondriacal adherence to medical advice. Meanwhile, we sublimate and exquisitely refine our sensuality so as to caress souls instead of bodies, giving the whole seductive process the name of spiritual direction. We may even learn to disguise the petulance of old age with elegance, modulating our manners and refraining from any show of emotion that might reveal our mood. A dispassionate spirit can also be a mask or even a shell: not only does it protect us from others, but it quells every torment within us before it can even arise.

With young people and our children, however, it is hard to fake "respectability." The young have a sort of sixth sense with regard to older folk. They respect some of them and feel close to them; they treat them with affection, seek them out, and ask their advice; they open their hearts to them in confession and enjoy sharing a meal with them. Some older folk, on the other hand, are ignored or scorned by the young. Youngsters would never think of approaching them of their own accord; their respect for them is only formal. They may not say so in so many words, but the young draw close to their elders or shy away from them as if by instinct.

We are "caught out" when we refuse to let go of the rudder, when our main concern is our image, when even in personal conversation we take no risks and hide our inner selves, when we are selfish or untruthful, when we say "yes" to everyone in order not to get burned, though in reality we are singed to a crisp within. Those "caught out" are basically persons who have no desire to transmit any legacy, because they really don't have one to transmit. Having administered a personal legacy to their own advantage, they have none to transmit to others. When they cease to be administrators, they are left with nothing. Such is the case of those in the Apocalypse who think themselves alive but in reality are dead. God has not been interiorized in their hearts. They continue to have a small-minded view of God as someone out there who will forgive their "sins" or peccadilloes—which we all have—but they have not discovered the God who lays claim to their hearts.

In his relationship to the youthful Timothy, Paul is the prototype of the admirable older person, "already being poured out as an offering" (2 Tim 4:6). He knows how to leave the younger man with a legacy. In writing to Timothy, Paul fondly remembers their parting in Ephesus: "Recalling your tears, I long to see you so that I may be filled with joy" (2 Tim 1:4). Paul is now an old man in the autumn of his life, a life full of struggle and persecution, but he keeps two things before his eyes: *his vocation*, for his faith in the One who called him to announce the promise of life in Christ Jesus is unshakable, and *his paternity*, for Timothy is his beloved son whom he remembers day and night in his prayers and whom he encourages to remain faithful.

Joy is the sign that our hearts have found what is good for them. But the ultimate good for our hearts does not consist in our domination of any situation; it does not consist in controlling what is done or said around us or even what happens within us. Our ultimate good lies in our love for concrete persons: for our neighbors, for our Lady, for Father, Son, and Holy Spirit. Over and above these concrete persons, there exists no ideal realm of values that merits our zealous efforts. Therefore, when we question ourselves about our joy in ministering, we should not pose the question in terms of efficiency or asceticism or quantities; rather, we should look at the true sources of joy, which are human hearts. And the questions we might ask ourselves are these: Are we ready to be "poured out as an offering"? Are we being converted into the pure and holy host worthy of entering into our God? Are we taking good care of our legacy, the children we have been given, and preparing them to receive the torch?

29. Philadelphia—Love among Sisters and Brothers

And to the angel of the church in Philadelphia write:
"These are the words of the holy one, the true one,
   who has the key of David,
   who opens and no one will shut,
   who shuts and no one opens:
"I know your works. Look, I have set before you an open door,
which no one is able to shut. I know that you have but little power,
and yet you have kept my word and have not denied my name. I
will make those of the synagogue of Satan who say that they are
Jews and are not, but are lying—I will make them come and bow
down before your feet, and they will learn that I have loved you.
Because you have kept my word of patient endurance, I will keep
you from the hour of trial that is coming on the whole world to test
the inhabitants of the earth. I am coming soon; hold fast to what
you have, so that no one may seize your crown. If you conquer, I
will make you a pillar in the temple of my God; you will never go
out of it. I will write on you the name of my God, and the name of
the city of my God, the new Jerusalem that comes down from my
God out of heaven, and my own new name. Let anyone who has
an ear listen to what the Spirit is saying to the churches." (Apoc
3:7-13)

THE LETTER TO PHILADELPHIA is victorious in tone
throughout; the only warning is to "hold fast to what
you have, so that no one may seize your crown" (Apoc 3:11).

Although it may seem hard to believe, we sometimes feel a certain resistance to consolation. An abundance of consolation frightens us and fills us with false fears, but Saint Paul urges us to run so as to win the prize, the crown of victory. The point is, though, not to hold on to our little crown but to let God's glory shine forth.

Symbols of the Lord's Majesty:
"the holy one, the true one, who has
the key of David" (Apoc 3:7)

Holiness and truth open every door wide. The Lord consoles the Church of Philadelphia and shows her the path to triumph. He urges her to be totally open to his grace, for he is the only one with the key that can unlock the gates of glory. No one will be able to shut the door that he opens, for he himself is the door: "I tell you, I am the door for the sheep" (John 10:17). Jesus is the open door to the apostolic mission, as Paul has experienced in his far-reaching journeys (cf. Acts 14:27; 1 Cor 16:8-9; 2 Cor 1:12; Col 4:3). The Lord promises that the enemies of the Church of Philadelphia will be humbled and she will be protected in her trials and tribulations. Philadelphia is a model of apostolic joy and success among all the seven churches to whom John writes. Like Smyrna, Philadelphia is a church that has remained wholly faithful; but whereas Smyrna is encouraged to bear her trials with fortitude and patience (*hypomonē*), Philadelphia is urged to move forward to "conquer" and win the "crown."

When they arrived, they called the church together and related all
that God had done with them, and how he had opened a door of
faith for the Gentiles. (Acts 14:27)

I will stay in Ephesus until Pentecost, for a wide door for effective work has opened to me, and there are many adversaries. (1 Cor 16:8-9)

Indeed, this is our boast, the testimony of our conscience: we have behaved in the world with frankness and godly sincerity, not by earthly wisdom but by the grace of God—and all the more toward you. (2 Cor 1:12)

At the same time pray for us as well that God will open to us a door for the word, that we may declare the mystery of Christ, for which I am in prison. (Col 4:3)

Despite her fidelity and success, Philadelphia also experiences temptations. Remember, for example, what happened with the apostles at the ascension. They were so overjoyed on beholding the risen Lord that they were incredulous and bewildered; they stood about confused, looking up to heaven when they should have been going forth to spread the good news. The door opened by the Lord cannot be shut, but we must enter and exit by it without being rendered ecstatic out of false humility. We have to trade with the talents given us, place our light on the lampstand, and let our city shine brightly on the hilltop. We must do good works so that people will believe. We must leave the upper chamber, where we have taken refuge out of fear of public opinion. What the Lord crowns cannot be "desacralized" or "secularized." What the Lord establishes as a "pillar in the temple" cannot be shaken; it must be firmly maintained and never moved from the sanctuary (such as for purposes of "religious tourism"). All the names of God are engraved in Philadelphia, and her own name means "love of our brothers and sisters." This is the love that sums up all that is written in the law and the prophets; it is the only sure sign we can give so that the world might believe: "By this everyone will know that you are my disciples, if you have love for one another" (John 13:35).

Even though possessing "little power," Philadelphia does not shrink back when the Lord opens the door. He urges the people to confront the deceivers with truth and not to indulge in false piety: "I will make them come and bow down before your feet, and they will learn that I have loved you" all the time you were being persecuted (Apoc 3:9). Even as "the hour of trial is coming on the whole world" (Apoc 3:10), the people of Philadelphia need not feel ashamed that the Lord is protecting them, for they are the church of "love among sisters and brothers," and that attribute of theirs can never be diminished or denied. To the contrary, it must shine forth in all its beauty and with all its might. What is love is love plain and simple, and such love is completely protected and guaranteed by the Lord. All the other qualities of the churches are relative, qualities such as the patience of Ephesus and her ability to discern. Relative also are the sins of the churches: those of Pergamum for being divided and not standing strong, those of Thyatira for her self-interested toleration of false prophets, and those of Sardis for appearing alive when she is really dead. What is absolute is love among sisters and brothers, the apex of charity, and the Lord blesses it with every prize. No one can remain neutral with regard to Philadelphia: whoever fails to love her and follow her lead will end up envying her. The Lord is with her—who will condemn her? She has her faults and has committed sins, but the Lord doesn't even bother to name them. Philadelphia will possess the fullness: the name of the Father, the name of Spouse (the New Jerusalem), and the dearest name of Jesus Christ.

30. Laodicea—True Friendship

And to the angel of the church in Laodicea write: The words of the Amen, the faithful and true witness, the origin of God's creation:

"I know your works; you are neither cold nor hot. I wish that you were either cold or hot. So, because you are lukewarm, and neither cold nor hot, I am about to spit you out of my mouth. For you say, 'I am rich, I have prospered, and I need nothing.' You do not realize that you are wretched, pitiable, poor, blind, and naked. Therefore I counsel you to buy from me gold refined by fire so that you may be rich; and white robes to clothe you and to keep the shame of your nakedness from being seen; and salve to anoint your eyes so that you may see. I reprove and discipline those whom I love. Be earnest, therefore, and repent. Listen! I am standing at the door, knocking; if you hear my voice and open the door, I will come in to you and eat with you, and you with me. To the one who conquers I will give a place with me on my throne, just as I myself conquered and sat down with my Father on his throne. Let anyone who has an ear listen to what the Spirit is saying to the churches." (Apoc 3:14-22)

THE DISTRESS of the Church of Laodicea results from its lukewarm condition. (The very name "Laodicea" is from the Greek words *laōn* and *dikē*, meaning "judgment of the peoples.") This Church is profoundly selfish, perhaps because it has never known true friendship. The Lord consoles her by showing her that his friendship with her is strong, both for correcting and for rewarding.

A "Lite" Church

Laodicea is what might be called a "lite" church—it's missing something. The Lord threatens to spit her out of his mouth. He reproaches her severely because he truly "loves" her; he wants to come to "dine" with her and to seat her on his throne. Clearly, Laodicea is a Church dear to the Lord; he wants her to be "with him": "I will come in to you and eat with you, and you with me.... I will give [you] a place with me on my throne" (Apoc 3:20-21). He admonishes her because he loves her.

The strength of the Lord's condemnation is evident in his harsh words: "I wish that you were either cold or hot. So, because you are lukewarm, and neither cold nor hot, I am about to spit you out of my mouth" (Apoc 3:15). Words like "spit out" become engraved in our memory. The act of spitting out implies discontent; we spit out something because it is distasteful. It's like when we're given tea to drink and it's only lukewarm; we take a good sip, but then we spit it out. The same happens when we swallow something (or someone!) that appears appetizing but is rejected by the palate. The Lord's palate is healthy, and we are loath to think that he who drank sour wine on the cross would spit anyone from his mouth. He makes these reproaches to a Church he loves dearly, for only a close friend can be told, "I prefer your hatred to your lukewarm indifference."

When dealing with strangers, we are surprised to encounter strong emotions, whether hatred or gratitude, but with friends it is different. We feel stunned when they are only lukewarm toward us. That is the great sin against friendship. A lukewarm attitude conceals the opportunistic types, those "eternally perplexed" persons who are always wondering whether to commit themselves or not. They are forever waiting as they make their precise calculations. They are irreproachable: nothing "bothers" them. The are selfish persons who *love things* ("I am rich, I have prospered, I need nothing") and *make use of persons*. What they should do instead is *love persons* ("if you hear my voice and open the door") and *make use of things* ("I counsel you to buy from me gold refined by fire so that you may be rich, and white robes to clothe you, ... and salve to anoint your eyes that you may see" (Apoc 3:17-18).

Being lukewarm is the opposite of bearing witness. That is why the Lord presents himself as "the Amen, the faithful and true witness, the origin of God's creation" (Apoc 3:14). He leaves no room for bewilderment because he has sown good seed in his field. That is why he has no patience with the deceptive façades or the eternal doubts of those who do not let themselves be corrected (that is, loved).

We need to ask ourselves what the signs are that the Lord is spitting us out of his mouth; we need to allow ourselves to be corrected now and not wait until the final judgment.

Spitting Out Grace

One sign of our being lukewarm is that we are forever falling into the same faults without true repentance: "the dog returns to his vomit," as we say. We feel comfortable with our lukewarm vomit. We can't stand grace. No sooner does the Lord fill our souls with his love, which we happily receive, than we get sick and spit it out and end up back where we started. Our souls regurgitate "false doctrines" and can't stomach the truth. As soon as someone speaks a strong word to us, we are startled— how could they!

Spitting Out Those Who Bear Witness

Another sign of our lukewarm condition is surrounding ourselves with other tepid souls and carefully avoiding people who might offer us correction. The lukewarm person cannot bear the testimony of the saints, for "fire pours from their mouth and consumes their foes" (Apoc 11:5). Those who do not give voice to their complaints end up vomiting them onto others. Spitting out grace is the opposite of "faithfully bearing witness." Vomiting on others is the opposite of accusing oneself in order to be justified by the Lord.

Diabolical Spewing

All vomiting of the things of God is rooted in the devil's own vomiting: "Then from his mouth the serpent poured water like a river after the woman, to sweep her away with the flood. But the earth came to the help of the woman; it opened its mouth and swallowed the river that the dragon had poured from his mouth. Then the dragon was angry with the woman, and went off to make war on the rest of her children, those who keep the commandments of God and hold the testimony of Jesus" (Apoc 12:15-17).

PART IV

Human Prayer

31. Drawing Close to All Flesh

MANY PARABLES OF JESUS speak of God's "coming." Matthew's last judgment parable tells of the day "when the Son of Man comes in his glory" (Matt 25:31-46), and Luke speaks of the man who "returned, having received royal power" (Luke 19:15). The Lord will indeed come again in glory, but that glory will not eclipse the reality of his first coming, for that was when he was revealed in the flesh (2 John 7). The Lord is not only spirit, as he insisted with his disciples: "Touch me and see; for a ghost does not have flesh and bones as you see that I have" (Luke 24:39). At the end of time, the risen Lord will return, drawing close to us in the flesh, and "all flesh shall see the salvation of God" (Luke 3:5-6; cf. Isa 40:5). The Word become flesh (John 1:14) will not judge us by abstract or purely "spiritual" ethical norms. He will judge us rather by those concrete norms that arise directly out of the way he lived and the path he traced out for us. He will judge us on whether we knew how to draw close to "all flesh" and recognize in it the Word of God.

> *And the Word became flesh and lived among us, and we have seen his glory, the glory as of a father's only son, full of grace and truth.* (John 1:14)

The Word made flesh redeems our sinful flesh through his passion, that is, by taking on himself the pain of all flesh. Jesus draws close to all tormented flesh and with his own flesh cancels the legal claims against us (cf. Col 2:13-14). He does not keep his distance, for he is the good Samaritan (Luke 10:31-32). In the end, we will all be judged on whether we have "become neighbors" of all flesh, on whether we have drawn close to suffering flesh.

Many do not draw near at all; they keep a distance, like the Levite and the priest in the parable. Others draw close by intellectualizing the pain or taking refuge in platitudes ("life's like that"). Still others focus their vision narrowly and see only what they want to see, or they join the ranks of those who cloak life's uncomeliness with cosmetics. Many are the ways we avoid drawing near to flesh in pain.

Drawing close to all suffering flesh means opening our hearts, showing compassion, touching the wound, aiding the injured. It also means giving the innkeeper two denarii and guaranteeing payment for whatever else is spent. It is for this that we'll be judged. "Understanding" all this is a matter of exercising not just our intellects but also our hearts and our feelings. We must cultivate in our lives not just ways of thinking but also attitudes and ways of proceeding that entail the following:

- loving justice with a desert thirst,
- preferring the wealth of poverty to the impoverishment produced by worldly wealth,
- opening our hearts with gentleness rather than inflaming them with ferocity,
- promoting peace as a value superior to all war and all evasive pacifism,

- having a clear vision that comes from a pure heart and that keeps us from falling into the greed of storing up riches for ourselves (Mark 12:40; Luke 12:21).

"They devour widows' houses and for the sake of appearance say long prayers. They will receive the greater condemnation." (Mark 12:40)

"So it is with those who store up treasures for themselves but are not rich toward God." (Luke 12:21)

If we do all this concretely, we will succeed in drawing close to all flesh, to the flesh that hungers and thirsts, to the flesh that is ill and wounded, to the flesh that is purging its offenses in prison, to the flesh that has no clothes to wear, to the flesh that feels that bitter corrosion of the loneliness born of disdain.

"When the king returns ..." The glorious king is none other than the slaughtered Lamb who desires to draw close to all suffering flesh. At the end of time, the blessed ones who behold the splendor of the Lord's glorified flesh will be those who know how to recognize it even now, when its glory is concealed beneath the sores and the grime that repel and disgust us. The blessed will be those who draw lovingly close to the Lord's flesh even as it dwells among us (John 1:14) in our brothers and sisters for they are able recognize its hidden glory. "Truly I tell you, just as you did it to one of the least of my brothers and sisters, you did it to me.... Truly I tell you, just as you did not do it to one of the least of these, you did not do it to me" (Matt 25:40, 45).

What we are trying to do here, then, is give our lives a sure direction. If we contemplate the Word hidden in all flesh, then we (who are flesh as well) will be truly contemplative, and all

215

flesh will see the glory of God. The task before us is to prepare our flesh for this vision, for we will be glorified in the same flesh with which we are moved to contemplate the Word of God in our neighbor: "What we have heard, what we have seen with our eyes, what we have looked at and touched with our hands, concerning the word of life ..." (1 John 1:1).

Preparing ourselves for this contemplation requires not only that we serve our neighbor but that we place our flesh in the presence of God, submitting it to the action of the Word and the Spirit for the glory of the Father. We must dedicate our flesh to service that leaves us frayed and exhausted; our flesh must become a poor pilgrim in exodus. Everything we do to place our flesh "in the presence of God" is prayer, and it is prayer that will guide us along the path, at once easy and difficult, of recognizing the Word in all suffering flesh and of surrendering our own flesh to God's will in order to live according to the Spirit. Only prayer will prepare our eyes to contemplate the person of the Word made flesh (now glorious) when he comes to judge us—to judge us on whether we have truly recognized him in the flesh.

For Prayer and Reflection

"But a Samaritan while travelling came near him; and when he saw him, he was moved with pity. He went to him and bandaged his wounds, having poured oil and wine on them. Then he put him on his own animal, brought him to an inn, and took care of him. The next day he took out two denarii, gave them to the innkeeper, and said, 'Take care of him; and when I come back, I will repay you whatever more you spend.' Which of these three, do you think, was a neighbor to the man who fell into the hands of the robbers?" (Luke 10:33-36).

32. Abraham: Learning to Let Go

PLACING OUR FLESH on the road of prayer means knowing how to take leave of ourselves and what is ours. "Knowing how to take leave" does not mean flight or dispersal but true "exodus" toward the Father, toward the promised land, toward those who will follow in our footsteps. Often this will mean a forced exile: "By the rivers of Babylon—there we sat down and there we wept when we remembered Zion. On the willows there we hung up our harps" (Psalm 137:1-2). As we take leave of ourselves, we encounter the flesh of our brothers and sisters, and we draw close to their flesh through service. When conflicts arise in consequence, we must take them to prayer.

Abraham is the prototype of those who take leave of themselves and their homelands and who journey "from place to place" (Gen 13:3) toward the promised land. Abraham sends his flesh into exile, becoming a poor pilgrim in exodus. Even in that life of wandering without permanent abode, conflicts arise about possession and control of the land. Even the nomadic life has its "sedentary" yearning, the desire to rest from the journey at an oasis, the urge to sing the hymns of the homeland in the midst of exile. We long to reach the horizon before time, deluding ourselves with our blinkered, myopic illusions. I am reminded of those priests who, when named to an administrative post, first create a fitting habitat; before anything else, they remodel the office, change the secretaries, carpet the floor, hang curtains, and acquire all the equipment an executive needs. This way of proceeding generates tension and conflict about possessions. Even Abraham, our model in taking leave of oneself to receive God's gift, experienced something of this. Since there was not enough space for him and his brother Lot to live together, Abraham sought to avoid conflict by telling Lot: "Is not the whole land before you? Separate yourself from me," and he allowed Lot to choose the land he wanted (Gen 13:6-9). For Abraham knew that the Lord had set a special land apart for him and would some day reward him abundantly. "Lift up your eyes," the Lord had told him, "and look from the place where you are, ... for all the land that you see I will give to you and to your descendants for ever." And the promise to Abraham would extend far into the future: "I will make your descendants as the dust of the earth" (Gen 13:14-16).

Those who set out on an exodus from themselves make a definite option: they prefer time to space. They are betting on time, for time always opens onto the horizon of eternity; it knows nothing of "competition" for space. But this journey in time is not without its hidden traps, for we sometimes camouflage space in the guise of time. We believe we are "on exodus" in the dimension of time, which is always God's domain (what Blessed Peter Faber calls the "Messenger of God"), but we unwittingly create domains of possession. That "great moment" we experience as something absolute and definitive is merely the result of our turning time into space. God is not there. We have settled down: it is our executive office disguised as the pilgrim's trail. Our movements are those of "sedentary" persons, kept well within our own domains. And since all reduction of realities is forced and violent, the space in which we travel as peers of the realm is nothing but a labyrinth. We think that we are journey-ing through the dimension of time, but we are only going about in circles, carried by the "momentum" of our permanence while we unconsciously hope for some future Ariadne to set us free. Such is the remorse that lies coiled up within the fiction of the journey.

The limits of our flesh are the origin of all conflicts waged for control of space. Yahweh teaches Abraham to take leave of his home and to renounce possession of the land through which he travels, land which is given him entirely in promise. What Abraham experiences as an exile in space endows him with the power of the promised homeland so that he becomes a perma-nent traveler ever ready to move on to new encampments.

Lot chooses the better land, but along with possession of the land he inherits its contradiction, for "the people of Sodom were extremely wicked rebels against the Lord" (Gen 13:13). Lot's wife also gets trapped in space: she does not know how to "take leave" but instead "looks back" and so is turned into a pillar of salt (Gen 19:26). There is much more to say about this "looking back." The scriptures relate it to the pernicious nostal-gia of the Israelites in the desert who long for "the onions and the garlic" of Egypt (Num 11:5-6; Exod 16:3; 14:11-12). Jesus himself declares that those who look back are unsuitable for the kingdom (cf. Luke 9:61-62). Looking back is another way of becoming "sedentary," now by means of memory. Memory undergoes a malignant metamorphosis when it disregards the mandate to "remember" in Deuteronomy (5:15; 8:2-20; 32:7; etc.). Instead of continually recalling our unmerited election by God or celebrating daily the Lord's passion and resurrection (cf. Luke 22:19; 1 Cor 11:23-26), memory is transformed into a seductive nostalgia that urges us to look backward. And this retrospection gives rise to the many laments of those wanderers who never accept being nomads in the Lord. Saint John of the Cross tells us about purification of the memory.

> *Remember that you were a slave in the land of Egypt, and the Lord your God brought you out from there with a mighty hand and an outstretched arm; therefore the Lord your God commanded you to keep the sabbath day.* (Deut 5:15)

> *Then he took a loaf of bread, and when he had given thanks, he broke it and gave it to them, saying, "This is my body, which is given for you. Do this in remembrance of me."* (Luke 22:19)

Abraham is thoughtful of Lot and lets him take the land he wants. In contrast, Lot suffers from a certain possessiveness or earthly greed, and with these he pursues his ambitions for the future, while his wife looks back in nostalgia toward the land that is lost. As a result, both remain subject to the tribulations of the flesh, that "space" surrounding Sodom and Gomorrah, whose sin was precisely a sin of the flesh.

For Prayer and Reflection

"As they were going along the road, someone said to him, 'I will follow you wherever you go.' And Jesus said to him, 'Foxes have holes, and birds of the air have nests; but the Son of Man has nowhere to lay his head.... Another said, 'I will follow you, Lord; but let me first say farewell to those at my home.' Jesus said to him, 'No one who puts a hand to the plow and looks back is fit for the kingdom of God.'" (Luke 9:57-58, 61-62).

33. Prayer as Obedience to Mission

A THEOLOGIAN OF OUR TIME tells us that our dialogue with God is of a precarious nature; it is basically just compensating for our lack of deeper communication and concord with God. If we had never sinned, then loving God and responding to his words would be something natural for us. It is precisely after that first sin is committed that God asks the question, "Where are you?" (Gen 3:9). Here begins the history of this dialogue we call prayer. In prayer, God makes it possible for us to draw close to him once again, for it is he who asks for us, it is he who calls out to us. We have seen in earlier reflections that this drawing close can happen only by way of the flesh: the good Samaritan "came near" the beaten man (Luke 10:29-37), and the very Word of God drew close to us by "becoming flesh" (John 1:14).

When the Word of God draws close to us, we see the essence of obedience: "Christ Jesus, though he was in the form of God, did not regard equality with God as something to be exploited, but emptied himself, taking the form of a slave, being born in human likeness. And being found in human form, he humbled himself and became obedient to the point of death—even death on a cross" (Phil 2:6-8). The letter to the Hebrews quotes Psalm 40 to show how this same obedience applies also to the incarnation: "Then I said, 'See, I have come to do your will, O God' (in the scroll of the book it is written of me)" (Heb 10:7). This is the obedience of Abraham's "Here I am!" (Gen 22:1-3), which reaches its culmination in the cry of Jesus in Gethsemane: "Yet, not what I want, but what you want" (Mark 14:36). In each case, flesh is required, for only flesh can be divested and passed through the crucible of contempt, dislodgment, derision, and humiliation. "Adam, where are you?" asks God, and it is Adam's flesh that must obey the command uttered in that first dialogue with God: "By the sweat of your brow you shall eat your bread" (Gen 3:19). The bread that Adam eats will be earned by the sweat of submitting his flesh to humiliation and deprivation. Flesh is required too in Abraham's "Here I am!" to which God replies, "Take your son—your only son, whom you love, Isaac" (Gen 22:1-2). Even Jesus prays, "Abba, Father, for you all things are possible; remove this cup from me; yet, not what I want, but what you want" (Mark 14:36).

If we observe carefully, we see that this prayer of Jesus is intimately linking with obedience to a mission. We might say that it is through prayer that Jesus first discovers and then reinterprets his own mission (cf. Mark 1:38; Luke 4:42-43; Mark 6:46; John 6:15; and the prayer in Gethsemane, as we just saw). Similarly, it is through prayer that Saint Paul's apostolic mission becomes effective (cf. 2 Cor 1:11; Rom 10:1; 2 Thess 3:1), and that is why he prays unceasingly (cf. Rom 1:9-10; Col 1:19-20; 2 Thess 1:3; 2:13). The first disciples also turn to prayer to discover the mission God is giving them, especially in difficult times (cf. Acts 4:24-30). The community does not ask God to punish the persecutors or even to stop the persecution but begs only for the courage to be obedient to their mission, which is to proclaim Christ to the world no matter what the opposition.

Our ability to seek out, discover, define, and orient our mission—and be obedient to it—comes to us and grows in us only through prayer. Nonetheless, a prayerful attitude is not something detached from reality; rather, it is deeply rooted in our prior experience of concrete reality. It is a constant, persistent *ritornello* even in the midst of difficulties; it requires confidence in God, for "who else will put up security for me?" (Job 17:3; cf. Job 16:19-20; 19:25). Despite vigorous protests and heated discussions with God, every believing soul possesses deep within itself a fidelity that keeps it true to its mission and a love for God's word that no opposition succeeds in destroying (cf. Jer 20:9). Even when persons of prayer experience pain and express lament, they feel at a deeper level the renewal of confidence that comes from joy, faith, and hope (cf. Jer 15:16; 17:14). This indestructible zone of fidelity within us gives us a serenity beyond all explanation; it is a basic experience that is key for all types of prayer and for discernment of spirits.

At daybreak he departed and went into a deserted place. And the crowds were looking for him; and when they reached him, they wanted to prevent him from leaving them. But he said to them, "I must proclaim the good news of the kingdom of God to the other cities also; for I was sent for this purpose." (Luke 4:42-43)

As you also join in helping us by your prayers, so that many will give thanks on our behalf for the blessing granted us through the prayers of many. (2 Cor 1:11)

After they were released, they went to their friends and reported what the chief priests and the elders had said to them. When they heard it, they raised their voices together to God and said, "Sovereign Lord, who made the heaven and the earth, the sea, and everything in them, it is you who said by the Holy Spirit through our ancestor David, your servant:

'Why did the Gentiles rage,
and the peoples imagine vain things?
The kings of the earth took their stand,
and the rulers have gathered together
against the Lord and against his Messiah.'
"For in this city, in fact, both Herod and Pontius Pilate, with the
Gentiles and the peoples of Israel, gathered together against your
holy servant Jesus, whom you anointed, to do whatever your hand
and your plan had predestined to take place. And now, Lord, look
at their threats, and grant to your servants to speak your word
with all boldness, while you stretch out your hand to heal, and
signs and wonders are performed through the name of your holy
servant Jesus." (Acts 4:24-30)

Your words were found, and I ate them,
and your words became to me a joy
and the delight of my heart;
for I am called by your name,
O Lord, God of hosts. (Jer 15:16)

"Hope does not disappoint," Paul tell us (Rom 5:3-5). It is to this conviction that we must have recourse. If we lose sight of this reference point, then we lose our stability. Our prayer becomes ever more "illusionary"; our flesh becomes "spiritualized" or "psychologized"; our obedience becomes caprice. "But to what will I compare this generation?" asks Jesus. "It is like children sitting in the market-places and calling to one another, 'We played the flute for you, and you did not dance; we wailed, and you did not mourn.' For John came neither eating nor drinking, and they say, 'He has a demon'; the Son of Man came eating and drinking, and they say, 'Look, a glutton and a drunkard, a friend of tax-collectors and sinners!' Yet wisdom is vindicated by her deeds." (Matt 11:16-19). Jesus calls this generation "adulterous" (Matt 12:39; 16:4) because it has lost its orientation toward fidelity; it has no solid foundation in hope to which it can refer doubt or suffering or persecution. The people of this generation are guided simply by their fancies, by their "likes" and "dislikes." Because they know nothing of prayer or obedience or oblation of the flesh, this generation is unable to recognize the "Word made flesh." They fabricate their own mission in life because their hearts are so unruly that they're incapable of receiving from the Lord a mission; they are unable to adore him in the immolation of obedience. These are the people whose "fulfillment" consists in becoming certified bachelors and spinsters, not in being consecrated to a God-given mission that impels them to empty themselves completely, starting with the dispossession that comes with prayer.

The obedience required for prayer affects our lives and wounds own flesh. Let me explain. The ordinary conception of prayer is "asking God for things" or "asking God to change situations that are difficult for us." No doubt, this is true prayer; even the Lord urges us to pray this way. But there is another basis for our prayer, arising from the certainty of our hope, as I mentioned above. Prayer touches the very depths of our flesh; it touches our heart. It is not God who changes; rather, it is we who change, through obedience and surrender in prayer.

The prophet Elijah went out in search of God. He was terrified and wished to die. But when he encountered God, his heart was changed (1 Kings 19:1-18). Such also was the case of Moses when he interceded for his people. It was not God who changed his mind but Moses. He had known the God of wrath, but now he knew the God of forgiveness. He discovered God's true face at this moment in his people's history: the face of fidelity and forgiveness. He learned how to take a just measure of his people's sin. Prayer is therefore the privileged place where God reveals himself; it is the space where we move from "what people think" about God to God as he truly is. Prayer is the place where silent faith grows before the revelation of mystery: "See, I am of small account; what shall I answer you? I lay my hand on my mouth" (Job 40:4). "I had heard of you by the hearing of the ear, but now my eye sees you" (Job 42:5). When God sent an angel to Elijah to encourage him to keep going (cf. 1 Kings 19:5-8), or when the stubborn Jonah saw everything as hopeless, the Lord's response was always the same: "Go back the way you came" (1 Kings 19:15). But this is not the turning back that results just from stagnant nostalgia or romantic restoration; rather, it is letting God's response shatter the discouragement and the uselessness we feel in carrying out our mission so that new possibilities are opened up toward the future. Restored by prayer, the prophet Elijah retraced his steps and found a more fruitful path: he called Elisha to assist him in his work (1 Kings 19:19-21). Prayer, by dispossessing us in obedience, makes us realize that we are suspended in constant tension between what is finished and what is beginning. For persons of prayer something is always ending and something else is always commencing—nothing ever stands still.

For Prayer and Reflection

"Then he withdrew from them about a stone's throw, knelt down, and prayed, 'Father, if you are willing, remove this cup from me; yet, not my will but yours be done.' Then an angel from heaven appeared to him and gave him strength. In his anguish he prayed more earnestly, and his sweat became like great drops of blood falling down on the ground" (Luke 22:41-44).

34. David: The Art of Surrender

T HE FIGURE OF DAVID in flight, as narrated in 2 Samuel
15 and 16, will help us to understand better what it means
to find ourselves in a precarious situation and then surrender to
God. King David is in a humiliating retreat, pursued by his own
son, Absalom, but, even in such straits, his humility and his
noble qualities stand out. David recognizes the sacred character
of his flight, which is truly a form of exodus, and so he proceeds
with utter calm, his heart surrendered to God's designs. His
situation is not unlike that of the Jews when they are carried off
to Babylon (cf. Psalms 14:7; 61; 77).

> *Hear my cry, O God;*
> *   listen to my prayer.*
> *From the end of the earth I call to you,*
> *   when my heart is faint.*
> *Lead me to the rock*
> *   that is higher than I;*
> *for you are my refuge,*
> *   a strong tower against the enemy.*
> *Let me abide in your tent forever,*
> *   find refuge under the shelter of your wings. Selah*
> *For you, O God, have heard my vows;*
> *   you have given me the heritage of those who fear your name.*
> *Prolong the life of the king;*
> *   may his years endure to all generations!*

May he be enthroned forever before God;
  appoint steadfast love and faithfulness to watch over him!
So I will always sing praises to your name,
  as I pay my vows day after day. (Psalm 61)

All the people of Jerusalem set out with the king, weeping loudly as they leave their homes and pausing sadly at the last house on the outskirts of town. When the king reaches Kidron Valley, he stops and remains standing as all the people file past him, heading toward the desert (cf. 2 Sam 15:17-23).

This exile is not a flight. It is a penitential procession that demonstrates the loyalty of the king's faithful servants and the dignity of a monarch who refuses to be rushed from his domain. He is directing the people's movement with prudence and good judgment. Some he allows to follow him, and others he sends back home. This is called leading, not controlling.

The king does not try to use God: he orders the Ark of God to be brought back to the city. He does not identify his fate (that is, his immediate fate) with that of the Ark. After graciously returning the Ark to Jerusalem, he bides his time and prepares for his own return there if God so wishes. But he is ready for anything: "If God should tell me, 'I do not take pleasure in you,' then he will deal with me in a way that he considers appropriate" (2 Sam 15:25-26).

David's exile is deliberate; he does not allow himself to be chased away; he realizes the limits of his situation, and he tries to be realistic about his hope for a possible return. He instructs Zadok the priest to return to the city but tells him, "I will be waiting at the fords of the desert until word from you reaches me" (2 Sam 15:28). He withdraws only as far as he has to. He is familiar with God's retreats and knows how to leave room for God. His strategy is like that of Jesus at the critical moment when his "hour" was near: he avoided public gatherings and spent his nights in Bethany.

David places his liberty at the service of God's designs and cooperates with God's desires. In so doing, he does not lose what he himself called "prudence," which is simply providing the human means that God requires and then letting God act. David cares for his people and does not abandon them. He does not burn the city; he does not cremate history. He leaves some followers in the city who will counteract the influence of Absalom's supporters (2 Sam 15:30-36). Complete surrender to God sets David's horizons and gives him greatness of soul. But his surrender is not passive servility; rather, it is the dedication of the astute servant who unfailingly places his talents at the service of his lord. In this case, David submits his talents to the will of his God, who wants to dispossess *him*, but not his people.

While journeying forth from the city, David is cursed and stoned (2 Sam 16:5-14). Despite the rocks thrown and the insults proffered, he does not let himself become discouraged. He has faith that God has loved him and continues to love him. He does not mourn or feel sorry for himself because of his misfortune; at most, he offers his distress to his God in search of remedy. The very way he handles his humiliation will bring about a change in his situation. He is able to see God's hand even in the most contrary signs. In this he is very different from Saul, for the more Saul tried to control God's designs, the less he achieved. This is a temptation to which David will also succumb later on, when he calls for a census of the nation. Forgetting that all his relations with the people are sacred acts, he will try to exercise undue control over the people (cf. 2 Sam 24:1-17). Here we see the two sides of David, one surrendering to God, the other seeking to control.

Our attempts to control and manage our commitment to the

mission God has given us sometimes take the form of magic—recall Saul's consultation with a soothsayer. In our own day, this magic takes different forms. There is, for example, the naïve, bucolic self-control of New Agers; there are various types of ideology and intellectualizing; and there are even attempts to submit the mystery of God to psychological and sociological analysis.

When we try to control the terms of our surrender, the tenderly personal experience of being children of God is lost to us. We may turn to ideologies; we may seek the balance of our being in ecological immanence; we may submit the mystery to psychoanalysis or sociological scrutiny—but none of these knows anything of tenderness. Their artfulness consists in manipulation, not caressing. It was at the moment of his supreme surrender that Jesus pronounced the word "Father" with the utmost human tenderness, and that is how he pronounces it in heaven.

For Prayer and Reflection.

"So the king left, followed by all his household.... The whole country wept aloud as all the people passed by; the king crossed the Wadi Kidron, and all the people moved on towards the wilderness.... Then the king said to Zadok, 'Carry the ark of God back into the city. If I find favor in the eyes of the Lord, he will bring me back and let me see both it and the place where it remains. But if he says, "I take no pleasure in you," here I am, let him do to me what seems good to him'" (2 Sam 15:16, 23, 25-26).

35. The Solitude of Prayer

AFTER UTTERING HIS FIRST PRAYER, Adam set out on the road of exile. He traveled far from paradise, but he did so in the hope that he might, by God's mercy, one day return to it. The exile of Adam is relived in the history of the Babylonian exile, which is interpreted with tragic overtones by the author of the letter to the Hebrews. That letter gives poignant expression to the Israelites' nostalgia for their abandoned homeland; it recounts the sacrifices the people made to remain faithful to their memory: "They confessed that they were strangers and foreigners on the earth, for the people who speak in this way make it clear that they are seeking a homeland. If they had been thinking of the land that they had left behind, they would have had opportunity to return. But as it is, they desire a better country, that is, a heavenly one" (Heb 11:13-16). For remaining true to their memory, these exiles "were tortured, refusing to accept release, in order to obtain a better resurrection. Others suffered mocking and flogging, and even chains and imprisonment. They were stoned to death, they were sawn in two, they were killed by the sword; they went about in skins of sheep and goats, destitute, persecuted, tormented—of whom the world was not worthy. They wandered in deserts and mountains, and in caves and holes in the ground" (Heb 11:35-38).

In its pilgrimage, our flesh feels nostalgia for the homeland, and it voices its longing deliberately and explicitly in prayer, in the presence of the glorious Lord, the Lord of that homeland we yearn for. Meanwhile, our flesh is caught between feelings and numbness, between grace and sin, between deference and rebellion. It feels the oppression of exile and dreads the long road it must walk; it struggles valiantly to defend its hope. The day that our nostalgia dies, our flesh will cease to pray. Seeking release from exile and from wandering in a strange land, it will make this world its homeland. It will tire of seeking after God. On that day the greatest gift that can be given to us is the one that was given to Elijah when an angel roused him from his sleep-inducing depression and told him: "Get up and eat, for otherwise you won't be able to continue on your journey" (1 Kings 19:7).

Those who consciously and willingly accept their exiled state suffer a twofold solitude. On the one hand, they feel isolated from other people; they are strangers on the road. On the other, they taste the bitterness of distance from God. This is also the twofold solitude of the person in prayer, who is essentially on the fringes, estranged both from God and from other persons, but at the same time unable to prescind either from God (because he seeks God and feels sought by him) or from others (because his mission puts him at the service of his sisters and brothers, whom he tries to love as he loves himself). This was the experience that Jeremiah felt in the marrow of his bones. For announcing what God had commanded him to say, he was accused of sacrilege and despised by all the people (Jer 15:10). Feeling isolated in that contradiction, Jeremiah complained that God had left him alone. He went so far as to curse the day he was born, but he never denied the nostalgic seduction of the face of God that was burning in his heart: "O Lord, you have enticed me, and I was enticed; you have overpowered me, and you have prevailed. I have become a laughing-stock all day long; everyone mocks me" (Jer 20.7). This is the prayer of a man who gave himself completely and asked no more than that God would take his side. In our own lives, though, it sometimes seems that God takes the other side. It would be good to read slowly the whole of Jeremiah's agonizing complaint (Jer 20:7-18).

Those who serve God faithfully experience both these aspects of their solitude as coming from the same source: the depths of their exile. Reality seems to make fun of believers. Where is the word of God? Why doesn't it come true? (cf. Jer 17:15). It seems that God has not fulfilled the promise he made Jeremiah when he chose him: "I will be with you to protect you" (Jer 1:8). It seems that God has nothing else to say to his chosen ones (cf. Jer 15:18; Job 6:15-20). The scorn heaped on those who have trusted in God reaches its climax on Calvary: "You who would destroy the temple and build it in three days, save yourself! If your are the Son of God, come down from the cross.... He saved others; he cannot save himself! He is the King of Israel; let him come down from the cross now, and we will believe in him. He trusts in God; let God deliver him now, if he loves him" (Matt 27:39-44). In this silence of God, our flesh once again undergoes a change: we discover that the obedient dialogue of prayer is not a "negotiation." God's faithful promise is very different from anything we imagine. Our heart keeps changing as we walk along this road.

When we experience the silence of God and of other human beings, we feel exiled from ourselves. We are stripped of all possessions as we sit by the rivers of Babylon; hanging our guitars on the willows, we feel too sad to sing the songs of the homeland (Psalm 137:1-4). This feeling of being exiled from oneself also finds its culmination in the Lord's passion, during the prayer in Gethsemane. This is the most human and most dramatic of all Jesus' prayers (cf. Mark 14:32-38; Matt 26:36-46; Luke

22:40-46). There is entreaty, sadness, and anguish, almost to the point of bewilderment (Mark 14:33-34). Feeling his Father to be far away, Jesus experiences the utter loneliness of exile. His grief is like the extreme melancholy of Jonah, who could not understand the plans of God (Jonah 4:8-9). "My God, why have you forsaken me?" (Matt 27:46).

> *They went to a place called Gethsemane; and he said to his disciples, "Sit here while I pray." He took with him Peter and James and John, and began to be distressed and agitated. And he said to them, "I am deeply grieved, even to death; remain here, and keep awake." And going a little farther, he threw himself on the ground and prayed that, if it were possible, the hour might pass from him. He said, "Abba, Father, for you all things are possible; remove this cup from me; yet, not what I want, but what you want." He came and found them sleeping; and he said to Peter, "Simon, are you asleep? Could you not keep awake one hour? Keep awake and pray that you may not come into the time of trial; the spirit indeed is willing, but the flesh is weak." (Matt 26:36-41)*

When we feel the depths of our exile and enter into prayer, we are led through a singular process of a purification. Our hearts raise question after question, but the dark night yields no answers. Still, we keep striving to comprehend something of the mystery. Our attitudes, our words, our thoughts keep alternating between contradictions: we experience exhaustion and resignation (Job 29:2-6), or we resort to bitter irony (Job 7:20), or we try to make God see reason (Job 10:8), or we assume an attitude of distrust (Job 10:2). But despite all our posturing and protest, we feel ourselves in exile, we recall our homeland, and we let our hearts yearn. Without negotiating or turning back, we keep moving forward, searching for God beyond the conventional sanctuaries. We stand helpless before our loneliness, our exile, our pain-filled world, and the uncomprehending silence.

This is the moment when God intervenes, not exactly with answers but with questions. He leads us by new paths to free us from false pretensions. Here again, we face the hard truth: it is not God who must change, it is we. That is the ultimate aim of prayer. Prayer is the privileged place of our exile, for it is in prayer that revelation takes place. It is in prayer that we experience the passage from what we think God is to what God truly is. We are led by God through the purification of exile, the dark night of the soul, and it is in this moment of crisis that we reach conversion. This is the exile of all flesh, feeling ourselves without a homeland, without mother or father, without even a dog to pet. We are exiled from ourselves because our hearts are in tune with nothing; all is dissonance. We are exiled from other persons and from God, for all are silent. But this is the exile that brings about the deepest conversion of our flesh, which becomes a wound that is "cured" by the "touch" of God.

For Prayer and Reflection

"By the rivers of Babylon—there we sat down and there we wept when we remembered Zion. On the willows there we hung up our harps. For there our captors asked us for songs, and our tormentors asked for mirth, saying, 'Sing us one of the songs of Zion!' How could we sing the Lord's song in a foreign land?" (Psalm 137:1-4).

36. Moses and the People: Intercession vs. Murmuring

WE HAVE SEEN how our flesh in exile feels nostalgia for the homeland, a nostalgia that at times becomes blighted as our longing for "the onions and the garlic" of Egypt (Num 11:5-6) makes us look back and lose hope. How do we become aware that we have changed our forward direction (like "those who shrink back" in Heb 10:39)? How do we distinguish good nostalgia from bad, the nostalgia by which we are "saved in hope" from that which seeks salvation by romantically transforming memory into mere memento? The signs of unhealthy nostalgia are resentful murmuring and the triumphalist striving that creates for itself false gods: "Make us gods that will go before us," the people tell Aaron. "As for this fellow Moses, who brought us out of the land of Egypt, we do not know what has become of him" (Exod 32:1). All triumphalism simply cloaks our desire to possess an idol we can adore. The God of memory gets transformed into the token of a god made to our measure.

Moses is the prototype of the person who prays in solitude before God, meditating and receiving the law of God for a people who has already sought another god. Sometimes when we pray, we feel that we are "arriving late," as if our message of salvation is being heard by people who have already been saved by another god—and they are in their own way, having traded in the gift for the negotiated deal.

What is interesting in this passage from Exodus is that God himself proposes a trade to Moses; he offers to exchange this stiff-necked crowd of Israelites for a better, more faithful people. God seems to be anticipating Moses' anger, for on other occasions Moses has told God how tired he was of the people's hard-heartedness and how he preferred to die than to be their leader. But when God proposes to give Moses a new people to lead, the prophet objects strongly and intercedes for Israel.

Here we see Moses' greatness of soul, for he renounces the dream of every leader; he refuses to have the people made to his own measure. Instead Moses reminds God of his promise and tells him that the promise is non-negotiable: salvation cannot yield to human triumphalism. Moses bids God remember Abraham, Isaac, and Jacob. He protests that God will himself be ridiculed by the Egyptians if he abandons his beloved people. It's almost as if God were faltering and being tempted to change his ways, from being the God of faithful memory to being a God kept as a quaint souvenir. Moses tells God that he wants him to remain the God of faithful memory (Exod 32:11-13).

> But Moses implored the Lord his God, and said, "O Lord, why does your wrath burn hot against your people, whom you brought out of the land of Egypt with great power and with a mighty hand? Why should the Egyptians say, 'It was with evil intent that he brought them out to kill them in the mountains, and to consume them from the face of the earth'? Turn from your fierce wrath; change your mind and do not bring disaster on your people. Remember Abraham, Isaac, and Israel, your servants, how you swore to them by your own self, saying to them, 'I will multiply your descendants like the stars of heaven, and all this land that

I have promised I will give to your descendants, and they shall inherit it forever.'" (Exod 32:11-13)

Only by understanding that prayer of intercession is truly a dialogue of love will we comprehend this "reversal of roles" by which each interlocutor uses arguments that belong in the other's mouth. This reversal of roles can also help us understand that difficult passage in the story about the wedding in Cana: Mary is able to discern the deepest sentiments of Jesus and intercede with him, even though Jesus' words seem to contradict his actions (cf. John 2:1-11). The praying person who intercedes for others is the one who has intuitively sensed God's deepest sentiments and holds fast to them despite all contrary indications, even when God's speech seems to be at variance with events.

What is at work in the book of Exodus is a kind of divine pedagogy by which God makes his servant into an intercessor: by exchanging roles and exaggerating the contradiction, God dissolves the angry reproach of Moses and brings forth the best from his worthy heart. The prophet understands that he should not be ashamed of his own flesh and blood. He realizes that by interceding he is not simply performing an obligatory function; rather, he loves his sisters and brothers as himself. He has thrown his lot in with this people, and, in so doing, he is becoming day by day more like God himself: "If we are faithless, he remains faithful—for he cannot deny himself" (2 Tim 2:13).

Moses' dialogue of intercession takes place despite the deep pain he feels at the stubbornness of this people who refuses to change. Nevertheless, Moses chooses this people as his own, and instead of living apart, he seeks to share in their opprobrium (cf. Heb 11:24-25).

It is against this background of intercession that we should understand the punishment that Moses then imposes on the people: the breaking of the tablets of the law and the slaughter carried out by the Levites (Exod 32:19-29). There follows a second intercession, in which the roles return to their customary pattern. Now it is Moses who offers to be wiped out of God's book instead of his people, and it is God who confirms him in his mission and approves the way he has led and punished the people (Exod 32:31-34).

> *So Moses returned to the Lord and said, "Alas, this people has sinned a great sin; they have made for themselves gods of gold. But now, if you will only forgive their sin—but if not, blot me out of the book that you have written." But the Lord said to Moses, "Whoever has sinned against me I will blot out of my book. But now go, lead the people to the place about which I have spoken to you; see, my angel shall go in front of you. Nevertheless, when the day comes for punishment, I will punish them for their sin."* (Exod 32:31-34)

For Prayer and Reflection

"On the third day there was a wedding in Cana of Galilee, and the mother of Jesus was there. Jesus and his disciples had also been invited to the wedding. When the wine gave out, the mother of Jesus said to him, 'They have no wine.' And Jesus said to her, 'Woman, what concern is that to you and to me? My hour has not yet come.' His mother said to the servants, 'Do whatever he tells you'" (John 2:1-5).

37. God Revealed in Weakness and Limitation

THE MORE WE ARE CALLED to greatness, the more we feel the weakness and limitation of our own flesh. Abraham was faithful: in obedience, he left his land without knowing where he was going (Heb 11:8). Even though greatly encouraged by God's promises, he felt the pain of his own limited humanity, which seemed to contradict all that he was promised. After all, he was childless, and his only heir was a servant (Gen 15:2-3). When our flesh truly *feels* its weakness and limits, the natural reaction is to rebel and make our prayer a form of complaint or lament. This experience, occurring almost daily, prepares us gradually for the critical moment when we realize with inescapable certainty that we have reached our utmost limit. "Naked I came from my mother's womb, and naked shall I return there; the Lord gave, and the Lord has taken away; blessed be the name of the Lord" (Job 1:21). At such a moment, the solid basis of our hope takes the form of resignation as we stand face to face with the limits of our finitude.

This sense of limitation also leads us by the path of the dark night to which I referred before. Even if Job is to some extent resigned, his prayer, rising as it does from the limits and weakness of all flesh, gives expression to profound bitterness and anguish (Job 10:1; 7:7-21; 9:28-31; 10:1-22; 13:20-21; 14:18-

22; 30:20-23). We feel aggrieved because, in addition to suffering the ridicule that others heap on us for "taking leave" of ourselves, we now see that the godless seem to be doing quite well for themselves. How can it be that they prosper as they do even as they scoff at God? Such questions make our limitations feel all the more painful; they make our weakness seem a sickness; they make us feel like foolish idiots in the face of life.

> *Remember that my life is a breath;*
> *my eye will never again see good.*
> *The eye that beholds me will see me no more;*
> *while your eyes are upon me, I shall be gone.*
> *As the cloud fades and vanishes,*
> *so those who go down to Sheol do not come up;*
> *they return no more to their houses,*
> *nor do their places know them any more.*
> *"Therefore I will not restrain my mouth;*
> *I will speak in the anguish of my spirit;*
> *I will complain in the bitterness of my soul.*
> *Am I the Sea, or the Dragon,*
> *that you set a guard over me?*
> *When I say, 'My bed will comfort me,*
> *my couch will ease my complaint,'*
> *then you scare me with dreams*
> *and terrify me with visions,*
> *so that I would choose strangling*
> *and death rather than this body.*
> *I loathe my life; I would not live forever.*
> *Let me alone, for my days are a breath."* (Job 7:7-16)

Only prayer can give us strength to pass the test: "Keep awake and pray that you may not come into the time of trial; the spirit indeed is willing, but the flesh is weak" (Mark 14:38). The flesh is weak. That is how we experience our weakness and the limits of all flesh. Saint Paul felt this in the depths of his being: "To keep me from being too elated, a thorn was given to me in the flesh, a messenger of Satan to torment me, to keep me from being too elated. Three times I appealed to the Lord about this, that it would leave me, but he said to me, 'My grace is sufficient for you, for power is made perfect in weakness.' So, I will boast all the more gladly of my weaknesses, so that the power of Christ may dwell in me. Therefore I am content with weaknesses, insults, hardships, persecutions, and calamities for the sake of Christ; for whenever I am weak, then I am strong" (2 Cor 12:7-10). Here Paul asks to be freed from the hindrance of weakness and limitation, and the response he receives is the logic of the cross: God makes himself present in weakness.

Our wounded flesh is the "gateway" for God's manifestation. We need simply to recognize this reality and by prayer "provide space" for the revelation of strength. Our limitation and our weakness can be transformed by prayer into a cross. This is the essence of the Pauline logic. In speaking of his limitations, Paul mentions how he is buffeted by temptation and feels constrained by external forces. It's the same with us. The problem is that when we concentrate only on external hindrances, we stop praying and start complaining. We are no longer servants of the Gospel but take on victim status. We canonize ourselves and seek to do away with all limitations. We learn to disguise our weakness with the incense of our saintly status. The victim is not Christ; it is myself. This is the beginning of all blasphemy, and blasphemy is the highest form of anti-prayer. As Leon Bloy used to say, "When we do not speak with God, then we speak with the Devil." There is no halfway point in the way we experience our weakness and limitation: either we pray or we blaspheme. Flesh that is accustomed to blasphemy, flesh that knows nothing of seeking help for its own sinful sores, is flesh that is unable to help with the sores of others. It will invidiously keep its distance from the other. It will never be a neighbor to anyone but itself. Even when it consecrates its life to God, it does so only to protect its cozy relation with itself; it remains fixed in the profound selfishness that makes it avoid every exodus, every sore, every weakness, every limitation, every encounter with the other. This is the aseptic attitude of the Pharisees—neither virus nor vitamin.

In describing the moment where one passes from the night of the senses to the night of the spirit, Saint John of the Cross speaks of tempests and labors. In the last verse of his first song, after mentioning the shameless *spirit of fornication* (which he calls the angel of Satan), the poet specifies that it is the *spirit of blasphemy* (or self-sufficiency) and the *spirit of confusion* (Isa 19:13-14) that rock the soul with every wind of doubt and scruple and obsession and insecurity. It is at the moment of greatest purification that the soul experiences these three limitations, these three sores, these three weaknesses. The reason for this is that prayer is openness to the gift of God, and we must feel the need for that gift in our own flesh.

For Prayer and Reflection

"Three times I appealed to the Lord about this, that it would leave me, but he said to me, 'My grace is sufficient for you, for power is made perfect in weakness.' So, I will boast all the more gladly of my weaknesses, so that the power of Christ may dwell in me. Therefore I am content with weaknesses, insults, hardships, persecutions, and calamities for the sake of Christ; for whenever I am weak, then I am strong" (2 Cor 12:8-10).

38. Job: Praying from Our Sores

JOB IS THE PROTOTYPE of the person who has reached the limits of suffering. The words of the local sages no longer satisfy him; he wants to talk face to face with God. If Job had been able to see Jesus on the cross, then he would have found a worthy interlocutor. Only Jesus can answer Job, for Jesus is the answer of a merciful Father wounded with mercy. The wounds of Jesus might make us think that the Father suffers from the "illness" of mercy. When the Father's unstinting gift of self, which is the Son, remains eternally wounded, then the way is opened for us to enter into a dimension of fatherly mercy that we can express only as "illness" in the sense that it is something the Father cannot resist, something before which he is defenseless.

That is why our own flesh wounded by sin (the flesh of prodigal sons and daughters) is the entryway into the flesh wounded by love (the flesh of Jesus), which opens for us the way to the Father of all flesh, who makes rain to fall on the righteous and on sinners, who covers with kisses and warmly embraces his returning wayward child.

At a dramatic point in his story, Job realizes that he needs to dialogue with God and not with other human beings: "Look, my eye has seen all this, my ear has heard and understood it. What you [wise men] know, I also know; I am not inferior to you. But I would speak to the Almighty, and I desire to argue my case with God. As for you, you whitewash with lies; all of you are worthless physicians" (Job 13:1-4).

244

Job prays at the risk of dying and therefore has the right to tell his counselors: "Refrain from talking, and I will speak" (Job 13:13-14). As a son who is suffering, he has the right to pray. He begs God not to remain silent: "Call, and I will answer; or let me speak, and you reply to me" (Job 13:22). Since we humans speak without understanding things too wonderful for us to know, we have no right to an answer from God, but we can still demand that God hear us when we speak from our wounds: "Hear, and I will speak; I will question you, and you declare to me" (Job 42:3-4).

It is this prayer out of suffering that makes the Father speak. And once his Word has come forth from his mouth, it cannot return to him until it becomes Word made flesh. "By his wounds we have been healed" (Isa 53:5). We do well to recall the liturgical hymn for the vespers of Wednesday of Holy Week.

> I come, Lord, to behold the fiery traces
> of your sacred luminous wounds;
> fivefold blossoming of imperishable roses,
> heavenly constellation of five bright stars.

> I come to touch your beautiful recesses,
> to study in their silent halls,
> and to drink with painful tenderness
> the bitter honey you put in them.

> When my unarmed courage wavers,
> when I sink deep in murky anguish,
> when I also see myself as wounded,
> then let your sweet wounds encircle me
> and hide me in their gracious cloisters
> and cure me with their godly gentleness.

The word of God has creative force, and once God speaks a word to us, it can only become Word made flesh. But to receive the gift of the Word made flesh, we must hear it from our fleshly neediness, from our wounds, from our own debility. Otherwise, the flesh would wax proud. That is why the Lord comes for the sake of the sickly and not the healthy; that is why he heals our frail flesh and becomes food to nourish it. Only by the flesh of Christ do we reach the Word.

In our exile and our woundedness, the Word provides consolation and hope (Psalm 119:49). The Word provides escape on the wings of a dove; it carries us off to a place where we are safe from the abusive cries of our foes (Psalm 55:1-8). By our wounds, through the Word made wound, we have access to the only One who is capable of embracing us in his mercy: "You have kept count of my exiles (my wanderings). Put my tears in your bottle!" (Psalm 56:8).

> *Give ear to my prayer, O God;*
> *do not hide yourself from my supplication.*
> *Attend to me, and answer me;*
> *I am troubled in my complaint.*
> *I am distraught by the noise of the enemy,*
> *because of the clamor of the wicked.*
> *For they bring trouble upon me,*
> *and in anger they cherish enmity against me.*
> *My heart is in anguish within me,*
> *the terrors of death have fallen upon me.*
> *Fear and trembling come upon me,*
> *and horror overwhelms me.*
> *And I say, "O that I had wings like a dove!*
> *I would fly away and be at rest;*
> *truly, I would flee far away;*
> *I would lodge in the wilderness; Selah*

246

I would hurry to find a shelter for myself
from the raging wind and tempest." (Psalm 55:1-8)

For Prayer and Reflection

Hymn of Holy Thursday

After they had shared
in the supper of the Lamb,
what seemed only symbol
began to be real.

To show his faithful people
his woundedness with love,
God unites his many mercies
into a single sign.

Taking into his hands
earthly bread and wine,
he gives us in their stead
his Body and his Blood.

If one bite caused our common death,
then life is also given by one mouthful;
if sin supplied the poison,
then God provides the antidote.

Make merry, heaven and earth;
rejoice, all creation,
for God who fills the universe
has found shelter in my soul. Amen.

39. Homeward Bound

WHEN ADAM LEFT PARADISE, he wasn't simply "kicked out." Certainly there was an aspect of punishment, but his exile was also self-imposed. Like the prodigal son, he set out with his inheritance (in Adam's case, knowledge of good and evil), but there was always the promise that he would return. From that day when Adam left paradise, the Father climbed up to the roof of history and looked far off into the horizon (cf. Luke 15:20). He knew the moment would come when his son returned; he knew with certainty when our flesh, now justified, would return home to his temple (cf. Luke 2:22-38). God is a Father and knows the impatience of a father's heart when the lives of his children are at stake. More than just observing, God the Father was anxiously awaiting the return of his lost child, all of humankind, to his embrace. Even when wandering far from home, the son felt in his bones the unsettling memory of the Father's house. Although a drifter, the son was gifted with a sense of direction, and, in obedience to that gift, he sought a re-encounter with his truer self. He found space for questioning and sought to correct the direction in which he was heading. He realized the significance of that guiding star within his heart, though he knew not whence it came nor where it led. That is, he prayed—and he prayed for his return. All flesh follows its own paths, and it is precisely in prayer that the meaning of its existence falls into place. It is only in prayer that our heart comes to see clearly where it's coming "from," what it's moving "toward," and where it presently stands.

When we ask ourselves these questions, God does not stand far off, just waiting for us. No, he "draws close" and walks beside us. God the Father "takes" us where we are, in our most humble circumstances, but he leads us toward other water and other bread (cf. John 4:7-15; 6:35-40). Our Father does not stand idly awaiting us, but rather incites in us the nostalgic desire to be "homeward bound." He leads us far beyond our feeble yearnings.

> *A Samaritan woman came to draw water, and Jesus said to her, "Give me a drink." (His disciples had gone to the city to buy food.) The Samaritan woman said to him, "How is it that you, a Jew, ask a drink of me, a woman of Samaria?" (Jews do not share things in common with Samaritans.) Jesus answered her, "If you knew the gift of God, and who it is that is saying to you, 'Give me a drink,' you would have asked him, and he would have given you living water." The woman said to him, "Sir, you have no bucket, and the well is deep. Where do you get that living water? Are you greater than our ancestor Jacob, who gave us the well, and with his sons and his flocks drank from it?" Jesus said to her, "Everyone who drinks of this water will be thirsty again, but those who drink of the water that I will give them will never be thirsty. The water that I will give will become in them a spring of water gushing up to eternal life." The woman said to him, "Sir, give me this water, so that I may never be thirsty or have to keep coming here to draw water." (John 4:7-15)*

Prayer is a way of letting ourselves be guided by God, of letting ourselves be led beyond our tranquility and our anxiety. If, as we've already said, prayer is a way of setting out in exodus from ourselves and enduring our exile and estrangement, now we can also say that prayer is a road back home that is "far beyond" any return route we might imagine.

Prayer is born out of history and life. To pray is to reread in the light of faith the history of every exile, every exodus, every road back home. The Pharisee in the temple (cf. Luke 18:9-14) was not praying out of his life; he was avoiding life and history. He was praying on the margins of life because, in declaring himself righteous, he thought himself non-historical. The book of Psalms (choose some favorite psalm for this meditation) is an example of what I mean by "praying from life." We find there in the psalms joy, praise, and thanksgiving; we also find lament, grief, and entreaty. The psalmist prays and reflects on the concrete problems of existence. We might also meditate on the Israelites' canticle of triumph in Exodus 15:1-19. This song tells of a great historical event and then describes the reaction of God's people, a reaction so rich in emotion that it can be expressed only in poetry, for poetry alone captures the totality of human feelings.

He also told this parable to some who trusted in themselves that they were righteous and regarded others with contempt: "Two men went up to the temple to pray, one a Pharisee and the other a tax collector. The Pharisee, standing by himself, was praying thus, 'God, I thank you that I am not like other people: thieves, rogues, adulterers, or even like this tax collector. I fast twice a week; I give a tenth of all my income.' But the tax collector, standing far off, would not even look up to heaven, but was beating his breast and saying, 'God, be merciful to me, a sinner!' I tell you, this man went down to his home justified rather than the other; for all who exalt themselves will be humbled, but all who humble themselves will be exalted." (Luke 18:9-14)

When we experience God's victory in our personal lives and feel the joy of his companionship and guidance (this is the moment of consolation in prayer), then our flesh experiences a new tension: the tension between being at peace and taking leave of itself. But this "taking leave of self" is quite different from the exodus from self we spoke of before; it is the ecstatic leaving of self that is proper to praise. In prayer, we experience a definite tension between inner repose and exuberant praise. In prayer, all our existence vibrates with faith, enthusiasm, joy, praise, wonder. That is why Jesus could not contain himself but broke out in praise: "I thank you, Father ..." (Matt 11:25-26).

In order for this to happen, however, we must keep in mind that our fidelity to history is dependent precisely on our memory. It was the people's *remembrance* of a long history of deeds performed by God that gave birth to the prayer of the psalms and the biblical canticles. At the same time, prayer goes beyond history, for it sees in God's historical deeds an ongoing theme that offers a key for reading the present and a promise that opens toward the future. Our history is full of tensions: between past and present, between present and future, between time and eternity. Memory engages us with that tension and learns to read the present situation in the light of God's saving power, and when read this way, the present is transformed into promise for the future. As a result, when human flesh settles down to pray, it rescues memory: our flesh is remembrance. And the memory of the Church is precisely the memory of the suffering flesh of God, the remembrance of the Lord's passion, the eucharistic prayer.

Precisely because prayer is historical, it tends to be "prayer of the people." Only in prayer do we have the extraordinary experience that what is most particular in oneself is united with what is most universal. What makes us truly persons and rescues us from individualism is precisely our experience of the tension between the particular and the universal. We are persons; I am totally responsible for my actions, but I belong to a people. When our flesh realizes its own responsibility and at the same time its oneness with the people, then "we pray in common" even when we are alone. As Jesus never tires of repeating, praying in common is especially efficacious (Matt 18:9). It is the prayer of exiled, banished flesh that is on the road toward the ultimate homeland, conscious of belonging to something beyond the limits of its skin, of belonging to the people of God.

The early disciples understood this; that is why they "were constantly devoting themselves to prayer" (Acts 1:14). During the most difficult moments of the primitive Church, prayer became the primary way of finding the way toward God: the community prayed over who would replace Judas (Acts 1:24, 26) and over the choice of the seven deacons (Acts 6:6); the Twelve devoted much of their time "to prayer and to serving the word" (Acts 6:2-4); the community prayed for the liberation of Peter and John (Acts 4:24-30); and Peter and John prayed for the converts who were baptized by Philip in Samaria (Acts 8:15). The book of Acts also relates the diverse circumstances in which Peter, the head of the Church (Acts 9:40; 10:9), and Paul (Acts 9:11; 13:3; 14:23; 20:36; 21:5-6) prayed.

> *About noon the next day, as they were on their journey and approaching the city, Peter went up on the roof to pray.* (Acts 10:9)

> *The Lord said to him, "Get up and go to the street called Straight, and at the house of Judas look for a man of Tarsus named Saul. At this moment he is praying."* (Acts 9:11)

> *And after they had appointed elders for them in each church, with prayer and fasting they entrusted them to the Lord in whom they had come to believe.* (Acts 14:23)

In the early Church, the people did not pray only at decisive moments or only to recall their history as God's people; rather, prayer became for them the very vehicle of community life, along with hearing God's Word, fraternal communion, and the breaking of the bread. By hearing the Word, practicing charity, and praying together, the early Christians kept alive their memory of the Lord's passion (Acts 2:42-48). By prayer, the memory of being God's people is recovered, and, by prayer, every single person feels united with the community's universal reach.

> *They devoted themselves to the apostles' teaching and fellowship, to the breaking of bread and the prayers. Awe came upon everyone, because many wonders and signs were being done by the apostles. All who believed were together and had all things in common; they would sell their possessions and goods and distribute the proceeds to all, as any had need. Day by day, as they spent much time together in the temple, they broke bread at home and ate their food with glad and generous hearts, praising God and having the goodwill of all the people. And day by day the Lord added to their number those who were being saved.* (Acts 2:42-48)

This molding of the community together into unity has no limits; it goes beyond anything foreseeable. That is why the Church is essentially far-reaching (outwardly, but also inwardly, toward the hearts of the faithful). We pray for the whole world, including our enemies and persecutors (Matt 5:44-45; Luke 6:27-28). The greatest example of this molding of the Church's universality is found in the priestly prayer of Jesus (John 17:1-26). There we find delineated the true horizons of the Church, which extend from trinitarian communion to the unity of humankind. In Jesus' prayer, universality reaches its supreme expression. Church unity is molded into universality following the pattern of the Father and the Son and the Holy Spirit. The I-Thou of Father and Son unfolds into a progressively expanding movement: from the disciples (John 17:11) to all believers (17:20-21) to the whole world (17:23). Jesus prays that participation in the divine I-Thou be extended to the Church (17:21, 23, 36) so that the community of believers becomes immersed in the trinitarian dialogue. Jesus prays not only that his disciples be united among themselves, but that their unity be prolonged visibly and historically in the communion of love that constitutes the mystery of God.

> *But I say to you, Love your enemies and pray for those who persecute you, so that you may be children of your Father in heaven; for he makes his sun rise on the evil and on the good, and sends rain on the righteous and on the unrighteous.* (Matt 5:44-45)

For Prayer and Reflection

"Now I am no longer in the world, but they are in the world, and I am coming to you. Holy Father, protect them in your name that you have given me, so that they may be one, as we are one.... I ask not only on behalf of these, but also on behalf of those who will believe in me through their word, that they may all be one. As you, Father, are in me and I am in you, may they also be in us, so that the world may believe that you have sent me. The glory that you have given me I have given them, so that they may be one, as we are one, I in them and you in me, that they may become completely one, so that the world may know that you have sent me and have loved them even as you have loved me" (John 17:11, 20-23).

40. Simeon: Led by the Spirit

OLD SIMEON'S FLESH is weary of life; it is flesh that has
retreated from passions and from attempts to control
God; it is flesh that lets itself be led by the Spirit, who promises it consolation. Simeon is the prototype of the person of
prayer who allows himself to be led by God. Luke stresses three
times that Simeon is a person "guided by the Spirit" (cf. Luke
2:25-27).

Simeon is the human face of the merciful Father. In the parable of the Prodigal Son, the father waits for his boy to return
from the sin into which he has voluntarily exiled himself, but in
Simeon we see the father who awaits not the return from exile,
but the coming of the new flesh of the Son, who voluntarily
exiles himself to save us (cf. Phil 2:5-11; Heb 1:3). We see incarnate in Simeon all the expectation of the prophets, especially
Isaiah, the indefatigable prophet of the people's new exodus.

*He is the reflection of God's glory and the exact imprint of God's
very being, and he sustains all things by his powerful word. When
he had made purification for sins, he sat down at the right hand of
the Majesty on high.* (Heb 1:3)

The flesh of that newborn baby is light for revelation to the
nations. How can flesh be light? Our image of the world, our
dreams, all our projections are linked with the history of our
flesh. Often, we find ourselves banished, living in chains in the

foreign land of our complexes; we have no energy or will to return to the point where sin began to darken our soul. But there is a sure way to return: in the flesh of Christ so free of complexes, in that flesh brought up by Mary whose smile was dimmed by no shadow of sin. In the flesh of Jesus we find the bright gateway that allows our flesh to return once again to what our Creator dreamed it should be: formed of clay, but in his image and likeness.

Flesh is the key to the reading of each person's life, and the flesh of Christ is the key to the reading of the whole of salvation history. Simeon sees the glory of God in the flesh of the Child Jesus, and there is nothing more he needs to see in this world: he can depart in peace. Simeon is both "leader" and "led," and that is how the liturgy presents him: *Senex puerum portabat, puer autem senem regebat.* "The old man was carrying the child, but the child was guiding the old man."

Simeon has been waiting for the consolation of Israel. His heart has aged, but not the promises he heard in the words of Isaiah: "'Comfort, comfort my people,' says your God. 'Speak kindly to Jerusalem'" (Isa 40:1-2). This is the great message with which Handel began his meditation on the Messiah—he understood something. And the composer, once purified by the tears of his long artistic reflection, serenely concluded his meditation with the confident assurance that consolation would come: "I know that my Redeemer liveth!"

"All flesh is grass.... The grass withers, the flower fades; but the word of our God will stand for ever" (Isa 40:6-8). In old Simeon, we see the fulfillment of Isaiah's promise: "The glory of God will be revealed, and all people will see it at the same time" (Isa 40:5).

Holding the Child Jesus in his hands, Simeon performs the first eucharistic gesture in Luke's Gospel, and thus he blesses the Father. He also addresses the heart of Mary: "Speak to the heart of Jerusalem" (Isa 40:2).

For Prayer and Reflection

"Now there was a man in Jerusalem whose name was Simeon; this man was righteous and devout, looking forward to the consolation of Israel, and the Holy Spirit rested on him. It had been revealed to him by the Holy Spirit that he would not see death before he had seen the Lord's Messiah. Guided by the Spirit, Simeon came into the temple; and when the parents brought in the child Jesus, to do for him what was customary under the law, Simeon took him in his arms and praised God, saying, 'Master, now you are dismissing your servant in peace, according to your word; for my eyes have seen your salvation, which you have prepared in the presence of all peoples, a light for revelation to the Gentiles and for glory to your people Israel'" (Luke 2:25-32).

41. The Mystery of Talking with God

CONSIDERATION OF THE TRINITY makes us reflect not only on the three divine Persons but also on the universality of the Church. Sometimes I ask people, "To whom do you pray?", and often enough the answer is, "To God." Behind that word "God" is, of course, the figure of the Father or Jesus himself. But there are also people who pray to God as if they were praying to the divine essence. This is not prayer. The prayer of Christians is unavoidably personal. It is person-to-person: we pray to the Father or to the Son or to the Holy Spirit. What is more, each one of the divine Persons relates to us differently when we pray.

First of all, we do well to keep in mind that it is God himself who inspires our prayer; it is the Holy Spirit who suggests to us what the Father wants to hear. The Spirit comes to help us in our weakness, suggesting the things we should ask for according to the divine designs (cf. Rom 8:26-27). By making us aware that we are truly children of God, the Holy Spirit frees us from fear and anxiety; it endows us with the boldness (*parrhēsia*) we need to call on God with the name of Father, as Jesus taught us to do and as he did himself (Gal 4:6; Rom 8:15). Praying in the Spirit means becoming fully aware both of our neediness and of the power of this divine presence within us. The precarious nature of our Christian existence makes us realize that we need to ask for help, and so we are given the Holy Spirit to guide us in our petition, adoration, thanksgiving, and contemplation.

> *In the same way, the Spirit helps us in our weakness. We do not know what we ought to pray for, but the Spirit himself intercedes for us through wordless groans. And he who searches our hearts knows the mind of the Spirit, because the Spirit intercedes for God's people in accordance with the will of God.* (Rom 8:26-27)

In the Gospels, Jesus says that the sin against the Holy Spirit is so serious as to be unforgivable (Matt 12:31). Why is this? It would seem to be the case that there is pardon for the sin against the Father (think of the parable of the Prodigal Son), and there is the forgiveness pronounced by Jesus on the cross (and the pardon of Peter's betrayal, etc.). Why, then, is the sin against the Holy Spirit unforgivable?

In searching for an answer, we might be helped by a passage in Luke where Jesus speaks of the need to persevere in prayer: "So I say to you, Ask, and it will be given to you; search, and you will find; knock, and the door will be opened for you. For everyone who asks receives, and everyone who searches finds, and for everyone who knocks, the door will be opened. Is there anyone among you who, if your child asks for a fish, will give a snake instead of a fish? Or if the child asks for an egg, will give a scorpion? If you then, who are evil, know how to give good gifts to your children, how much more will the heavenly Father give the Holy Spirit to those who ask him!" (Luke 11:9-13). The Holy Spirit is the gift of the Father and the Son, promised and sent to the community that constantly devotes itself to prayer (Acts 1:14). To sin against the Holy Spirit means to sin against the gift of the Father and the Son, against the gift par excellence. It means sinning against the infinite generosity of

God's love, revealed as a Person. It means rejecting the need for the very love that enables us to exist; it means believing that we can obtain what we need by ourselves; it means daring to ask to be justified by God because "we are not sinners like those publicans." It means seeking to live without prayer or else to make prayer a form of commerce with God, just one more business transaction in our lives. What we are talking about is basically blasphemy, because what we are saying to the Father and the Son is this: "Thanks for creating me, and thanks for redeeming me, but now I'm on my own. With this stock of capital I've received, I now address you as equals—because I can do so." Herein lies the blasphemy because, as Paul tells us, "no one can say 'Jesus is Lord' except by the Holy Spirit" (1 Cor 12:3).

Praying in the Spirit, therefore, means being fully convinced that prayer is a great gift given by the Father. We are able to pray only by opening ourselves up to that gift, like children on Christmas morning: the children's hearts are open to receiving gifts because they know how little they have and they know that they will be given much. Praying in the Spirit means believing that God will pour his Spirit out upon all flesh (cf. Acts 2:17).

> *In the last days, God says,*
> *I will pour out my Spirit on all people.*
> *Your sons and daughters will prophesy,*
> *your young men will see visions,*
> *your old men will dream dreams.* (Acts 2:17)

That is why we pray to the Father, by the Son, in the Holy Spirit. In all his letters (except perhaps in 2 Cor 3:7-8 and Eph 5:18-20), Paul addresses his prayers ultimately to the Father, while giving Christ an essential place in the prayer as mediator. Praying "in the name of the Lord Jesus" (Col 3:17; Eph

5:20) is more than commending ourselves to Jesus or invoking his name. It means praying with Jesus, as sons and daughters in the Son, lovers of the one and only Beloved. This is what Jesus means when he tells us to pray in his name (cf. John 14:13-14; 15:16; 16:14-26). Such prayer assumes a real connection with Jesus, a connection that is not just notional or sentimental but life-giving, like the branch on the vine (cf. John 15:1-8). Praying in Jesus' name implies our participation in the life of Jesus, a participation that is realized concretely in mutual love (John 15:16). We are called to be united with Christ and to be like Christ, knowing that we are loved by the Father as the Son is loved (John 16:26-27). While the force and the potential of all prayer lies precisely in letting ourselves be assisted by the Spirit, the concrete setting of prayer is this identification with Christ Jesus. In him we have access to the Father, and we call to the Father as Jesus did: "Father, Abba" (Mark 14:35-36). Thus, Christian prayer can only be filial prayer. In prayer, our flesh, now identified with the flesh of the Word and moved by the Spirit, experiences nostalgia for the Father, for he is the mystery that is revealed in prayer. Only in prayer is revealed the mystery that promises us unique communion with the Father in the Spirit and by the Son, the mystery that makes us share in that marvelous exchange by which the Son takes on our flesh and we receive his Spirit.

Through this communion in prayer, we are released from all servitude and liberated from all fear. We are free, and our liberty inspires us to return home from our exile. We return in freedom because we have understood the strength of God's word. We realize that even though we "have sinned against heaven and before you" (Luke 15:18, 21), God still organizes for us a party. Beneath our wounded flesh, the Father beholds his Son, who was wounded for our sake. The reach of this freedom of ours extends even farther, for once we realize that we have been "accepted," we grant even more space to the Spirit. In turn, the Spirit inspires in us the intercessory prayer that shows that we are truly free children of God, rightful heirs of his kingdom. We cannot be fully aware of this intimate relation we have with the Father (being part of his family and his household) unless we pray frequently as intercessors.

All the great men and women of God have been intercessors. Intercession has the character of yeast, and that is why Jesus asks us to be like yeast in the midst of the world (Luke 13:20-21). Intercession is like yeast in the bosom of the Trinity. Abraham interceded for Sodom: dust and ashes coming face-to-face with the Rock—and they conversed (Gen 18:23-32)! Only faith makes it possible for humans to converse with God with such insistence and familiarity. Moses prayed the same way. Recall the times when he prayed with his hands raised during the victory over the Amalekites (Exod 17:8-13) and the times when he interceded for the sin of his people in the desert and begged for pardon (Exod 32:11-14, 30-34; Num 14:10-20; 16:22; 21:7). Moses' intercession in Exodus 32 was especially dramatic; it was almost a wrestling match between God and the prophet. Moses used classical arguments to "convince" God to be merciful; he appealed to God's love (this nation is your people), to God's fidelity (remember your promises), and to God's glory (what will other nations say if you abandon this people that belongs to you?). In the end, Moses' prayer won the day: "the Lord relented over the evil that he had said he would do to his people" (Exod 32:14). Here I would like to repeat what I said before: it is not God who changes his mind, it is human beings who change their understanding. By prayer they come to realize that God is not a God of wrath but a God of forgiveness. Moses has discovered the true face of God, which is fidelity and forgiveness, and he has learned how to understand his people's sin in just measure. Intercession opens the way for the revelation of God's face, the true face he wants us to seek out.

By intercession, we gain access to the Father and discover new facets in concrete situations that allow us to change them. We can truly say in human terms that "God's heart is moved by intercession," but in reality he is always far ahead of us in movements of the heart, for "he has loved us first." What our intercession makes possible is greater clarity of revelation: God's power, love, loyalty, and fidelity can never change, since he is always faithful—but they can become more creatively manifest to us in our world.

That is why intercession assumes familiarity with God and the ability to address God with that bold discourse (*parrhēsia*) of which we spoke before. Moses spoke to God "as though he saw him who is invisible" (Heb 11:27). And in reality he did see him: God spoke to him face to face as a friend, as a confidant (Num 12:5-8; Exod 33:11; Deut 34:10-11). Someone wrote that "prayer is being present to God so as to discover the profound sources of love, even in situations where the logic of history tells us the schemas of sin, curse, and punishment should be working." Jesus himself gives us many examples of intercession; he intercedes for Peter so that his faith will not fail (Luke 22:31-32); he intercedes so that the Father will send the Spirit (John 14:16); he intercedes for those who have crucified him (Luke 23:33-34). And he insists that it is only by intercessory prayer that we are able to free persons of evil spirits (Mark 9:25-29).

The Lord would speak to Moses face to face, as one speaks to a friend. Then Moses would return to the camp, but his young aide Joshua son of Nun did not leave the tent. (Exod 33:11)

In Russian icons, intercession is called "supplication" (Greek *deēsis*), and it is represented in the figure of Mary (the Church) standing with her head slightly bent before the lordship of Christ Pantocrator, who holds a book open. She hold her hands out, open to God's gift, asking to be filled with the Holy Spirit.

The touchstone for proving the authenticity of intercession is praise, for intercession takes place through praise. When praise is lacking, we need to fear that our "requests" may not truly be intercession; behind our petitions may be lurking a type of hypocrisy that seeks to conceal insatiable greed with lengthy prayers (Mark 11:24-25). Praise is a way of guaranteeing the gratuitous nature of our intercession. It is the air that we must breathe so that with childlike confidence we can approach the Father in the Spirit and through the Son.

> *"So I tell you, whatever you ask for in prayer, believe that you have received it, and it will be yours.*
> *"Whenever you stand praying, forgive, if you have anything against anyone; so that your Father in heaven may also forgive you your trespasses."* (Mark 11:24-25)

There are two canticles of Isaiah (42:10-17; 45:20-25) that can help us enter into the spirit of praise. Since authentic praise is marked by an awareness of gift, it includes a contemplative dimension, as does all prayer. In the psalms of praise, nothing is requested; rather, the psalmist expresses joy, surrender to God, and thanksgiving for the mere fact of existing. God is the Creator who made human beings and all that exists (Psalms 8 and 114). God watches over his faithful ones (Psalms 33 and 92). God cares for his flock (Psalm 23); he defends his people (Psalm 27); he does justice (Psalm 77); he constantly reveals his love for human beings (Psalm 103). Praise inspires us to imitate the gratuitous generosity of God. That is why praise makes our flesh grow lighter and rise higher; it become more contemplative and less utilitarian—it simply sings. That is why Paul begins most of his letters with a profound hymn of praise, for praise is the basis of all that follows; it creates the atmosphere that Christians breathe.

The greatest praise we can give the Father is the offering of the passion of his Son. Our sinful, exiled flesh offers God the wounded flesh of the Word so that our praise takes the form of blessing (in Greek, *eulogia*) and Eucharist (cf. Mark 6:41; 14:23). In blessing, we acknowledge the gift and give thanks for it. The blessing is born of the conviction that everything is a gift from God, and it leads us to affirm our solidarity as fellow believers. By pronouncing a blessing, we renounce proprietary rights over the things that surround us. We relinquish exclusive possession of property because the true proprietor is God: "I thank you (*exhomologoumai soi*), Father, Lord of heaven and earth, because you have hidden these things from the wise and the intelligent and have revealed them to infants" (Luke 10:21; Matt 11:25-26). The Greek word *exhomologein* means acknowledgment, thanksgiving, amazement, joy, praise. Jesus is rejected by the wise and the prudent, but he is accepted by the simple folk. As he did when he raised Lazarus (John 11:41-42), Jesus praises the Father and attributes his power to him. The prayer of praise rises only in those who know how to discern, in their very own history, the presence of God who works wonders.

Taking the five loaves and the two fish, he looked up to heaven, and blessed and broke the loaves, and gave them to his disciples to set before the people; and he divided the two fish among them all. (Mark 6:41)

Access to the Father is wide open. Our flesh, justified by the passion of Christ and buoyed by the Spirit, enters with great confidence (with *parrhēsia*) into the sanctuary. Now the veil has been drawn back; everything is open to view. What happens with prayer is similar to what happens with conversion. I recall Paul Claudel's words: *Je vois l'Église ouverte, il faut entrer*—"I see the Church open; I must enter in." The letter to the Hebrews especially helps us to understand better the real meaning of this free access of all flesh to the Father.

For Prayer and Reflection

"Sing to the Lord a new song, his praise from the end of the earth! Let the sea roar and all that fills it, the coastlands and their inhabitants. Let the desert and its towns lift up their voice, the villages that Kedar inhabits; let the inhabitants of Sela sing for joy, let them shout from the tops of the mountains. Let them give glory to the Lord, and declare his praise in the coastlands. The Lord goes forth like a soldier, like a warrior he stirs up his fury; he cries out, he shouts aloud, he shows himself mighty against his foes.... I will lead the blind by a road they do not know, by paths they have not known I will guide them. I will turn the darkness before them into light, the rough places into level ground. These are the things I will do, and I will not forsake them" (Isa 42:10-13, 16).

42. Judith: Speaking Freely with God

JUDITH REPRESENTS the true daughter of Israel, a strong woman who embodies the destiny of her people and leads them forward in the midst of the vicissitudes of history. She is a woman free in spirit, and she speaks out boldly (with *parrhēsia*). The sacred writer introduces Judith after describing a situation that threatens the future history of the Jewish people. The Assyrian army of Holofernes is besieging the mythical city of Bethulia, a type of Macondo.[16] Deprived of access to water, the people call a meeting and demand that their leader, Uzziah, seek terms of surrender. Uzziah, however, tries to convince the people not to give in to the enemy; he pleads with them to continue the struggle a while more: "Have courage, brothers and sisters! Let us hold out for five more days.... If these days pass by, and no help comes for us, I will do as you say" (Jdt 7:30-31).

Judith is described as a widow of exceptional beauty and dignity whose husband died of heatstroke. In her grief, she dwells in a tent on the roof of her house and from there witnesses all the problems and the protests of her people. Judith's moral authority becomes manifest when she summons the city elders and tells them that their human prudence is foolishness to God: "Do not try to bind the purposes of the Lord our God; for God is not like man, to be threatened, nor like a human being, to be won over with pleading." She then advises them enigmatically: "While we wait for God's deliverance, let us call upon him to help us, and he will hear our voice if it pleases him" (Jdt 8:10-19).

The reason for Judith's hope is that the people of Israel faithfully recognize Yahweh as the one and only God, and they do not worship other gods. The people's acknowledgment of Yahweh is not just an intellectual assent; it is a vivid memory branded into their flesh, as Judith reminds them: "Remember what he did with Abraham, and how he tested Isaac, and what happened to Jacob in Syrian Mesopotamia, while he was tending the sheep of Laban, his mother's brother. For he has not tried us with fire, as he did them, to search their hearts, nor has he taken vengeance on us; but the Lord scourges those who are close to him in order to admonish them" (Jdt 8:26-27). The memory that this woman evokes is more than just recollection: it is a hidden treasure that takes on flesh and reveals to her the path the people must follow. Judith reinterprets the present moment in the light of enfleshed memory, which we might call "catholic" in the sense that it is memory of the past that opens new spaces for God in the future. By making salvation history a present reality, Judith discovers good reasons to encourage the people to continue hoping. Both her prayer and her action are saturated with memory. Indeed, she has access to the living God precisely because she is a woman with memory-soaked flesh.

Judith declares that the people of Bethulia cannot afford to negotiate with the Assyrians, for if this stronghold falls, so will all Judea. Bethulia must set an example for the rest of the nation, "for their lives depend upon us, and the sanctuary and the altar and the temple rest upon us" (Jdt 8:24). What the sacred writer has earlier explained in "sociological" terms, Judith now reinterprets from the perspective of her faith, which reveals to her that in this crisis God is testing those who draw close to him.

Uzziah agrees that Judith's understanding of the situation is accurate and judicious, but he says that her advice will be effective only if Judith herself intercedes for her people and risks her own neck. If she does not intervene personally, her analysis, as inspired as it may be by faith and memory, will remain at the level of good intentions.

After asserting her authority before the city elders, Judith cries out to the Lord as a poor widow, asking him to remember the outrages committed against the people (Jdt 9:1, 4-6) and beseeching him to crush the enemy's pride by the hand of a woman (Jdt 9:10). And when she goes forth to meet the enemy general Holofernes, she is gentle as a dove and wise as a serpent.

Judith is the prototype of the person who knows how to speak freely with God and with others. She practices *parrhēsia* by telling the full story with confident courage and by dealing openly with one and all. She corrects and instructs her own people even as she adroitly deceives the enemy with adulation but without deceit, for she always refers to God as "my Lord" (Jdt 11:5-6).

> Judith answered Holofernes, "Accept the words of your slave, and let your servant speak in your presence. I will say nothing false to my lord this night. If you follow out the words of your servant, God will accomplish something through you, and my lord will not fail to achieve his purposes." (Jdt 11:5-6)

Judith prays even while in action: both before and after she beheads Holofernes, she calls upon the Lord. Her action is truly dramatic, for the truest drama is that which takes places between our freedom and God's (Jdt 13:4-10). There is no question here of the self-sufficiency of Tosca's lethal kiss (*questo è il baccio*) or of Macbeth's debate with himself about killing the king. The sufficiency here is in the tragedy. What we see in Judith is true salvation history, the struggle between freedom and grace.

Finally, Judith is the model of the person who praises God. Her praise becomes contagious among all the people and leads them to victory in God (Jdt 13:11-17).

Judith believes neither in quietism nor in deal-making. She does not isolate herself in self-sufficiency, nor does she retreat into insecurity. What cries out to God and lets God act is simply her memory-filled woundedness. By letting God lead, she feels free to embark on whatever action God inspires in her. Her plain and simple courage in the Spirit empowers her to reinterpret events in the light of salvation history, and so she is able to envision actions that inspire hope in the people. Praise to the One who is strong in our weakness!

For Prayer and Reflection

"Who are you to put God to the test today, and to set yourselves up in the place of God in human affairs? You are putting the Lord Almighty to the test, but you will never learn anything! You cannot plumb the depths of the human heart or understand the workings of the human mind; how do you expect to search out God, who made all these things, and find out his mind or comprehend his thought? No, my brothers, do not anger the Lord our God.... Do not try to bind the purposes of the Lord our God; for God is not like a human being, to be threatened, or like a mere mortal, to be won over by pleading. Therefore, while we wait for his deliverance, let us call upon him to help us, and he will hear our voice if it pleases him" (Jdt 8:12-14, 16-17).

43. Entering into the Humanity of Jesus

"THEREFORE, MY FRIENDS, since we have confidence to enter the sanctuary by the blood of Jesus, by the new and living way that he opened for us through the curtain (that is, through his flesh), and since we have a great priest over the house of God, let us approach with a true heart in full assurance of faith, with our hearts sprinkled clean from an evil conscience and our bodies washed with pure water. Let us hold fast to the confession of our hope without wavering, for he who has promised is faithful. And let us consider how to provoke one another to love and good deeds, not neglecting to meet together, as is the habit of some, but encouraging one another, and all the more as you see the Day approaching.... But we are not among those who shrink back and so are lost, but among those who have faith and so are saved" (Heb 10:19-25, 39).

This text from Hebrews can serve as an introduction to some reflections that will help us in our prayer today. The passage tells us about confidence, the true heart, the assurance of faith, the confession of hope, the motive of mutual love. We are told that our confidence should be founded on the flesh and the blood of Jesus. This week, when we are celebrating the Lord's Passover, is an ideal setting for contemplating the mysteries of his passion and resurrection, that is, the mysteries of his flesh at once despoiled and glorified. By meeting together as family and celebrating the Passover, we defend ourselves from the chaos of sin and the frenzied splintering of our sinful conscience—such was the custom of the nomadic tribes of Israel's ancestors. The Passover rescues us from the chaos outside. In our midst, we have the flesh of the Lamb, who was slaughtered (Apoc 5:8-9), who nourishes us (cf. John 6:35), who assures us of courage and constancy, and who defends us from the cowardice that is the fruit of the chaos of sin.

When Saint Ignatius treats of the mysteries of the passion in his Spiritual Exercises, he tells us to ask for "sorrow, regret, and confusion, because the Lord is going to his passion for [our] sins" (SpEx 193). He also recommends that we request "sorrow with Christ in sorrow, a broken spirit with Christ so broken, tears and interior suffering because of the great suffering that Christ endured for [us]" (SpEx 203). Our meditation will lead us to "consider what Christ our Lord suffers in his human nature, or desires to suffer," and we "should begin here with much effort to bring [ourselves] to grief, sorrow, and tears" (SpEx 195). Ignatius asks us to reflect on the fact that "his divinity hides itself"; we should consider "how he could destroy his enemies but does not, and how he allows his most holy humanity to suffer cruelly" (SpEx 196).

Like Saint Teresa, Saint Ignatius understands that the only sure way to gain access to divinity is by the sacred humanity of our Lord. When meditating on the passion, we must enter into this humanity, into this man Jesus, who is God but who suffers as man, in his body and in his psyche. This is not some quaint piece of folklore; it is something real; it is the only viable, tangible path by which we can contemplate the Father, who is revealed in the Son. We must contemplate the reality of the passion in the flesh of Jesus and in our own flesh. There is no other road to travel if we want to proclaim that Jesus is risen and alive, walking now with the same flesh and with his wounds open to the transcendence of the Father's face. In contemplating the passion, we must consider how the Lord enters into it. As his followers, we have to learn what it means to "enter in patience." What does this mean, and how will it help us to know him better so as to "love him more intensely and follow him more closely" (SpEx 104)?

God made his Son "perfect through suffering" (Heb 2:10). Jesus had to share in our flesh and blood "so that through death he might destroy the one who has the power of death, that is, the devil, and free those who all their lives were held in slavery by the fear of death" (Heb 2:14-15). By God's grace, Jesus tasted death on behalf of all of us (Heb 2:8-9), and now he is crowned with splendorous glory because of the death that he suffered. "You are worthy to take the scroll and to open its seals, for you were slaughtered and by your blood you ransomed for God saints from every tribe and language and people and nation; you have made them to be a kingdom and priests serving our God, and they will reign on earth" (Apoc 5:9-10). "Worthy is the Lamb that was slaughtered to receive power and wealth and wisdom and might and honor and glory and blessing!" (Apoc 5:11-12).

In order to save us, Jesus "enters in patience." In the pages that follow, I will reflect on what this "entering in patience" meant for Jesus. First, it was his way of undergoing death; second, it signified the totality of his surrender; third, it involved his failure from a human point of view; and fourth, it had a priestly dimension. Finally, I offer some reflections on how all this relates to us and our consecrated life.

44. Freely Embracing Death[17]

J ESUS TOOK HIS DEATH seriously, as he did his life. Anointed by the Spirit, he was able to discern the signs of the times and was therefore perfectly aware that his "hour" would soon come (cf. John 2:4; 7:30; 13:1; Matt 26:45). Paradoxically, however, we find that Jesus at times "hid himself" to escape public notice and persecution (cf. John 7:1; 8:59). Jesus was no coward, but neither was he suicidal. He was hiding from the police, from the assassins, from his enemies, because his hour had still not arrived. The thought of death distressed him (John 12:27), but he accepted the divine will; he left everything in the hands of his Father. He knew that he was going to die, but he did not hand himself over recklessly. He defended his life until "the hour" arrived and so stayed out of sight. This circumstance makes us aware of the painful inner tension that afflicted the heart of Jesus, a tension that became visible at the culminating moment of Gethsemane.

> *Now before the festival of the Passover, Jesus knew that his hour had come to depart from this world and go to the Father. Having loved his own who were in the world, he loved them to the end.* (John 13:1)

> *Then he came to the disciples and said to them, "Are you still sleeping and taking your rest? See, the hour is at hand, and the Son of Man is betrayed into the hands of sinners."* (Matt 26:45)

"Now my soul is troubled. And what should I say—'Father, save me from this hour'? No, it is for this reason that I have come to this hour." (John 12:27)

The death of Jesus was carried out by human beings, but it was according to God's designs—it was a human deed "worked over" by God. "The Son of Man is to be betrayed into human hands, and they will kill him, and three days after being killed, he will rise again" (Mark 9:31). The words "betray" and "kill" have a technical meaning in the scriptures. "Kill" refers to the slaying of a righteous person, and it designates human beings as the ones responsible for the death. In Greek, on the other hand, the verb "betray" means the same as "hand over" or "give up"; it is used to indicate that God is the one who does the "handing over," as Saint Paul tells us: "He did not withhold his own Son, but gave him up for all of us" (Rom 8:32).

When we hear that Jesus was "handed over" by Judas and the chief priests, we should understand that they are agents of the divine will. When Jesus is finally handed over, that is "the hour," as he himself says: "This is your hour, and the power of darkness" (Luke 22:53). At the same time, it is the hour of his glorification (cf. John 12:23-24).

At all times, Jesus acts with freedom, alternately appearing in public and disappearing from view—and eventually allowing himself to be taken captive. He makes his strategy clear: "For this reason the Father loves me, because I lay down my life in order to take it up again. No one takes it from me, but I lay it down of my own accord. I have power to lay it down, and I have power to take it up again. I have received this command from my Father" (John 10:17-18). His freedom is such that he accepts both the plan of the Father (being handed over) and the instrument used (being killed by specific persons in a particular way). As we behold the splendor of Christ's dignity so manifest here, we are moved to exclaim, "Worthy is the Lamb!" (Apoc 5:12). This is the dignity of the person who surrenders in obedience to the Father's will and allows that will to determine how the deed will be done. All of this Jesus does with the utmost freedom.

All dignity is founded on both freedom and surrender. At first sight, the two concepts seem opposed: freedom means the ability to decide for oneself, while surrender suggests leaving the decision in someone else's hands. Nevertheless, freedom's deepest root entails voluntary abandonment because only thus can we find that for which we have been created, and this is called worthiness in the Worthy One, true lordship in the Lord.

For Prayer and Reflection

"The hour has come for the Son of Man to be glorified. Very truly, I tell you, unless a grain of wheat falls into the earth and dies, it remains just a single grain; but if it dies, it bears much fruit" (John 12:23-24).

45. The Totality of Surrender

S AINT PAUL LEAVES no doubt about the completeness of Jesus' destitution: "He humbled himself and became obedient to the point of death—even death on a cross" (Phil 2:8). The previous verse speaks of Jesus "emptying himself"; indeed, Jesus' self-divestment is total; he is left with nothing for himself. His mere presence provokes consternation in others (cf. Wis 2:12-22); even without doing or saying anything, he is a living reproach. It is precisely his flesh that confounds and unsettles Satan, who keeps challenging him: "If you are the Son of God...." But this diabolical questioning does not end in the desert (cf. Luke 4:13), for Jesus encounters it at every turn in his life: in healing the possessed and the infirm; in debates with the Pharisees and the Sadducees; in the zeal of the disciples who would call down fire from heaven; in the doubts of the Essenes, who would have him withdraw to a contemplative life in the desert; in the taunts of the soldiers; in the betrayal of Judas; in the challenge to come down from the cross. Satan is troubled by this flesh that threatens him, and he in turn troubles the hearts of human beings. Satan wants to know—he wants the satisfaction of gnosis—but his incurable skepticism leads him ultimately to defeat. Like Herod, he plays his last card by "killing." He thinks that in this way he will vanquish the flesh of Jesus and consume it. But for Satan that flesh turns out to be a deadly bait, for it conceals the poison that will slay him once and for all: divinity.[18]

Jesus provokes all kinds of persecution just by his presence, but where is it that we see the totality of his destitution? Saint Paul tells us that it is in his "death on a cross" (Phil 2:7-8). Jesus is recognized as a prophet (Matt 21:11; Luke 7:16; John 4:19; 9:17), and a prophet cannot be killed outside of Jerusalem (Luke 13:33): "Jerusalem, Jerusalem, the city that kills the prophets and stones those who are sent to it!" (Matt 23:37). Nevertheless, Jesus does not die in Jerusalem, nor is he stoned to death. He dies as one accursed, "hung on a tree" outside the walls of Jerusalem (cf. Deut 21:22-23). The punishment imposed by Jewish law for a false prophet and a blasphemer is stoning, but Jesus does not die as a prophet. Rather, he is put to death as a conspirator, a zealot, a guerrilla fighter against Roman power. As a contemporary theologian puts it, Jesus' enemies robbed him of his rightful death. Not only did they take away his life with a "legal" murder, but they denied him the meaning that he personally gave to his life and his death. Jesus' total divestment includes the manner of his death on the cross: he did not even have the final satisfaction of dying in a way that bore witness to the true meaning of his existence.

The crowds were saying, "This is the prophet Jesus from Nazareth in Galilee." (Matt 21:11)

Fear seized all of them; and they glorified God, saying, "A great prophet has risen among us!" and "God has looked favorably on his people!" (Luke 7:16)

The woman said to him, "Sir, I see that you are a prophet." (John 4:19)

"Yet today, tomorrow, and the next day I must be on my way, because it is impossible for a prophet to be killed outside of Jerusalem." (Luke 13:33)

When someone is convicted of a crime punishable by death and is executed, and you hang him on a tree, his corpse must not remain all night upon the tree; you shall bury him that same day, for anyone hung on a tree is under God's curse. You must not defile the land that the Lord your God is giving you for possession. (Deut 21:22-23)

Faithful discipleship means following Jesus in his way of destitution and crucifixion. His true disciples follow this path out of love for their Lord. The temptation to turn apostolic zeal into a "business" does not recognize the saving power of walking this path of torment on the cross. We should remember that crucifixion was a punishment inflicted only on those who were not Roman citizens. Consequently, the disciples of Jesus must take into account the likelihood of being judged "criminals" as he was, of being considered "antagonistic" to the common good. Saint Paul contemplates this mystery of suffering destitution out of love for his Lord, and he is willing to be himself accursed in order to save his brothers and sisters: "I am speaking the truth in Christ—I am not lying; my conscience confirms it by the Holy Spirit—I have great sorrow and unceasing anguish in my heart. For I could wish that I myself were accursed and cut off from Christ for the sake of my own people, my kindred according to the flesh" (Rom 9:1-3).

Saint Ignatius shared this same sentiment. To those making the Spiritual Exercises and deciding about how to lead their lives, he proposes that they "choose poverty with Christ poor rather than wealth, contempt with Christ laden with it rather than honors" (SpEx 167)—all this for the sake of following Jesus Christ more closely. This proposal of Ignatius is not a debatable spiritual opinion of a particular epoch; it is not just a "corollary" that can be more or less negotiated according to circumstances. It is of the very essence of the destitution of Christ: if we do not accept it in the total way that Ignatius proposes, then we are not wholeheartedly following the Master. The totality involved in this commitment has been affirmed by contemporary saints, such as the founder of the Servants of the Sacred Heart, Saint Rafaela María. Mediocrity consists in accepting the cross "halfway" or "to a certain point." That is not really dying on the cross; at most, it will be death in a high-tech clinic.

For Prayer and Reflection

"Christ Jesus, though he was in the form of God, did not regard equality with God as something to be exploited, but emptied himself, taking the form of a slave, being born in human likeness. And being found in human form, he humbled himself and became obedient to the point of death—even death on a cross" (Phil 2:6-8).

46. The Failure of Jesus

ALL THESE REFLECTIONS are concerned with the Christian theology of hope and failure, and any such theology must begin with consideration of the passion and death of Jesus.[19] What is more, the historical failure of Jesus and the frustration of the hopes of so many people ("We had hoped ..." [Luke 24:21]) are the royal road for Christian hope, for they are the way God reveals himself to us in Christ as he works out our salvation. Jesus himself foretold it: "Those who want to save their life will lose it, and those who lose their life for my sake will find it" (Luke 9:24; Mark 8:35). The possible failure of the work of salvation was already apparent, in a partial and less intense way, when the Israelites left Egypt in search of the promised land. Moses must certainly have feared failure when he was standing on the banks of the Reed Sea, in the midst of an unruly people with the Egyptians on their heels. He was left with few options: surrendering to the Egyptians, working out a deal with them, committing suicide, or trusting God. He opted for the last, and God made himself powerfully present there in the midst of total human incapacity. The situation was similar later on, when the Israelites were murmuring because they lacked food and water. God made them understand how helpless they were at the human level, and then he intervened to save them.

But we had hoped that he was the one to redeem Israel. Yes, and besides all this, it is now the third day since these things took place. (Luke 24:21)

The failure of Jesus is part of this same dynamic: when everything seems lost, when all his friends desert him ("I will strike the shepherd, and the sheep of the flock will be scattered" [Matt 26:31]), then God intervenes with the power of the resurrection. The resurrection of Jesus Christ is not the climax of a movie; it is God's intervention in the total impossibility of human hope. The resurrection is God's declaration that the crucified one who accepted failure so that divine power might be revealed is now glorified as "Lord."

Our human tendency is to disguise all evidence of the reality that most frustrates us: death. We need only look at the cemeteries, the gravestones, the monuments to understand the ways in which we seek to embellish our mortality and banish from our minds this ultimate failure of our humanity. Sometimes we even resort to "canonizing" our dead. After Saint Peter's Square, the place where most people are canonized is at wakes: usually the dead person is described as a "saint." Of course, he was a saint because now he can't bother us! These are just ways of camouflaging the failure that is death. We use subterfuge to situate our hope outside the sphere of failure, and so we fail to place our hope in God. Pure hope in God occurs at the moment when, as in the case of Jesus, we are overwhelmed by the sense of having failed completely. This means something more than not being able to see any way out; it is the sure conviction that there is no way out, that the case is closed.

Jesus lost all hope of being able to escape from the infamy of public execution; he felt his mission had failed. But he knew that he had reached that point precisely because he had been the kind of person the Father wanted him to be. Nothing was more important for him than doing the will of his Father: "My food is to do the will of him who sent me and to complete his work" (John 4:34).

This reflection on failure focuses our attention on the "flesh" of Jesus. In Gethsemane, Jesus was still instinctively hoping to avoid the prospect of utter failure. Only his certainty about the Father's love enabled him to overcome his fear. As we consider the failure of Jesus, we would do well to recall the recommendations of Saint Ignatius that I mentioned at the beginning. We need to "touch" the flesh of Jesus. Our certain sense of "politeness" may tempt us to avoid what seems "scandalous," but in so doing we would be denying the role of Jesus' flesh in his failure. We would simply be adopting a form of the enlightened neo-Docetism[20] that is found so often these days among our ecclesiastical elites, our agnostic leftists, and our unbelieving rightists. Our Catholic "elites" miss the point of the Beatitudes, which Jesus proclaimed precisely for those times when we experience failure: "Blessed are those who take no offense at me" (Matt 11:6; Luke 7:22-23). In pronouncing the Beatitudes, Jesus was speaking mostly about the failures that humble folk experience, since it was to them that he addressed this message, but when our privileged elites hear the same message, they turn up their nose at the thought of failure and are scandalized. They prefer to have the Church use categories based on "common sense" rather than on the failure of the cross. They are neo-Docetists because they basically do not believe that Jesus the Christ is bodily alive, is truly risen. At most, they accept a spiritualist idea of resurrection, something closer to what Bultmann proposed, and they do so simply because they refuse to accept the reality of Christ's failure and so deny his flesh.

And he answered them, "Go and tell John what you have seen and heard: the blind receive their sight, the lame walk, the lepers are cleansed, the deaf hear, the dead are raised, the poor have good news brought to them. And blessed is anyone who takes no offense at me." (Luke 7:22-23)

The most painful failure Jesus experiences at the level of human friendship is with his disciples, and above all with Judas, who does not see the mercy in the Master's eyes. The final moments Jesus spends with his disciples are marked by a terrifying isolation: an abyss has been created. Jesus is not able to get through to them, and they have no idea what their Master is going through. This is the beginning of the terrible solitude and the profound rejection that Jesus experiences on the cross, where he feels abandoned even by his Father: "Father, why have you forsaken me?" (Matt 27:46).

It is there on the cross that Jesus feels the full force of failure and evil, and it is there that he transcends them. It is there that he reveals the unfathomable depths of his love because only the greatest of lovers possesses the peace and vitality of spirit needed to embrace failure. In the crucified Jesus, we see the culmination of all those ancient failures that we read of in the Old Testament in particular times and places. Hebrews tells us that the Israelites "all died in faith without having received the promises" (Heb 11:13)—that is, they died with some sense of failure. In his death, Jesus assumes and fulfills all these failures scattered across the history of salvation. Now only one solution remains: the divine solution, which in this case is resurrection as revolutionary ferment. This means that Christians today must incorporate into their daily lives the conviction that Jesus Christ is fully alive and walking in our midst. Otherwise, their Christianity will be a pseudo-failure. If they try to evade the scandalous failure of the cross, which appears to be the total negation of human hope, then they have not truly "hoped against all hope." If their hope fails, they will seek out a more acceptable kind of failure, failure that can coexist elegantly with universal, all-purpose values. Such is the failure of religion without devotion, religion that knows nothing of the healing font of all devotion, Jesus Christ risen from the dead and living among us.

For Prayer and Reflection:

"Then Jesus said to them, 'You will all become deserters because of me this night; for it is written, "I will strike the shepherd, and the sheep of the flock will be scattered." But after I am raised up, I will go ahead of you to Galilee.' Peter said to him, 'Though all become deserters because of you, I will never desert you.' Jesus said to him, 'Truly I tell you, this very night, before the cock crows, you will deny me three times.' Peter said to him, 'Even though I must die with you, I will not deny you.' And so said all the disciples" (Matt 26:31-35).

47. Jesus Christ the Priest

Thus Jesus "enters in patience," with his flesh, in his flesh, and through that flesh he is constituted priest. "Therefore he had to become like his brothers and sisters in every respect, so that he might be a merciful and faithful high priest in the service of God, to make a sacrifice of atonement for the sins of the people. Because he himself was tested by what he suffered, he is able to help those who are being tested" (Heb 2:17-18). In his total destitution and acceptance of failure, he offered "a single sacrifice for sin" (Heb 10:12-13), a sacrifice he performed not with words but with his flesh and blood: "But when Christ came as a high priest of the good things that have come, then through the greater and perfect tent (not made with hands, that is, not of this creation), he entered once for all into the Holy Place, not with the blood of goats and calves, but with his own blood, thus obtaining eternal redemption. For if the blood of goats and bulls, with the sprinkling of the ashes of a heifer, sanctifies those who have been defiled so that their flesh is purified, how much more will the blood of Christ, who through the eternal Spirit offered himself without blemish to God, purify our conscience from dead works to worship the living God!" (Heb 9:11-14). "For it was fitting that we should have such a high priest, holy, blameless, undefiled, separated from sinners, and exalted above the heavens. Unlike the other high priests, he has no need to offer sacrifices day after day, first for his own sins, and then for those of the people; this he did once for all when he offered himself. For the law appoints as high priests those who are subject to weakness, but the word of the oath, which came later than the law, appoints a Son who has been made perfect for ever" (Heb 7:26-28). We have drawn close to this priest, who is the mediator of a new covenant, for the cleansing torrent of his blood speaks louder than that of Abel (cf. Gen 4:8-11).

The priesthood of Christ is exercised at three moments: in the sacrifice of the cross (and in that sense it was "once and for all"), in his present intercession with the Father (cf. Heb 7:22-25), and at the end of time when Christ hands all creation over to the Father (but "not to deal with sin" [Heb 9:27-28]). In the second moment, the present time, Jesus the Christ exercises his priestly intercession through us: "He holds his priesthood permanently, because he continues for ever. Consequently he is able for all time to save those who approach God through him, since he always lives to make intercession for them" (Heb 7:24-25). Jesus Christ is alive and is interceding with the fullness of his humanity and divinity: "Since, then, we have a great high priest who has passed through the heavens, Jesus, the Son of God, let us hold fast to our confession. For we do not have a high priest who is unable to sympathize with our weaknesses, but we have one who in every respect has been tested as we are, yet without sin" (Heb 4:14-15). In the mystery of the resurrection, Jesus, now constituted Lord, appears bodily to the disciples and has them touch the wounds of his flesh (see John 20:19-20, 27; Luke 24:36-39, 40-42). That body, those wounds, that flesh—all are intercession. What is more, there is no other way of access to the Father except this one. It is in beholding the flesh of the Son that the Father grants salvation. It is through the wounds of Christ that we encounter the Father. Fully alive in his glorified flesh, Christ is bringing forth life in our midst as we take part in his flesh and enter in patience into his passion so as to share also in his glorification. Such is the substance of that crucial statement in the letter to the Hebrews: "We have an altar from which those who officiate in the tent [the priests of the former covenant] have no right to eat" (Heb 13:10). That altar is Christ, with his body suspended on the cross.

> *When it was evening on that day, the first day of the week, and the doors of the house where the disciples had met were locked for fear of the Jews, Jesus came and stood among them and said, "Peace be with you." After he said this, he showed them his hands and his side. Then the disciples rejoiced when they saw the Lord.* (John 20:19-20)

> *While they were talking about this, Jesus himself stood among them and said to them, "Peace be with you." They were startled and terrified, and thought that they were seeing a ghost. He said to them, "Why are you frightened, and why do doubts arise in your hearts? Look at my hands and my feet; see that it is I myself. Touch me and see; for a ghost does not have flesh and bones as you see that I have."* (Luke 24:36-39)

For Prayer and Reflection

"For it was fitting that we should have such a high priest, holy, blameless, undefiled, separated from sinners, and exalted above the heavens. Unlike the other high priests, he has no need to offer sacrifices day after day, first for his own sins, and then for those of the people; this he did once for all when he offered himself" (Heb 7:26-27).

48. Holding Back Nothing

THE TEXT with which I first introduced this theme of Christ's self-emptying contained allusions and exhortations regarding our own conduct. I would like now to speak of how we personally relate to what was said about the immolation of Jesus and about his priesthood. I have already said something about this in passing, but I would like now to stress what I consider to be the true backbone of Christian behavior, and I do so without using adjectives, as if the simple fact of "being Christian" was not enough. We experience in our daily lives a certain inability—even a certain resistance—to take on ourselves all that is implied in Jesus' "entering in patience." The letter to the Hebrews warns us: "We must pay greater attention to what we have heard, so that we do not drift away from it" (Heb 2:1). The inability I speak of comes from our failure to discover the glory of God in the mystery of the living Jesus Christ. The patient, devastated Christ is God's glory. The risen Christ, glorious in flesh and spirit, is God's glory. Our inability to appreciate this glory is what makes it difficult for us to draw out the consequences of what we have seen and heard. Jesus told his adversaries: "I do not accept glory from human beings. But I know that you do not have the love of God in you. I have come in my Father's name, and you do not accept me; if another comes in his own name, you will accept him. How can you believe when you accept glory from one another and do not seek the glory that comes from the one who alone is

God?" (John 5:41-44). Here is the origin of the rejection of the mystery of Jesus the Christ, whether the rejection be blatant or craftily camouflaged. Our hearts are more prone to accept glory from others than to give glory to God; we are more ready to receive those who come in their own name than those who come in God's name. We prefer to converse and discuss rather than to pray and proclaim.

Hebrews encourages us to let "our hearts be strengthened by grace," as were the hearts of our ancestors, so that we are not "carried away by all kinds of strange teachings" (Heb 13:9). We are warned: "Take care that none of you may have an evil, unbelieving heart that turns away from the living God" (Heb 3:12). The debilitated heart is a cowardly heart, an unfeeling heart; we are urged to shake our hearts free of every useless weight (cf. Heb 12:1). We are encouraged to renounce every form of paralyzing "quietude." We are asked to "run" courageously. But run where? Toward the test that is set before us, and that test is bearing witness to Jesus the Christ, the one who "entered in patience" and who now is alive among us, giving us new life. That is why we are exhorted to "look to Jesus the pioneer and perfecter of our faith, who for the sake of the joy that was set before him endured the cross, disregarding its shame, and has taken his seat at the right hand of the throne of God. Consider him who endured such hostility against himself from sinners, so that you may not grow weary or lose heart" (Heb 12:2-3). As we look upon Jesus who "suffered outside the city," we are asked to "go to him outside the camp and bear the abuse he endured" (cf. Heb 13:10-16). The contemplation of Jesus, who has been constituted Lord for having entered in patience, helps us to correct our vitiated attitudes: "Now, discipline always seems painful rather than pleasant at the time, but later it yields the peaceful fruit of righteousness to those who have been trained by it. Therefore lift your drooping hands and strengthen your weak knees, and make straight paths for your feet, so that what is lame may not be put out of joint, but rather be healed" (Heb 12:11-13). The spirit's lameness ends up separating us from our body: in the long run, all lameness numbs and paralyzes us.

When I speak of lameness, I am thinking of the halting way in which "conventional" attitudes treat the passion and resurrection of Christ. Such attitudes are definitely disincarnate because they lead us to consider Christ as not having entered in patience and as not being glorified in his body. They, therefore, portray a risen Christ who is not a living person but just a hopeful idea or at best a religious or cultural "value" unrelated to the true history of the Father's love for human beings.

There exists a tendency among us to "make things easy." We find it easier not to spend too much time considering seriously what the fleshly suffering of Jesus, man and God, was like. The same thing happens with the glorious body after the resurrection. Even Jesus' disciples had doubts about the reality of his body: "they thought they were seeing a ghost" (Luke 24:36-37). There is a line in Luke's Gospel that may give us some insight: "They still could not believe it (because of their joy) and were amazed" (Luke 24:41). Their faith was hobbled by fear of new frustrations, and so they preferred to believe that they were seeing only the spirit of Jesus and not Jesus resurrected in the flesh. Something similar can happen with us: we are filled with joy at the thought that Jesus, Christ and Lord, is alive among us, but the joy becomes so great that it scares us. As a result, we camouflage the resurrection, preferring a type of formulaic preaching that fights shy of the vital message that gives us life: Jesus Christ is risen! We need to apply that saying of Saint Teresa, "a sad saint is a sorry saint," not just to the "sad saint" but also, and perhaps more commonly, to the "half-happy" saint. When we as consecrated persons follow the path of "carefully moderating" the joy produced by Jesus' resurrection, then we run the risk of compensating for our lack of joy by promoting a multitude of "efficient" pastoral projects. In so doing, we may become simply impresarios of the Gospel, so many "executives" of the kingdom.

The letter to Hebrews encourages us to reflect on our own bodily nature so that, being fully aware of it, we may understand how close God is to us in the flesh of the Savior when we are close to those who suffer (Heb 13:1-4). We are encouraged to go in search of our suffering sisters and brothers and to "enter in patience" with them by sharing their fate. We should do this without any desire to hold back anything for ourselves (Heb 13:5), just as Jesus held back nothing even though "he was in the form of God" (Phil 2:7-8). As we consider our own flesh and the flesh of Jesus, we are exhorted to be courageous, to speak out boldly (with *parrhēsia*): "Let us therefore approach the throne of grace with boldness, so that we may receive mercy and find grace to help in time of need" (Heb 4:16). And in case we experience fear, we are told, a bit ironically: "In your struggle against sin you have not yet resisted to the point of shedding your blood" (Heb 12:4).

> *Let mutual love continue. Do not neglect to show hospitality to strangers, for by doing that some have entertained angels without knowing it. Remember those who are in prison, as though you were in prison with them; those who are being tortured, as though you yourselves were being tortured. Let marriage be held in honor by all, and let the marriage bed be kept undefiled; for God will judge fornicators and adulterers. Keep your lives free from the love of money, and be content with what you have; for he has said, "I will never leave you or forsake you."* (Heb 13:1-5)

For Prayer and Reflection

"Therefore, since we are surrounded by so great a cloud of witnesses, let us also lay aside every weight and the sin that clings so closely, and let us run with perseverance the race that is set before us, looking to Jesus the pioneer and perfecter of our faith, who for the sake of the joy that was set before him endured the cross, disregarding its shame, and has taken his seat at the right hand of the throne of God. Consider him who endured such hostility against himself from sinners, so that you may not grow weary or lose heart. In your struggle against sin you have not yet resisted to the point of shedding your blood" (Heb 12:1-4).

Notes

1. References to the Spiritual Exercises (SpEx) are taken from George E. Ganss, S.J., *The Spiritual Exercises of Saint Ignatius: A Translation and Commentary* (Saint Louis, MO: Institute of Jesuit Sources, 1992).

2. Saint Ignatius and his first companions were very conscious of these two rival projects of faith. They taught us that the project of the evil spirit is divisive because it promotes individualism and does away with the mediation of institutions; it even suffocates religiosity at the level of the state. In this regard, the Society's option was simple but decisive in its aims: (1) consolidation of the ecclesial institution (of which the principle and foundation was the fourth vow to the Pope); (2) consolidation of the training of pastors (in seminaries and colleges such as the Roman College and the German College); (3) evangelization with true inculturation in Asia and America. In this evangelization, the missionaries worked with a real sense of universality that was quite different from the selfish goals of political absolutism or the abstract goals of Protestantism. Their universality was truly a *versus in unum* born of the reality of the concrete universal constituted by the earth's peoples. That is to say, the response of the Church and the Society of Jesus to the project of the evil spirit was militant in its very essence. Our faith is struggle.

3. "Non disse Cristo al primo suo convento:—Andate e predicate al mondo cience—ma diede il verace fondamento; e quel tanto sono nelle sue guance si ch'a pugnar, per acceder la fede, de l'Evangelio fero scuto e lance" (*Paradiso*, Canto 29, 97-117).

4. "Si que le pecorelle, che non sanno, toman del pasco pasciute di vento e non le scusa non veder lo danno" (ibid.).

5. "The enemy conducts himself like a woman. He is weak when faced with firmness but strong in the face of acquiescence. When she is quarreling with a man and he shows himself bold and unyielding, she characteristically loses her spirit and goes away. But if the man begins to lose his spirit and backs away, the woman's anger, vindictiveness, and ferocity swell almost without limit. In

the same way, the enemy characteristically weakens, loses courage, and flees with his temptations when the person engaged in spiritual endeavors stands bold and unyielding against the enemy's temptations and goes diametrically against them. But if, in contrast, that person begins to fear and lose courage in the face of the temptations, there is no beast on the face of the earth as fierce as the enemy of human nature when he is pursuing his damnable intention with his surging malice" (SpEx 325).

6. "Similarly the enemy acts like a false lover, insofar as he tries to remain secret and undetected. For such a scoundrel, speaking with evil intent and trying to seduce the daughter of a good father or the wife of a good husband, wants his words and solicitations to remain secret. But he is deeply displeased when the daughter reveals his deceitful words and evil design to her father, or the wife to her husband. For he easily infers that he cannot succeed in the design he began. In a similar manner, when the enemy of human nature turns his wiles and persuasions upon an upright person, he intends and desires them to be received and kept in secrecy. But when the person reveals them to his or her good confessor or some other spiritual person who understands the enemy's deceits and malice, he is grievously disappointed. For he quickly sees that he cannot succeed in the malicious project he began, because his manifest deceptions have been detected" (SpEx 326).

7. E. Pironio, *Meditación para tiempos difíciles*, p. 2.

8. Ibid.

9. Some of the liturgical hymns cited by the author are from the Spanish Breviary.

10. Romano Guardini, *El Señor* (Madrid, 1958), pp. 315ff.

11. Ibid., pp. 317-18.

12. Hans Urs von Balthasar, "Revelación y belleza," in *Verbum Caro* (Madrid, 1964), p. 153.

13. Guardini, *El Señor*, p. 321.

14. Ibid., pp. 322-23.

15. Ibid., p. 324.

16. Macondo is the remote fictional town that provides the setting for the novel *One Hundred Years of Solitude,* by Gabriel García Márquez.

17. On these two themes, how Jesus underwent death and the totality of his abandonment, I have taken some ideas from chapter 15 of Hughes Cousin, *Los textos evangélicos de la Pasión: El Profeta Asesinado* (Navarra: Editorial Verbo Divino, 1981).

18. Cf. Saint Maximus Confessor, Abbot, *Centuria* 1.8-13, *Patrologia Graeca* 90.1182-86.

19. On this theme of the failure of Jesus, I have taken some ideas from chapter 3 of the work by John Navone, *Teología del Fallimento* (Rome: Pontificia Universitá Gregoriana, 1988).

20. Docetism was a heresy that held that Jesus was not truly human: his body was not real, but only apparent (editor's note).

About the Translator

JOSEPH V. OWENS S.J. worked for over thirty years in the Caribbean and Central America. He is the author of *Dread: The Rastafarians of Jamaica* and has translated the theological work of Antonio González. He is currently translating the six volumes of Archbishop Oscar Romero's homilies.

About the Publisher

The CROSSROAD PUBLISHING COMPANY publishes CROSSROAD and HERDER & HERDER books. We offer a 200-year global family tradition of books on spiritual living and religious thought. We promote reading as a time-tested discipline for focus and understanding. We help authors shape, clarify, write, and effectively promote their ideas. We select, edit, and distribute books. With our expertise and passion we provide wholesome spiritual nourishment for heart, mind, and soul through the written word.